*(continued from front flap)*

nation was frequently in doubt. For a decade, the home isles were wracked by civil wars. Continental nations were poised threateningly beyond the channel. King clashed with Parliament, country with court, and Scotland and Ireland were in continuous revolt. Attention was, of necessity, turned inward. During these periods of non-supervision, strong feelings of self-reliance developed in the colonies. The people had to deal with small issues and large, questions of which leader to trust. Political and economic fortunes seesawed. These, then, were the "seeds of anger": officials were corrupt, laws favored the powerful, rights were ignored, the voice of the people was not heard. A timely subject, for these concerns are relevant in today's world.

Well researched and highly readable, *Seeds of Anger* provides a lively account of these early American uprisings and the people involved. Like her previous books, *The Women of '76* and *The Witches of Early America*, this book will be of great interest to students and historians, political scientists, economists and sociologists, and those who want a good story of other times.

# SEEDS OF ANGER

# SEEDS OF ANGER

*Revolts in America,*
*1607–1771*

by

SALLY SMITH BOOTH

HASTINGS HOUSE    *Publishers*    New York

*Library of Congress Cataloging in Publication Data*

Booth, Sally Smith.     Seeds of anger.

  Bibliography: p.
  Includes index.
    1.  United States—History—Colonial period, ca. 1600–1775.  2.  Government, Resistance to.  3.  Great Britain—Colonies—America—Administration.  I.  Title.
E188.B74     973.2       77-7117
ISBN 0-8038-6742-5

Published simultaneously in Canada by
Saunders of Toronto, Ltd., Don Mills, Ontario

*Printed in the United States of America*

*To Lloyd and Charlotte*

# *Contents*

Introduction      ix

I   Turmoil at Jamestown     3

II   Religion Stirs Foment     22

III   Revolt on the Chesapeake     50

IV   Dutch Rule Threatened     64

V   Bacon Takes Virginia     85

VI   Trouble in Carolina     114

VII   Riot or Rebellion?     132

VIII   New England's Union Upset     156

IX   Leisler Humbles New York     182

X   Maryland's Catholics Imperiled     201

XI   Carolina Lords Overthrown     219

XII   The Black Rebellions     229

XIII   Violence on the Frontier     254

XIV   Regulators Confront Tryon     271

Selected Readings     287

Index     293

# Introduction

ARMED REBELLION, a violent tactic for an angry people, early on found a home in colonial America. From the first days of settlement, passive acceptance of governmental decisions was as alien to New World pioneers as the primitive land that surrounded them. Revolt against crown authority was an important aspect of political tradition in the "plantations." Since the first adventurers waded ashore at Jamestown, Americans of all persuasions let their guns be heard when their voices in protest were ignored.

Nearly a century and a half before Washington's army drove the appointees of George III homeward, Virginians forcibly expelled a royal governor. In Maryland, attempts to overthrow the lawful administration of the Lords Baltimore became so common that insurrection was virtually accepted as a legitimate way in which to pass the idle days between harvest and planting. The Massachusetts saints showed no reluctance in rebelling against the mother country when it appeared that the religious utopia on the Bay might be imperiled by English dictate.

It was perhaps inevitable that conflict should mark the attempt of Britain's elegant lords to impose absentee rule on the rugged individualists of the provinces. The cabins of America were separated from the conference rooms of Whitehall by an ideological gulf far wider than the Atlantic. Strategies devised in the Isles for use in the colonies were more often suitable for urbanites in Leeds or Bath than for the western castaways who suffered "starving times", battled marauding pirates and raised the sport of eye gouging to a fine art.

In the primitive land where the strongest rather than the most loyal or obedient survived, the flow of royal proclamations, Privy Council directives, Parliamentary statutes, crown instructions and proprietary orders seemed ludicrous. No national armies stood by to enforce the will of English authorities. No great bureaucracy of sheriffs and constables was available to stifle unrest by locking dissenters into impregnable dungeons. In the provinces, adherence to law was achieved only through the voluntary cooperation of the people: common folk who far outnumbered the meager flock of foreign appointees.

Fortunately for the English, most colonists held a deep respect for authority and recognized that order was essential if the vulnerable settlements were to be preserved. Citizens prefered to file petitions of grievances, dispatch agents to London or use political maneuvering to bring about change in unfavorable policies. However, when it seemed that channels of peaceful protest had been closed, provincials unhesitatingly resorted to violent means to achieve redress.

Despite the sense of individualism and the freedom of action that physical isolation produced, those in the plantations did not lightly elect to challenge established government. Penalities were harsh for political deviates whether their crime was known as treason, mutiny, insurrection, revolt or rebellion.

Who were these Americans who so frequently move through the pages of colonial history with violent steps? What prompted leaders and followers to risk beheading, hanging, burning, drawing and quartering? What were the reasons that compelled them if not to separation, then to repeatedly test the tenuous bonds that held them to Mother England?

To Samuel Johnson and many other Britishers, residents of the provinces were a "race of convicts" unworthy of consideration. According to the contemptuous Doctor, the colonials should have been grateful for anything offered by the English "short of hanging."

Felons and other "Newgate Birds" were indeed transported to America in large numbers, but in an age when more than three hundred crimes were punishable by death, the forced immigration did not result in establishment of a hardened criminal class. Joining the miscreants in involuntary exile were debtors, prostitutes and enemy soldiers captured in battle. Ironically, these "dregs" of the Old World shared a common bond with such upstanding denizens as the sober Puritans in Massachusetts and the pious Catholics on the Chesapeake: all had gone beyond the mainstream of English life. By choice or chance, each of the immigrants had been unable to assimilate into accepted patterns of behavior and as a result, had been rejected by society. Americans, by nature, were a discontented people, penalized by established authority.

Like the Bay Puritans, Pennsylvania's Quakers and South Carolina's Huguenots immigrated to find a refuge where unorthodox religious precepts could be practiced without intervention from the official church. Political dissenters from Scotland, Ireland and the German Palatinate sought relief from constant warfare and the vengeance of invading armies. Yeomen and tenant farmers came for land, unavailable in Europe where soil was a privilege of the wealthy few. Workers and artisans, exploited by industrial barons, arrived with hopes for a greater share of the wealth.

A unifying thread joined the expectations of the first Europeans who became Americans. This tie was a common search for self-improvement and personal freedom in a fluid society where individuals were not frozen for life into predetermined status. The men and women of the plantations left not only their native land behind. Also rejected were the ancient institutions that declared all of humanity must accept assigned stations in economics, politics, religion and society.

Radically differing ideas of America's promise were held by those who did not immigrate—the powerful elite who were secure in British society. In most cases, the New World was seen as an untouched treasure chest lying ready for use by the mother country.

Industrialists visualized profits: provincials could be made captive consumers of English-made goods and could be compelled to supply raw materials at cheap rates. Military minds saw an almost limitless supply of naval stores needed to make Britain queen of the seas. Borough officials, confronted by poor riots and mounting urban debts, concluded that the west might serve as a dumping ground for the idle, vagrant, orphaned and aged who lived at public expense.

Landed aristocrats saw the virgin continent as a safety valve which would ease the hostility of peasants being expelled from large estates as a result of the enclosure movement. Anglican churchmen viewed the territory as an opportunity to spread the gospel and counteract the threat of Popery created by France's presence in Canada. In the Privy Council, the colonies were seen as a means of counterbalancing the power of Spain, Holland and Portugal. For the King, sovereign of all English liegemen, the provinces were a tool to use against the rising power of Parliament. Customs and duties from the plantations could fill royal coffers and reduce the monarchy's dependence upon the tight-fisted Commons. Great tracts of land could be deeded to favorites as rewards for services to the crown.

The conflicting expectations between those east and west of the Atlantic, were not conducive to the creation of stable relations, but the first years of settlement were not plagued by extreme discord between America and the mother country. For at least five decades after the initial settlement, the colonials considered themselves indisputably British subjects and therefore bound by historical traditions of loyalty. In addition, the unceasing labor necessary for survival in a primitive environment left little time for pondering resentments caused by philosophical differences. Lives were short. Survival was perilous at all times. The most efficacious way of dealing with offensive English policy was simply to ignore unacceptable orders.

The inability of English leaders to give attention to the provinces on a continuous basis was equally important in preserving the peace. The 1600's were a critical time for Britain, an era in which the very survival of the nation was frequently in doubt. For a decade, the home isles were wracked by civil wars. Continental nations were poised threateningly beyond the channel. King clashed with Parliament. Country with court. Scotland and Ireland were in continuous revolt. Attention was, of necessity, turned inward.

During these periods of non-supervision, strong feelings of self-reliance developed in the colonies. Citizens became accustomed to the perquisites of semi-independent government that emerged in the absence of continuous British rule. Local institutions, adapted from English models, became vastly more important in everyday life than the establishment east of the Atlantic.

Immigrants from other nations began filtering into the population, bringing with them different values and attitudes. Concentrations of wealth emerged as economic ventures began to develop. A relaxed confidence replaced the anxieties of the harsh days of early settlement. Instead of remaining transplanted Europeans, the residents of the plantations were gradually becoming Americans. The rigid ways of the Old World were being replaced by the pragmatic customs of the new.

The Restoration Stuarts' attempts to reintroduce close administrative supervision were not welcomed by provincials who had been left to their own resources for so long. The question of royal prerogative or Parliamentary supremacy versus colonial self-government became the critical issue in American life: a problem resolved only by the American victory in 1783.

The eighteenth century brought new problems. As available land along the seacoast was taken up, great waves of immigrants began moving into the back country. Citizens on the Atlantic often scorned the frontiersmen in much the same manner as the English government had treated the first colonists. The east-west conflict that resulted from this attitude emerged as a divisive element from New York to Georgia.

At the same time, slavery became a critical factor. The indentured servitude system had proved inadequate to meet the labor needs of an agricultural society, but white provincials soon learned that bondage for life was damaging to the master as well as the slave. An atmosphere of quiet dread settled over the provinces as slave owners discovered that black workers harbored the same "rebellious" longings for independence that were felt by freemen.

For more than one hundred and fifty years, English and plantation governments were bombarded with a never ending series of petitions, grievances and remonstrances from quarrelsome and dissatisfied colonists. Black or white, farmer or city dweller, dissidence and rebellion seemed bred into all early Americans.

# SEEDS OF ANGER

# CHAPTER I

# *Turmoil at Jamestown*

M AY OF 1607 was a time of optimism for the 105 men of the Virginia Company's first expedition. Lured to the New World by tales of riches, most of the gentlemen adventurers and their servants intended to stay only briefly in America. Like the Conquistadores on the Spanish Main, the Englishmen planned to harvest treasures of gold and jewels, and then move on. Like their Elizabethan forebearers, the explorers were reapers of spoils, not sowers of permanent colonies.

Despite the common goal of self-enrichment that brought the party together, squabbling marked the venture from the earliest days. Even before Britain's coast was left to stern, internal dissension began to destroy the fragile ties of cooperation which bound the group. The situation worsened during the five month voyage and by landfall, a series of competing cliques had emerged in a fierce struggle for leadership.

Differences faded slightly in the adventurers' haste to begin the rush for wealth. Anchors were dropped in a swampy cove forty-five miles upriver from the mouth of the James, a careless selection for which a heavy toll would be levied. Not only was the site a poor defensive position, but the murky waters teamed with germs of disease as dangerous as human enemies.

Few of the men scrambling ashore recognized the magnitude of the hazards that surrounded the beachhead. Marauding pirates and rival sea powers anxious to halt England's western expansion might raid the unprotected village at will. Indian federations, capable of fielding armies equal to mighty European princes, could hardly be expected to stand passively by while their homeland was invaded. Unknown plagues might render the tiny settlement helpless in a day. Without crops under cultivation, survival depended upon the successful transportation of supplies from the Old World.

Even the most perceptive adventurer could not conceive of the vast, silent land that spread beyond the eastern shore. The first foothills, reached only by crossing a virgin forest, lay farther away from Jamestown than the French coast was from London. Beyond the eastern peaks stretched plains, mountains, deserts and canyons undreamed of in seventeenth century Europe. Yet much of the enormous land bore the name of Virginia.

One of the voyagers, an experienced man capable of surmounting the obstacles and leading the colony to survival, was not among those who eagerly fled the odorous ships. Although chosen by London officials to the expedition's governing Council, this low-bred traveler had not been allowed to take his seat among the ranking "gentlemen." Instead John Smith, adventurer and captain, battler of the Turks and soldier of fortune, remained aboard, a prisoner under restraint. Accused of mutiny, Smith had become the first Englishman in colonial history to be charged with conspiracy to overthrow a legitimate government.

The supposed plot had been discovered after the three ship convoy left the Canary Islands in late February. The design was indeed threatening: Smith, it was concluded, had masterminded a scheme aimed at murdering members of the Council, usurping the government and naming himself king. A band of confederates, ready to strike, were said to be poised on each of the vessels. Before the rebellion could be raised, the ringleader was put under arrest.

Smith was uncontestably an ambitious man with few of the genteel refinements that characterized other leaders of the expedition, but it is unlikely that even circumstantial evidence supported the allegations lodged against him. The soldier's most glaring error had probably been to align himself with an unpopular or unpowerful faction, thus alienating the entrenched appointees of the Virginia Company. In the high stakes game of seventeenth century exploration, however, political maneuvering was often a life or death proposition. Those who miscalculated could be assessed the ultimate penalty.

In early April, the expedition put in at the West Indian island of Nevis so that passengers who had fallen ill might recover. Here a pair of gallows was made ready for Smith, but the structure went unused. According to contemporary accounts, the prisoner could not be ''persuaded'' to use them.

Hostility against the Captain lessened after the party reached Virginia and attention turned to the immediate necessity of establishing Jamestown. Smith was released and on June 20 was installed on the seven-man Council. Supporters later claimed that the Captain had been the victim of a conspiracy by enemies who spread false rumors. The plan was supposedly thwarted when Smith's impeccable conduct under guard made his innocence evident to all. The settlement's officials appeared content to overlook the entire episode, but Smith had not forgotten the three month imprisonment.

Reports by previous explorers described America as a paradise, but on May 26, less than two weeks after disembarking, a work party was rudely introduced to the realities of the primitive land. Hostile Indians, caring little for the Company's letters patent, attacked the Britishers. Among the casualties was Edward-Maria Wingfield, president of the Council, who was shot through the beard with an arrow but escaped serious harm. The incursion was not an isolated one. The woods and rivers surrounding James Fort were no longer safe for any Englishman.

The newly arrived contingent should have begun to realize that Virginia was not an Eden, and that survival would depend upon incessant toil rather than divine providence. This simple and most basic fact of New World life, however, had yet to be learned.

The departure of the transport vessels severed all ties between the British outpost and Mother England. Retreat was impossible. Only a small, shallow-draft pinnace was left behind. But instead of planting crops and fortifying the vulnerable garrison, Jamestowners plunged into the hunt for treasure. Particularly important was the search for a northwest passage believed to link the Atlantic to the Pacific or Indian Oceans. If such a strait could be found, England's merchants would become masters of the Orient trade. In London, it was said that the waterway was just beyond the seacoast.

By July, the community's food supply was nearly depleted and the urgency of the situation finally penetrated the Council. A strict rationing system was imposed to extend the remaining stores. Each day, every man was allotted one cup of wheat and barley, but even this meager fare was substandard. The grain supply was riddled with worms hatched during the ocean crossing.

Soon the deaths began. Typhoid, malaria and dysentery, a sickness known as the ''bloody flux'' carried away the weakened explorers. Much of the contamination probably came from the slimy waters of the James River from which the adventurers drew drinking supplies. Without a nourishing diet, the illnesses reached epidemic proportions.

At one point, not five healthy men could be roused to defend the village. Fields remained unsown and malnutrition emerged as the major terror. George Percy, a survivor of the tragedy, explained: ''Our men were destroyed with cruel diseases, as swellings, flixes, burning fevers, and by wars, and some departed suddenly; but for the most part, they died of mere famine. There were never Englishmen . . . in such miserie as we were in this new discovered Virginia.'' Smith's account noted: ''Had we been as free from all sins as glottony and drunkeness, we might have been canonized for saints.''

As the deaths increased, unrest mounted. Rumors sprang up that Wingfield was stealing food from the common store to sustain himself and his cadre. John Martin claimed that the President neglected official duties to concentrate upon tending his ''pott, spit and oven.''

Before the grumbling could become incitive, a temporary respite occurred when friendly Indians relieved the famine with corn and fish. By September 10, the situation had again deteriorated and members of the community moved to overthrow the Company-appointed President. Wingfield was arrested and charged with a series of crimes including conspiring with the Spanish to destroy the settlement and withholding food from the dying.

Captain John Ratcliffe, who had been instrumental in deposing Wingfield, was sworn in as the new leader, but the second President found his authority immediately challenged. During an argument, Ratcliffe struck blacksmith James Read, a man who might have been plotting the President's removal. Read retaliated by attempting to hit his attacker, but self-defense was not considered sufficient cause for laying hands on an official of the Company. The blacksmith was convicted of mutiny and sentenced to hang.

Read, whose services were far more valuable to the village than most of the helpless gentlemen, managed to extricate himself. Just before the execution was scheduled to begin, the artisan accused Captain George Kendall of conspiring against the colony. The allegation was startling, for Kendall, probably a spy for British Secretary of State Lord Salisbury, was one of the original Councillors chosen by London investors to govern Jamestown.

In a quick reversal, Read was set free and a court was convened to weigh the charges against Kendall. The evidence proved convincing. The Captain was found guilty of plotting to steal the pinnace, sail to Europe and sell information concerning the community's weaknesses to England's enemies. Without further delay, Kendall was shot to death in punishment.

Hunger returned to Jamestown. The coming of winter found the once proud adventurers huddled desperately in primitive shelters attempting to ease the agony of their empty bellies. Without the charity of local Indians who brought gifts of food, the entire contingent would have perished. Even with the warriors' aid, only 38 of the original 105 voyagers remained alive when the relief ships appeared on January 4, 1608.

General discontent was promoted by the arrogant attitude that settlement leaders continued to exhibit. Shared hardships did not produce a mutual respect or a leveling of classes. The gentlemen continued to deport themselves as if in royal court. According to Wingfield:

> . . . it is familiar for the President, Counsellors, and other officers to beat men at their pleasures. One lyeth sick till death, an other walketh lame, the third cryeth out of all his bones . . . Were this whipping, lawing, beating and hanging in Virginia, known in England, I fear it would drive many well affected minds from this honorable action of Virginia.

Spurred by dissention and unrelenting hunger, the adventurers once again rose up against the incumbent leadership. During July, an abortive attempt was made to depose Ratcliffe and install John Smith as head of the colony. Two months later, the plan succeeded. To justify the ouster, Ratcliffe was charged with inadequate control over the food supply and frivolously insisting that a presidential "pallas" be built to the detriment of projects that would have benefited the entire community.

The new President of Jamestown boasted a checkered past which some may have considered disreputable rather than commendable. John Smith had served as a mercenary in several foreign armies, invented an incendiary bomb dubbed the "firey dragon" and proved to be an unpredictable man of extremes. His conquests as a hero were matched by periods of severe defeat. In one reported debacle, Smith served as a slave, but managed to gain his freedom by slaying three Turkish warriors in a marathon match. Each of the losers was decapitated in the process and to commemorate the triumph, Smith was awarded a coat of arms on which a trio of severed heads was emblazoned.

The resilience that characterized his entire career sustained Smith in Virginia. He emerged as the dictatorial leader necessary to bring the failing colony to attention. The Captain instigated a forced work program designed to strengthen the village's defenses and turn thoughts away from food. He devised an unalterable system of rationing and dispersed the settlers into small groups so that foraging would be more effective.

During periods of starvation, Smith negotiated with Indians for grain, using force when persuasion failed. Despite the vigorous efforts, however, deaths remained commonplace. The explorers, ever watchful for the next supply ships, became receptive to proposals of mutiny. Two Dutchmen were arrested for urging the inhabitants to abandon Jamestown, join the Indians and serve Powhatan as King. The pair was sentenced to be executed, but was reprieved. The brush with death did not lessen the men's agitation.

Hatred turned against Smith. Critics alleged that the President was purposely attempting to destroy the community. He was charged with planning an Indian ambush in which several Jamestowners had been slain. It was said that he had poisoned opponents with rat bane. The Captain's friendship with Emperor Powhatan was viewed with particular suspicion. Some suggested that Smith intended to use Indian forces to establish himself as king over a combined English-native confederacy with Pocahontas as Queen. Those who opposed the arrangement would be annihilated.

Smith managed to retain control despite the growing turmoil, but in June of 1609, a serious challenge to his authority arose when the annual relief convoy arrived from England. News of the Jamestown disasters had shaken London investors. Instead of the expected gold and jewels, the financiers had received only cries for more assistance. In an attempt to salvage their original expenditures, company stockholders demanded that both the Company and the American government be reorganized.

Instead of a President elected by the Council, it had been decided that the community would be administered by a Company appointed "Lord Governor and Captain-General" who would possess almost total authority. Orders authorizing the change, however, could not be produced when the annual supply reached America. The vessel on which written verification had been placed, had become separated from the main convoy during a hurricane in the Atlantic passage. Presumably both the courier ship and her company were lost at sea.

Though unable to show written authorization, three newly arrived Company representatives ordered Smith to relinquish control of government. Smith, suspecting a conspiracy to take over the settlement was afoot, refused to step down without formal instructions. Supporters of the President, believing that the newcomers intended to kill Smith and enslave the population, prepared for war.

It would later be charged that Smith tried to organize an Indian attack against the new supply and that the calamity was averted only when disaster struck the President. Although proof of a plot did not surface, ill fortune did indeed render the Captain helpless. During an upriver canoe expedition, Smith's powder bag exploded in his lap and set his clothes afire. In an effort to douse the flames, the Captain leaped overboard and only narrowly escaped drowning. He was rushed back to Jamestown in critical condition from a burn nearly ten inches square. As the beleaguered President lay incapacitated, the claimants assumed control of government. Reportedly, the officials sought to assure that no further opposition would be made by devising an assassination plot against Smith, but the scheme was not successful.

In early October, John Smith returned to England with the ships of the Third Supply, while life in Virginia disintegrated under the reorganized administration. The winter of 1609–1610 brought conditions even more appalling than the famine of 1607. During this "Starving Time," citizens became so desperate that guns and amunition were traded to the Indians in exchange for corn. Some ate boots, acorns and rats. Settler William Simmons maintained that the famished Englishmen exhumed the body of a dead Indian and stewed the corpse with roots and herbs. Even this repast did not satisfy the gnawing hunger of one unidentified adventurer. According to Simmons:

> . . . one amongst the rest did kill his wife, powdered her, and had eaten part of her before it was known; for which he was executed, as he well deserved. Now whether she was better roasted, boiled or carbonado'd, I know not; but of such a dish as powdered wife, I have never heard of.

Just seven months after Smith had departed only 60 of the nearly 500 settlers remained alive. The survivors agreed to abandon the outpost, but the exodus was halted on June 8, by the arrival of a new supply under Lord De la Warr, the colony's first Lord Governor and Captain-General.

Again the Virginia Company was forced to reorganize government in America. Visions of quick wealth had proved an illusion. More and more English pounds were needed merely to keep the settlement afloat. A return on investment seemed only a distant dream.

The permissiveness and haphazard management of men and supplies that had nearly destroyed Jamestown could no longer be tolerated. If Virginia was to be made productive and therefore profitable, an authoritative state was required. In May of 1611, a new code of conduct, called the *Articles, Lawes and Orders Divine, Politique and Martiall for the Colony in Virginia,* was adopted. This guiding charter for the province was far different than traditional English common law.

Strict regimentation was the sole intention of the *Orders Divine,* a document that made even minor offenses such as the failure to elevate a bedstead at least three feet above the ground, a crime triable in court martial. Punishments akin to those inflicted during the brutal days of medieval Britain were declared justifiable for seemingly minor infractions. "Weeders" assigned to the fields could be sentenced to death for willfully plucking up roots, herbs or flowers. Disobedience to a company official was also a capital crime and perpetrators of simple errors could be sentenced to slavery in irons.

Death by hanging or shooting was the most common form of execution, but more inhumane means such as burning at the stake were allowed in special circumstances. Several men attempting to steal a boat and return to England were shot, then hanged and finally broken on a wheel. A settler who had stolen a small amount of oatmeal received an equally painful death. After his tongue had been pierced with a bodkin, the miscreant was chained to a tree and starved to death. Those who were unable to work because of illness received no food allotment but were allowed to die of malnutrition.

Attempts were also made by the new regime to eliminate threats posed by Indians living near the community. Retribution imposed during a night raid on a Paspahegh village indicated that brutal treatment was not reserved only for whites. After the native community had been vanquished, the tribe's warriors were taken for slaves. The Paspahegh queen, whom some Britishers wished to burn at the stake, was killed with a sword. The royal children were thrown into a river and shot in the head as they surfaced for air.

The cruel discipline imposed under the *Orders Divine* helped to preserve Jamestown. Gradually the settlement was transformed from a collection of indolent individuals into a cohesive community. Women and children began to immigrate in large numbers. Their inclusion in the colony was a novel departure from European practice, for New World enclaves had traditionally been viewed as military strongholds fit only for soldiers and exploiters.

A different type of male colonial also appeared. Instead of gentlemen adventurers, the new Virginia arrivals were yeomen farmers or artisans who sought to achieve self-advancement through permanent work rather than spoils. The need for such persevering workers had become vital, for treasure had indeed been found west of the Atlantic. The riches, however, were not precious metals, but tobacco leaves. Since 1565 when John Hawkins returned from Florida with a sample of the "scurvey weed," smoking had progressively become a near mania in the London court.

By 1614, John Rolfe's experiments with the cultivation of tobacco had succeeded so well, that four barrels of the leaf could be shipped to Britain. Markets for the product developed quickly and soon even the streets of Jamestown were planted. In 1617, 20,000 pounds of the crop were harvested. Two years later the demand had so increased that a single farmer could confidently expect to earn £200 sterling from his annual harvest, a princely sum to those who had experienced the deprivations of England.

Development of a cash crop to provide employment and a basis for trade assured Virginia's permanence, but concentration on the weed doomed cultivation of less profitable crops that could have provided economic stability. The export of sassafras, for example, became insignificant despite European demand for the product, thought a cure for syphilis.

Rolfe contributed more than tobacco research in the drive to insure that Britain's American possessions would survive. On April 14, 1614, the planter married Pocahontas, Powhatan's young daughter. The proud father-in-law reigned as leader of at least thirty tribes in the tidewater, and was capable of crushing the English settlement at will. For eight years after the marriage, however, an uneasy truce prevailed between red and white. The British were able to strengthen their foothold and concentrate upon peopling a new continent without the distraction of continuous warfare.

Each season brought changes and improvements in the quality of Virginia life. Starving times became horrors of the past. The *Orders Divine* were relaxed, and on July 30, 1619, the first representative assembly in America was summoned to the "quire" of the Jamestown church. Twenty Burgess, the Governor and six Councillors were present.

The legislature passed laws condemning drunkenness, cursing and idleness. Residents were forbidden to revive "ancient" quarrels with the Indians. "Gaming" at dice and cards was prohibited. In other action, the Burgess regulated tobacco cultivation, Indian trade, indentured servitude, taxes and wearing apparel. After only six days, the assembly was forced to adjourn because of extreme heat. Though uncompleted, the session had established a tradition of citizen participation in government that would serve as a keystone in Virginia.

Other, less constructive evidences of permanence also evolved. In August of 1619, a Dutch man-of-war bartered approximately twenty black slaves to the colony in exchange for badly needed foodstuffs. Meanwhile, the importation of orphans, felons and kidnapped laborers increased in response to the insatiable demand for workers to till the tobacco fields.

The American experience took a dreadful toll on the expendibles that were herded toward Virginia. Vast numbers of immigrants who left England's ports were not strong enough to survive the voyage. In 1621 alone, more than 1,000 passengers died en route and the following year, the deaths increased by twenty percent. Even those who lived through the crossing contracted unknown ailments that routinely carried away "unseasoned" newcomers.

In March of 1622 a disaster more feared than pestilence struck the colony without warning. On Good Friday morning, Indians swept down on pioneer settlements all along the frontier. Despite laws decreeing death for anyone furnishing guns or ammunition to the red men, the warriors had been able to procure arms. Three hundred and fifty colonists, most of whom were surprised in the fields, were slain before the day ended. The massacre had been instigated in retaliation for the death of a popular tribesman killed by white traders in revenge for the death of an Englishman.

Again an imperiled Virginia was plunged into chaos. Heavy coats of armour, relics from England's middle age, were taken from the Tower of London and shipped to the colony to ward off enemy arrows. The English emerged victorious in the bloody confrontation, but the cost was dear. Of the thousands of Europeans who had poured into the colony since its founding, only hundreds survived.

The massacre of 1622 was the beginning of the end for the Virginia Company. Begun as a joint stock arrangement to supply amounts of capital too great for individual investors, the organization had proved inadequate for operating a thriving settlement an ocean away. Trial and error management was insufficient. Resentment against absentee owners could not be abolished by official dictate.

The financial success that had resulted from the tobacco trade was a second important factor undermining the Company's hold. Bountiful crops of the brown Orinoco leaf transformed the colony from a distasteful burden into a tempting plum. The change had not gone unnoticed by the crown.

In 1607, James I had used the auspices of the Virginia Company as a means of colonizing North America without lending official sanction that might inflame Spain. By 1624, the situation had altered. Badly in need of revenue, the monarch acted decisively to take the old colony as his own. On May 24, a writ of *quo warranto* against the corporate charter was upheld by the King's Bench. No longer would private interests reap benefits from the monarch's dominion. Virginia was officially placed under the aegis of the crown.

The change from a corporate to a royal colony did not drastically affect everyday life in Virginia, but some benefits did accrue. Peace with the Indians was facilitated by more cohesive policies, and the assurance that British forces stood ready to protect the settlement was a deterent against aggression from foreign powers. The introduction of crown appointed leaders no doubt reassured residents that the arbitrary justice that had prevailed under the *Orders Divine* would not be reimposed.

The Burgess continued to meet as usual and into the assembly's ranks came settlers of all stations. Former indentured servants became legislators and in some instances, men who had earlier bound themselves were named by the King to sit on the Governor's Council, a powerful body that provided advice to the chief executive.

Although some citizens had accumulated relatively large amounts of wealth, Virginia remained a socially mobile, nonaristocratic community of small farmers. Assigned status based on birth or riches was not an important factor in the society. Because survival was a shared struggle, the New World environment had created a closeness between residents that was unknown in the mother country.

It was into this intimate climate that Sir John Harvey, the royally appointed Governor, arrived in March of 1630. Harvey, described as a proper and somewhat "choleric" individual, was little prepared for the independent spirit that had been bred in the Virginians. Quickly, the regally-bent official became involved in a hateful, personal feud with Dr. John Pott, a local who had been serving as Acting Governor.

Pott's background was far different than that of the elegant Governor. The physician had not only been accused of conspiring to poison local Indians, but had been summoned into court on malpractice charges filed by Elizabeth Hamer. The settlerwoman alleged that she had suffered a miscarriage because of Pott's refusal to provide her with pieces of hog's flesh. The court found for Pott, suggesting that it was impossible that he could have known that Goodwife Hamer had "a longing" for the pork.

Attempting to silence his outspoken rival, Harvey charged Pott with felony in office by "pardoning wilfull murder, marking other men's cattle for his own and killing up their hogs." A speedy verdict of guilty was returned and the doctor's entire estate was confiscated on the Governor's order.

Virginians did not take kindly to Sir John's treatment of the colony's only physician, a man said to possess invaluable skills in curing the unique diseases of the planters and distilling strong waters. Elizabeth Pott was even more enraged and departed for England to seek redress for the harm imposed on her husband.

The public grumbling no doubt deterred Harvey from further abuse, for the Governor relented and suggested that Pott be given a royal pardon. In London, Commissioners for Virginia were unwilling to acknowledge that such forgiveness was necessary. Declaring that the physician had been poorly treated, the officials directed Harvey to rescind the confiscation decree and return what remained of the victim's property.

The unfavorable ruling did not prevent Harvey from alienating large segments of the plantation society and quarreling constantly with the Council. The Privy Lords, occupied with more pressing demands, grew weary of the incessant clashes. Sir John and the advisers were instructed to settle their differences and concentrate upon promoting the King's interests.

For a time, relations seemed to improve. On December 20, 1631, the feuding parties issued a joint communique announcing that all involved had agreed to "swallow up and bury" their disagreements. Despite the avowed intentions, the reconciliation was brief. Achieving a balance between the rights of royal government and the privileges of the people, Council and assembly, was not a simple task. The inherent conflict between crown prerogative and civil rights was a crucial issue that would trouble not only seventeenth century Virginia, but all American colonies from initial settlement until the 1776 revolution.

As a staunch royalist, Harvey did not see himself as a minor administrative officer appointed merely to enforce English directives. Instead, Sir John believed that governors were literally the "King's substitutes" who represented the monarch in absentia. This interpretation was consistent with the Stuart belief in the divine right of rulers. Although the absolutist theory was under attack in England by growing parliamentary opposition, many in the court party still clung to the philosophy that the King had been sacredly chosen to rule absolutely.

The rugged self-determinists of Virginia rejected the idea that a line of authority, that should not be questioned, ran from Harvey to the King to God. Instead of quietly acceding to Sir John's every wish, the people and Council grew increasingly irritated by the arrogance with which the official conducted his duties.

According to Councillor Samuel Mathews, government in the colony degenerated into Harvey's will. Justice was not that assured by the Magna Carta, but whatever exigency suited the King's substitute. Charges mounted against Sir John. It was alleged that his administration was arbitrary, corrupt and had resulted in the creation of widespread fear. In addition, it was charged that Harvey had illegally seized servants, disregarded property rights and usurped the powers of the assembly.

He purportedly infringed upon the privileges of the Burgess by confiscating correspondence between the legislature and the King. It was claimed Sir John had concluded an unwise peace with the Indians, imposed illegal taxes, demanded exorbitant fees and set excessive fines. Perhaps most offensive of all was Harvey's supposed assault on Councillor Richard Stephens, a popular Virginian whose teeth had been dislodged by the cudgel-wielding Governor.

Several criticisms against Harvey involved policy decisions made by the official that were far from illegal. The Governor's consistent support of a British monopoly over the province's tobacco trade was decried because of the severe economic losses that would result from the elimination of foreign competition. Second, Sir John had openly aided Lord Baltimore's settlers in nearby Maryland, a ''crime'' deemed most heinous by Virginians who deplored establishment of the Catholic colony. Jamestown Anglicans not only harbored fears of ''Papist plots,'' but believed that Baltimore's charter illegally appropriated territory that had been originally deeded to Virginia.

The Council's hostility against Baltimore was so ingrained, that when a royal order demanding cooperation between the two Chesapeake colonies was read in chambers, Mathews threw his hat to the floor, stomped upon it and shouted a curse on the sister province.

To the anger of subjects in the old colony, Sir John openly welcomed the Catholic arrivals, volunteered to send aid in times of difficulty and promised livestock so that new herds could be bred. Several advisers in Jamestown, notified of the order, vowed to kill their hogs rather than see the animals used by Popish agents who might rise up and massacre the Virginians at any moment.

Criticism of official policies such as the tobacco monopoly and the Maryland question was construed by Harvey as impudence bordering upon sedition. To condemn the King's substitute for implementing crown orders was a serious challenge to royal authority and the safety of the plantation. Discord reached a critical stage in the spring of 1635. Under the leadership of Francis Pott, brother of the physician, a series of public meetings was held at various plantations. During a gathering at York on April 5, citizens formalized their complaints by signing a list of grievances against the administration. According to some reports, participants at the meeting suggested that Harvey was conniving with the Indians to organize a massacre of white dissidents.

Reasoned compromise by both sides might have produced a peaceful solution to the problems that vexed the unhappy province. Mathews conceded that the dissidents had met in an "unlawful" manner, but the Councillor disclaimed that rebellion had been intended or even considered. The people, he suggested, had subscribed to the petition only in order to publicize their complaints.

Harvey chose to reject any action that might be construed as administrative surrender to public clamour. Arrest warrants were immediately issued against three leading opponents including Francis Pott. The trio was apprehended and clamped into irons at Jamestown. When the prisoners demanded to hear the charges against them, the enraged Governor curtly replied that they would learn of the accusations at the gallows.

Probably realizing that he would be unable to secure convictions in open court, Harvey brought the men before the Council on April 28. He demanded that the advisers endorse summary execution of the accused, as rebels. Such drastic waiving of civil rights was possible only during periods of martial law, an emergency situation that could be legally imposed by the Governor only in cases of imminent danger. The Councillors refused Harvey's ultimatum and instead began discussing the grievances that had brought about the citizens' unhappiness.

Sir John would not tolerate consideration of the people's complaints. The Council meeting deteriorated into rancor and an adjournment was called to quiet the heated atmosphere. When the group reconvened, there was no improvement in temper. As Councillor George Menefie discussed Harvey's infringement on the Burgess' prerogatives, all pretense of civility ended.

The Governor lashed out at Menefie, shouting that the Virginian was under arrest for treason against the King. Adviser John Utie leaped into the fray by arresting Harvey on similar charges. Other Councillors began wrestling with the Governor.

In the midst of the disarray, a band of fifty armed men under Captain William Pierce surrounded the chamber and the Governor was physically subdued. The rowdly session ended only when Sir John agreed to give up his post and return to England.

Details of Harvey's treatment following the stormy confrontation were subject to conflicting accounts. According to Mathews, Harvey requested that a guard be appointed for the "safety of his person." The council graciously complied with the plea and provided official protection so that the executive could leave Jamestown for The Mills, a plantation owned by William Brockas. Gossips suggested that Goodwife Brockas was more intimate with Sir John than was proper for a married woman.

Harvey disagreed with Mathews' version of events. In a letter to the Commissioners for Foreign Plantations, Sir John claimed that he had been unexpectedly attacked by a "mutinous company" of rogues that included his own Council. Not only was he rudely assaulted, but he was kept prisoner and rendered incapable of exercising any official duty. Harvey explained:

> . . . they caused guards to be set in all ways and passages, so that no man could travel or come from place to place, nor had I means or power to raise any force to suppress this meeting, they having restrained men and set a guard upon me.

The Governor had no intention of capitulating. While passage to England was being arranged, he attempted to undermine efforts being made to bring the Burgess into the quarrel on the side of the Council. When the assembly met to consider the situation, Harvey ordered the group to disperse on penalty of death for treason. The house refused and instead, approved a list of complaints against the deposed official together with an explanation of why the Governor had been "thrust out." It was decided that the documents would be taken to England and submitted to the Lords Commissioners as evidence that the removal of Harvey was not intended as rebellion against the crown.

The Virginians then turned attention to more practical matters of establishing a working government. On May 7, Captain John West, brother of Lord De la Warr, was chosen to act as interim Governor until a permanent successor could be named by Charles I. In a more militant maneuver, armed rangers were posted throughout Jamestown and on roads leading to the capital in case a counter revolt was attempted by Harvey's small circle of favorites.

In May, the Governor sailed for England aboard the same ship that carried Francis Pott and Thomas Harwood, a Virginia agent entrusted with the Burgess' correspondence. In addition to presenting the colony's complaints to English officials, Harwood would attempt to defend the province against any unfavorable reaction.

The Virginians did not act as decisively as the deposed Harvey. As soon as the vessel docked in Plymouth, Harvey arranged for the arrest of Pott and Harwood on charges of rebellion. The Burgess' resolutions and the people's grievances were confiscated by Sir John, who then set off to launch a campaign at court against the American dissidents.

To the Lord Commissioners, Harvey presented a self-serving narrative of the dismissal. The incident was described not as a limited action against Sir John Harvey, but as a revolt that threatened the very foundation of British rule. Each Councillor was labeled as a despicable rascal who acted for personal revenge or profit. Because no accusers appeared to refute the description or press legal charges against Harvey, the Governor was completely exonerated.

The King and Privy Council were probably less than elated with Harvey's administration. Whatever the Governor's defense, his actions in the plantations had created dissention, a condition often associated with a decline in royal revenues. Under routine circumstances, the official would have been replaced by a more capable appointee, but the forced deportation of the Governor had violated the most fundamental principle of royal supremacy. Not even the Governor of a colony was free to leave his assigned post without the expressed consent of the monarch. For a popular body to assume the power of expelling a crown designee was an insubordination that could not be ignored. It was imperative that the right of the crown over all officials be established without question. As a result, Sir John was given a new commission to return to Virginia as Governor. In addition, he was empowered to arrest those who had participated in the thrusting out.

Harvey arrived in America during January of 1637. Heeding threats that he would be shot on sight in Jamestown, the official established a temporary capital at Elizabeth City. Office-holders believed to be in sympathy with the so-called insurgents were dismissed from their posts and warrants were issued for the arrests of West, Menefie, Utie, Mathews and Pierce. After the men were apprehended and dispatched to London for trial, Sir John ordered the rebels' estates taken for the crown. Special attention was given to Mathews' holdings, worth an estimated £200,000. Harvey ordered that the livestock producer was to be left not "worth a cow's tail."

Defeat of the anti-Harvey faction encouraged the Governor to take punitive action against others who did not openly support the reestablished administration. Particularly tawdry was the prosecution of Anthony Panton, an Anglican clergyman who was tried on several bizarre charges including calling the Governor's secretary a "jackanapes." Because the secretary was assigned as Panton's prosecutor and judge, the churchman was found guilty. In punishment he was fined £500, banished from the colony on pain of death and sentenced to forfeit his entire estate.

In England, the accused rebels had managed to gain release on bond and joined by Panton, began publicizing their version of the Virginia controversy. The resulting propaganda was effective in making the Privy Council even more suspect of Harvey's behavior. Added to the Counsellors' protestations, were complaints by British merchants that trading ships were being charged illegal fees in the old colony.

Within months, all pretense of support for the royal appointee had eroded. Harvey was directed to return property taken from the supposed traitors. The Virginians were allowed to return home and Sir Francis Wyatt was named to replace Harvey as Governor.

Wyatt's arrival in Jamestown was greeted with great pleasure, an emotion that was magnified when Sir John was summoned into court to answer civil charges for damages brought by offended citizens. As a result of unfavorable verdicts, much of the ex-official's property was attached. In the spring of 1640, he notified an English friend: "I groan under the oppressions of my prevailing enemies . . . who are now advanced to be my judges, and have so far already proceeded against me as to tear from me my estate."

During Sir Francis' period in residence, a firm, mutual trust was established between the Governor, Council, Burgess and people. General confidence in English rule was restored and the future seemed bright for Britain's distant plantation. The outlook, however, was not as optimistic north of the Potomac.

# CHAPTER II

# Religion Stirs Foment

G EORGE CALVERT, the first Baron of Baltimore, did not intend that the founding of Maryland should create discord. Instead, the Irish peer hoped that his New World domain would be a haven of peace for all Christians unjustly persecuted for religious beliefs.

Service to mankind was an important, driving force for Calvert, a man of humble origins who had achieved high honors by diligent work for Britain, rather than through influential friends at court. In 1625, Calvert announced his conversion to Catholicism, and to avoid embarrassing James I, voluntarily resigned as Principal Secretary of State. He remained a trusted adviser of the King and an influential member of the Privy Council.

Upon succeeding to the throne, Charles I requested that Baltimore remain on the Council. Lord George refused, sensing that a tide of "anti-popery" was rising menacingly in England. Fearing that his presence might cause jealousies that would disrupt the body's effectiveness, the peer withdrew to devote full time to his blueprint for colonization.

The hazards of governing a province by absentee rule were well-known to Baltimore who had helped finance the Virginia Company. Calvert intended to insure that his own colony would not be rent by

resentment of foreign domination that had almost shattered Jamestown. To eliminate possible friction, Calvert planned a radical departure from accepted policy; he would move to America and live among
his provincials.

The site initially selected for Baltimore's experimental settlement
was an undeveloped tract called Avalon in what is now Newfoundland. By 1628, George Calvert was ready to join the small group
of settlers already located in the area. The stay of Baltimore and his
family was brief. A harsh winter and difficulties with neighboring
Frenchmen made colonization an impractical dream. In disappointment, Baltimore abandoned plans for Avalon after spending an estimated £30,000 on the project.

Hoping to discover a more suitable location for the religious utopia,
Baltimore went south to Jamestown during October of 1629. Word of
the peer's colonization plans preceded him and resentment was obvious at all levels. Thomas Tindall was sentenced to spend two hours in
the pillory for threatening to assault the Lord and members of the
Council were not above casting insults. When Baltimore refused to
take an oath acknowledging the King as the spiritual head of the nation, he was ordered to leave the province.

The sojourn had not been entirely unproductive. Calvert had become convinced that the mid-Atlantic area could easily sustain the
type of retreat he envisioned. He returned home, asking that a letters
patent be issued for a large block of uninhabited land north of the Potomac. The territory had originally been included in the Virginia Company grant, but had reverted to the crown when the corporation's
charter was revoked in 1624.

Objectors swiftly moved to protest the application. Virginians contended that the Maryland tract was irrevocably part of the old colony
and could not be redeeded. The Privy Council disagreed with the interpretation, but objected to the grant on the grounds that Baltimore's
charter delegated to the holder near regal powers that could be enjoyed
only by the King.

Charles rejected all arguments. The charter was sent on its way
through the tedious process of passing under various seals of state.

The decision to issue the charter was a pyrrhic victory, for neither
Baltimore nor his wife would return to the plantation christened Maryland in honor of Charles' queen Henrietta Maria. Lady Baltimore

passed away soon after leaving Virginia in 1631. A year later, George
Calvert died on April 15, just two months before the charter received
final verification.

By right of primogeniture, the land grant passed to George's eldest
son, Cecil Calvert. Despite the earlier objections, the final Maryland
charter retained what could have been interpreted as gross infringements upon the royal prerogative. Of greatest significance was the
inclusion of the "Bishop of Durham" clause, an instrument curiously
out of date in seventeenth century England.

The clause delegated to the holder, quasi-supreme powers of government and almost total ownership of land. When endorsed under the
Great Seal, the authorizations could not be checked by either King or
Parliament. The clause had been originally devised during the four-
teenth century when England's northernmost counties of Durham,
Lancaster and Chester were subjected to constant invasion by the
Scots. So that local authorities might cope with emergencies without
awaiting instructions from London, the presiding Bishop was given
near total authority to act in the place of the King. The investiture included such privileges as raising armies, conducting war, levying
taxes and controlling citizens under martial law. The possessor of such
powers became a virtual feudal lord.

To leave no doubt as to where authority was bestowed, the Maryland charter proclaimed Baltimore and his heirs as "True and Absolute
Lords and Proprietors," granted "free, full and absolute power."
Legal writs and processes were to be issued in the name of the Calverts, not of the King. The stipulation was more than a technicality,
for the allowance indicated that justice and law flowed from the Lords
Baltimore rather than from English customs or institutions.

Appeals from provincial decisions and confirmation of colonial
laws were placed under Calvert's jurisdiction, not under that of
Charles, Parliament or the English court system. In all legal cases,
decisions were to be made on the side most "beneficial, profitable and
favorable," to the Proprietor. Calvert was also empowered to establish
all courts, churches and towns. He could pardon any offense, grant
titles of nobility, raise armies, declare war, levy duties, impose taxes
and dispose of all land. He could, at will, call, adjourn or prorogue the
representative assembly.

The rights of soil conveyed by the charter were as extreme as the delegated rights of government. In a sweeping allowance, Baltimore was accorded:

> . . . all and singular the ports, harbors, bays, rivers and straits belonging to the region or islands aforesaid, and all the soil, plains, woods, mountains, marshes, lakes, rivers, bays and straits, or being within the metes, bounds and limits aforesaid, with the fishings of every kind of fish, as well of whales, sturgeons, or other royal fish . . . all veins, mines and quarries, as well opened as hidden, already found or that shall be found . . . of gold, silver, gems and precious stones . . . or of any other thing, or matter whatsoever. . . .

Only three clauses modified the absolute investiture of power. First, it was decreed that the laws of Maryland could not be repugnant nor contrary to British custom. If possible, statutes should be "agreeable" to those enacted by Parliament to govern the home isles. Second, although Baltimore was empowered to make laws, any measure involving life, limb or property was to be framed with the advice, consent and approbation of the majority of freemen or their representatives. Finally, Baltimore and his heirs were required to present the crown with one-fifth of all gold and silver mined in Maryland. As an act of obedience, the Proprietor was ordered to send a pair of Indian arrows to Windsor Castle each year on the Tuesday of Easter Week.

Cecil Calvert shared his father's hope that the province would become a shelter for the oppressed, but he did not agree that it was necessary for the Proprietor to live in the colony. Accordingly, the second Lord Baltimore named his brother Leonard as resident Governor. Leonard Calvert was given strict warning that under no circumstances was the colony to be torn by religious controversy. To insure that unity and peace prevailed, Catholics preparing to immigrate were instructed to worship privately and be silent in any discussion involving religion. The non-conformists were also ordered to give as little offense as possible to the Protestant majority. More practically, Leonard Calvert was warned to keep his ships out of range of the Virginia shore batteries.

Not all of those watching the preparations for colonization were solicitous of religious liberties. Opponents spread the alarm that the Marylanders might ally themselves with Catholic France or Spain to work against England's interests in the New World. Political intrigues

against the expedition were so blatant that it was feared the first immigrant ships would be sabotaged. Baltimore suggested that both the
passengers and the crew be questioned as to any plots that might have
been instigated by the proprietor's adversaries.

Baltimore's enemies were unable to prevent the departure of the
vessels *Ark* and *Dove,* but the November 1633 sailing did not go
unchallenged. Passengers were commanded to take an oath of allegiance to Charles I, and when it appeared that all had not been
sworn, the entire expedition was waylaid at Gravesend until the remaining colonists could be given the oath.

The extreme hardships that had hampered the 1607 adventurers did
not confront Maryland's first settlers. During the quarter century
separating the founding of the two colonies, regular supply routes had
been established between America and England. Adequate food and
supplies could be accurately projected, but more significant were the
attitudes of the later provincials. Unlike the Jamestown treasure seek-
ers, the Maryland pioneers were psychologically prepared for the toil
needed to survive in the New World.

A sheltered cove off of a Potomac tributary was chosen as the site
for St. Mary's, the colony's major village. Resident Yaocomicoe Indians, preparing to abandon the site, befriended the new provincials
and eagerly agreed to sell their farmlands and dwellings. Leonard Calvert and his charges assiduously obeyed Baltimore's admonition that
native Americans should be treated with dignity and respect. In accordance with the policy, Marylanders gave fair value for the property in
axes, rakes, cloth and hatchets.

A mutual feeling of honor was cemented that would last for decades. The good will that developed between English and Indian was
additionally fostered by Jesuit missionaries who left St. Mary's to
settle among the tribes.

It was soon clear that a white, rather than a red man constituted the
most immediate danger to Maryland. Unmistakably obvious was the
unfriendly presence of William Claiborne, a Virginia trader whose agitation and rebellion against Baltimore would disrupt the colony for
nearly thirty years. The basic cause of the dissident's machinations
never changed. Claiborne was convinced that the Chesapeake territory
was his and that Baltimore was merely an illegal encroacher.

In 1621, Claiborne arrived in Jamestown from England with a commission as Surveyor-General. The post was an important and lucrative one, secured with the help of powerful interests in court circles. Scientifically measured boundary lines were largely unknown in the old colony and disputes over land titles were of growing concern. The imminent lifting of the Virginia Company's charter made it even more imperative that clear demarcation be established in the tidewater.

Claiborne's rise in society was rapid. Within three years, the surveyor had been named to the Governor's Council. In 1626, he received a royal appointment as Secretary of Virginia.

Despite his success in the political world, economic prosperity eluded Claiborne. He decided to aim for greater rewards than surveying fees could provide and chose as an avenue to riches, the field of Indian trade, an area where high profits often sprang from modest investments. Claiborne envisioned himself as the master of a vast commercial empire comprised of frontier stations where Indians from distant tribes could barter otter, beaver, mink and muskrat pelts. In exchange for the furs, the red men would be offered an assortment of truck such as glass beads, rings, nails, pins, mirrors and fishhooks. The furs would be shipped to England and sewn into garments to protect the gentry from the icy British winters.

From 1627 to 1631, Claiborne received several licenses from Virginia governors to conduct trading operations in remote areas. After a series of trips to the outlands, he selected Chesapeake Bay as the most promising location. He decided to establish outposts along the waterway, and lure the Susquehannoch trade from the Dutch in New Netherlands.

Things progressed well for the surveyor. Other traffickers also had designs on the Bay, but these competitors lacked the political connections in Virginia that were needed to obtain trading monopolies. Claiborne, who remained on the Council, was able to secure the choicest locations.

But just as the Englishman's fortune seemed assured, rumors began circulating that the Chesapeake might be granted by the King to Lord Baltimore. Claiborne left for Britain in early 1630 in an attempt to halt approval of the Maryland charter and secure title for himself. Despite well-placed connections, he was unable to prevent issuance of the deed. He did, however, secure backing for his trading venture from the London firm of Cloberry and Company and managed to obtain a commercial monopoly issued under a minor government seal. The authorization was of little import when contrasted with Baltimore's charter embossed with the Great Seal.

In August of 1631, Claiborne arrived back in America with a large cargo of Indian truck and a group of indentured servants. His strategy was to establish an impregnable garrison in Maryland before Baltimore's claim could receive final approval. If a working plantation could be set up, its boundaries might be exempted from Baltimore's jurisdiction if the charter specifically excluded "hactenus inculta" or land already under cultivation.

Claiborne landed his party at Kent Island, a strategically placed isthmus halfway up the Bay. After purchasing the tract from local Indians, he frantically began constructing buildings and clearing fields. The task of taming the wilderness was not a simple one. Fire destroyed a storehouse in which trade goods were kept. Threats from unfriendly tribes necessitated a constant guard. Malaria swept through the laborers, depleting the work force.

Other developments were more favorable. The Virginia Council declared that Kent Island was part of the old colony and thus not subject to Baltimore's control. The Burgess accepted a representative from the Island and recognized Kent as a Virginia "hundred." In 1632, Harvey arrested Claiborne's chief rival, Captain Henry Fleet, for illegally trading in the Chesapeake. The master of Kent Island was now left in control of the Bay, but Fleet would soon seek revenge.

While Claiborne was busily preparing for the arrival of Maryland's first colonists, the Proprietor was considering the most effective means for subduing the uninvited tenant. Baltimore concluded that the intiial strategy should be a conciliatory one.

Leonard Calvert was instructed to send a polite message to Kent Island as soon as possible after the *Ark* and *Dove* had dropped anchor. Claiborne was to be courteously assured that his land title would be accepted and his trading privileges recognized as soon as he swore allegiance to Baltimore. In addition, Calvert was authorized to bestow on the trader the Lord's total love and affection.

Bouquets of admiration were of little concern to the former surveyor who refused all overtures and denied that the Proprietor possessed any rights of control over either Kent Island or commerce on the Chesapeake. Claiborne contended that the Island was historically and legally a part of Virginia and was his by right of Indian purchase. As further proof of ownership, he put forth the English trading authorization.

Baltimore had anticipated such a negative response and had instructed Governor Calvert to ignore the interloper for one year. Calvert turned to more immediate problems, but within months William Claiborne once again became the center of controversy.

Friendly relations between Marylanders and local Indians were unexpectedly imperiled by rumors that the Patuxents were preparing for war against the whites. Instead of automatically arming for battle, Calvert dispatched an emissary to the tribe so that the reasons for the sudden aggressiveness could be discovered.

Captain Henry Fleet was selected for the task. Fleet had been of invaluable help to the colonists and was particularly well chosen for the role of Indian ambassador. In the early 1620's, Fleet had been captured on the Potomac by the Anacostans and held for ransom. During the years in which he lived with the tribe as a prisoner, the trader became thoroughly familiar with the customs and languages of most native Marylanders.

After interrogating the Patuxents, Fleet returned to St. Mary's with disturbing news. According to the Captain, William Claiborne had been spreading false reports among the tribe and urging the warriors to rise up against the capital. Claiborne had supposedly insisted that Baltimore's colonists were Spanish fiends come to steal Indian goods, take land and commit widespread atrocities. As proof, the wily trader had pointed to the similarities between the religious rites of the Maryland Catholics and those of the Spanish.

Fellow trafficker Thomas Yong corroborated the notion that a plot existed and implicated high office holders in Virginia. John Harvey, who was rapidly becoming disenchanted with Claiborne agreed that a joint Virginia-Maryland commission should be organized to investigate the entire matter.

In June of 1634, the Patuxents were examined by the commissioners who arrived at a far different finding than that of Captain Fleet. Instead of condemning Claiborne for deception, the investigators accused Fleet of manipulating the facts to gain revenge on his old adversary.

Despite the exoneration of the Kent Islander, the incident proved damaging to Claiborne's reputation and career. In December he was replaced as Secretary of Virginia, and in Maryland he came under even closer scrutiny, for many believed him guilty of conspiring to inflame the Patuxents. Baltimore's patience, too, came to an end. Leonard Calvert was ordered to arrest Claiborne and take control of the encroacher's plantation, but before the instructions could be implemented, the Governor confiscated the Kent Island pinnace *Long Trail* for illegally trading in proprietary waters. Although the ship was retained, its captain, Thomas Smith, was released.

Claiborne retaliated by arming the vessel *Cockatrice* and ordering skipper Ratcliffe Warren to capture all boats putting out from St. Mary's. The action escalated. Calvert dispatched the *St. Helen* and the *St. Margaret* to halt Warren's raids. On April 23, 1635, the three vessels met in the Pocomoke River on the eastern shore. Results of the engagement were mixed. Claiborne's ship was taken. Warren and two other Kent Islanders were killed. The battle, however, breathed new life into the insurgents.

On May 10, the *St. Margaret* was captured by Thomas Smith in a Claiborne-owned raider. The boat's rich cargo of pelts and trading goods was confiscated as a prize of war and during the confrontation, a loyalist crewman was slain by the attackers.

The Virginia Council continued to endorse the rebellion against St. Mary's. Maryland was beginning to provide economic competition and Jamestowners believed that the large concentration of Catholics constituted a dangerous menace. Land speculators, resentful that such a potentially profitable tract had been removed from their grasp, joined in opposition. Baltimore's authority under the charter to declare war also prompted resentment in the old colony. It was feared by the Virginians, bound by traditional policy that only the King might wage foreign war, that the old colony would be unwillingly involved in one of the Proprietor's private intrigues.

As might have been anticipated, Governor Harvey applauded Baltimore's repression of Claiborne. Sir John was determined to enforce royal orders calling for cooperation in the region and he announced that all who refused to comply with the directive might be called to London to explain their disobedience. Several Councillors retorted that if the King was dissatisfied with their behavior, then he would have to come to Virginia to change it.

Despite continued resistance, Governor Calvert gradually gained ascendancy in the Bay. Claiborne was forced to flee to Jamestown where local authorities refused Maryland's requests for extradition. When the situation cooled in the north, Claiborne returned to Chesapeake waters and resumed trading.

A new face appeared on the scene in December of 1636 with the arrival on Kent Island of George Evelin, agent for Cloberry and Company, the English investors in the local trading operation. Evelin, a man of great ambition, attempted to unseat Claiborne, but was unable to gain the support of island residents. The Britisher appealed to Harvey for assistance and the Virginia Governor was eager to move against the trader who has assisted in the 1635 "thrusting out." In June, Harvey authorized Evelin to confiscate Claiborne's boats and goods in satisfaction of debts owed the London stockholders. The timing of the order was propitious, for Claiborne had departed for England to press claims against Baltimore.

Again Evelin was unable to win the loyalty of the Kent Islanders. When inhabitants refused to acknowledge Evelin as head of the plantation, he appealed to Leonard Calvert for help. Like Harvey, Calvert was anxious to provide aid, for Evelin appeared to be the means of ending the on-going rebellion that had for too long diverted attention from more important matters.

In December, Calvert with a band of musketeers, crossed the Bay, captured Claiborne's plantation and announced that henceforth, challenges to the Proprietor's rule would not be tolerated. Evelin was issued a commission as Commander of the island, and residents were forced to elect delegates to the St. Mary's assembly.

The peace was only temporary. By spring it was obvious that the rebels would accept neither Evelin nor Baltimore. Calvert learned that Thomas Smith of the *Long Tail,* and John Boteler, Claiborne's brother-in-law, had gone to Palmer's Isle at the head of the Bay to rouse the Susquehannochs into attacking St. Mary's. The Governor set out again, and was able to apprehend the troublemakers. Both men were paroled, a leniency that proved a major error. Within weeks, rebellion had broken out again on Kent Island.

A third expedition was organized. This time the Proprietor's force was successful in imposing Maryland rule on the Chesapeake plantation. Thomas Smith was apprehended and hanged for piracy and murder in connection with the *St. Margaret* incident. The assembly, labeling Claiborne as a ''notorious and insolent'' rebel, attaindered the Kent Island property for Baltimore.

On April 4, Claiborne received an additional blow when the Commissioners of Foreign Plantations rejected his claims and upheld Baltimore's title to Maryland's land and trading privileges. The arena of action moved to the English courts in a tangle of lawsuits involving Baltimore, Claiborne and Cloberry. On October 29, 1639, the London investors submitted documents showing that much more than principle had been involved in the Chesapeake arrangement. During the six years of operation, investments in trading truck had totaled £1,571. By bartering these goods, Claiborne had been able to obtain pelts and other Indian merchandise worth more than £5,000. In addition, significant profits had been made in New England where several thousand pounds of Indian corn had been sold. Despite constant warfare with Baltimore and extended periods in which trading had been suspended, the return on investment had been nearly five hundred percent.

Claiborne temporarily gave up the struggle to have Baltimore's charter annulled. He returned to Virginia in the spring of 1640 and settled near Elizabeth City. The trader, however, had no intention of forgiving the supposed wrongs committed by the owner and the Governor of Maryland. His rebellion was just beginning.

Tolerance of dissent, such as that shown by Baltimore during the early days of Claiborne's disturbances, was unknown on the rocky coast of the north. Leaders of New England showed no sympathy for citizens who deviated from the official way. Disagreement was not condoned. The government was indisputable. New England's saints refused to allow the faithful to become infected by words of rebellion.

Immigrant Puritans had created a private utopia in Massachusetts Bay, a holy experiment under the protection of God rather than the English government. Citizens believed that authority in the corporate province was derived from the consent of the governed and that the people's covenant would remain long after temporal leaders in London had passed away.

Because government and religion were inextricably bound in philosophy, a challenge to one was considered a threat to the other. It was imperative that both remain unquestioned if the vital work of the enclaves was to be accomplished.

From the first, the Massachusetts saints believed that God had led them to America on a sacred mission. Their outpost would always be under divine oversight and would serve as an example to Europeans of how life should be lived. Naturally, the religious state would be governed by laws formulated through the vote of "elected" church members, not by imposition of Parliamentary statutes. The divine right of Anglican kings had no place in Massachusetts ideology where only God ruled without the approval of the people.

Puritan ministers and officials constantly preached the moral necessity of citizen government. John Winthrop wrote: "No commonwealth can be founded, but by free consent." Reverend John Cotton echoed the theme by declaring: ". . . there is a covenant and oath between prince and people." It was obvious that if the oath was broken by the prince, then the people were under a sacred obligation to rebel and form a new, more holy arrangement.

Only a tiny minority did not share the stern message of the Puritans. Those who deviated from the saints' concepts were quickly punished as opponents to both the government and the church. Suppression of dissension was simpler in New England villages than in the South where residents were scattered among remote plantations and often immune from government supervision.

Thomas Morton, known as the "Lord of Misrule," was one of the first to feel the heavy hand of Puritan control. Morton's initial infraction was not open rebellion, but merely the encouragement of revelry at his Merrymount plantation.

The raucous cavorting that took place at Merrymount between Morton's disciples offended distressed onlookers at nearby Plymouth. William Bradford was particularly disgusted when the celebrants set up a Maypole and began: "drinking and dancing about it . . . inviting the Indian women for their consorts, dancing and frisking together (like so many fairies or furies rather), and worse practices."

More unsettling were suggestions that Morton was financing the bawdy affairs by selling guns and powder to local Indians. Despite warnings to desist, Morton refused to curtail either the festivities or the Indian traffic. In desperation, the saints ordered militia Captain Miles Standish to eliminate the threat by force.

Morton would not consider peacefully submitting to the dictates of officials who lacked legal jurisdiction over Merrymount. As the Puritan force approached, the chief celebrant retreated into his house, and according to Bradford stood "stiffly in his defense, having made fast his doors, armed his consorts, set divers dishes of powder and bullets ready on the table. . . ."

As both sides surveyed the situation, Morton made a quick change of strategy. Instead of remaining on the defensive, the merrymakers poured from the house ready for battle. Fortunately for the Puritans, the carousers were so "steeled with drink," that none was able to raise his heavy gun into firing position. Only a single casualty occurred. A member of the Merrymount contingent nearly cut off his own nose by staggering into a sword held by a companion.

Standish successfully scattered the erstwhile rebels and arrested Morton, suggesting that the prisoner was a dangerous insurgent who should be hanged. Instead, Morton was shipped back to England and the detested Maypole was chopped down. When the exile returned to renew the festivities in 1629, Merrymount was set afire. Morton was deported for a second time.

Equally severe punishment was meted out to those who verbally challenged established authority. For speaking "wickedly and boldly against the government and the governor," servant Philip Ratcliff was whipped, fined 40s and mutilated by having both ears cut off. Job Tyler, who declared he "car'd not a fart" for official directives, was whipped until his back was bloody. Physician Robert Child was imprisoned on charges of sedition for merely submitting a remonstrance of complaints against the arbitrary administration.

Predictably, the saints who so firmly repressed even the slightest indication of dissent, showed no hesitation in challenging undesirable policies of the British government. As a result, it was the Massachusetts theocrats, not the rugged Virginians or Catholic Marylanders, who emerged as the first group of colonials to rebel against England.

The persecution imposed on religious dissenters in Britain left an unhealed wound on the Puritans. As a result, the New Englanders cherished their 1629 charter for Massachusetts Bay as an almost holy document that guaranteed religious conscience could never again be denied. The patent, issued to twenty-six individuals, became symbolic that British interference in the affairs of the colony would not be tolerated.

The almost obsessive reliance upon the patent created an ambiguity that most Puritans chose to ignore. In theory, Massachusetts leaders denied that temporal English power could be imposed on the covenant. In practice, the Puritans relied upon just such authority to defend local rights of government and religion. In 1634, this contradictory ideology was put to the test when the Privy Council embarked on a course of confrontation that ultimately forced the Bay residents into authorizing war against the mother country.

Allegations of misrule in Massachusetts had reached English officials soon after the first footholds were taken in New England. As early as December 19, 1632, the Privy Council directed that the Massachusetts charter should be examined to determine if abuses had occurred or if the King's interests had been harmed as a result of its issuance. Critics alleged that the Puritans were plotting to rebel against the crown and cast off allegiance to Britain. It was said that agitation by the clergy lay behind the political unrest.

By direction of the King, all complaints were dismissed. Charles also refused to order rites of the Anglican church imposed on residents of the Bay. Stuart publicly based his decisions on the historical principle that it was just such restrictions that had prompted the immigrants to leave their homeland. A more practical rationale was that Massachusetts was becoming profitable to England. It was in the best interests of the crown, that the province's hard-working citizens be kept contented and gratified at the generosity of the monarch.

Tensions between Puritans and foes of the theocratic state continued to build. On February 21, 1634, the Privy Council ordered that several shiploads of immigrants bound for the Bay should be held on the Thames. Behind the embargo was the London belief that the colony was already a hotbed of "ill-affected and discontented" persons who needed no new disruptive influences. In an effort to improve provincial government and end the confusion, Massachusetts leaders were instructed to return the 1629 charter so that the document could be studied for possible modification.

Governor John Winthrop refused to surrender the patent and explained that only the colony's General Court could authorize such an important step. Until that body could consider the matter, Winthrop was compelled to reject the British command. Local radicals saw the Privy Council's announced intention as a subterfuge to conceal the fact that a plan had already been formulated to revoke the charter and unite

New England under a single governor. Such a maneuver, of course, would doom the Puritan experiment.

Physical possession of legal documents was considered essential during the seventeenth century. Although a primitive system of record keeping had been developed, original charter documents were vastly more credible than copies. Massachusetts officials may have believed that the only existing record of the charter was that held in the Bay. Without being able to examine the instrument, English courts would be unable to legally justify revocation of the document. Whatever the cost, it was deemed vital that the saints keep the charter in America and out of the hands of the British.

The imprint of the Great Seal assured that colonial charters, such as the Massachusetts patent, were immune from capricious demands or arbitrary revocation by either the crown or Parliament. The instruments could be overturned only after a court of justice found that the person to whom the charter had been issued had not complied with its terms, or that the document itself had been illegally issued. When such a ruling was handed down, the parchment could be declared vacated under a writ of *quo warranto*.

The General Court, meeting in September, proved as unwilling to give up the document as had been Governor Winthrop. Instead of complying with the British order, the body began preparing for war. It was declared that forts should be erected in Charlestown, Dorchester and on Castle Island in Boston Harbor. Militia officers were directed to begin rigorous training of soldiers. Government officials were instructed to "consult, direct and give command" for battle tactics that would be necessary if hostilities broke out. Plans for maintaining a central arsenal were undertaken.

The show of belligerency was met with silence in England, but the colonials did not interpret the lack of response as a sign of capitulation on the issue of charter recall. Efforts to strengthen New England's defenses were accelerated. Men were impressed to work on forts. A beacon was set up at Boston to alert the militia in case an English invasion fleet was sighted. Guns were ordered mounted at the Castle fort. A freeman's oath to support the province was extracted from all eligible males. A military commission was established to coordinate all war efforts.

In January of 1635, the rebellion was formally recognized when the

Governor and Assistants voted to resist with violence, all British attempts to seize the charter and impose a royally appointed governor.

Official John Endecott was not satisfied with the martial measures being taken and insisted that the cross of St. George should be cut from the King's ensign. According to the somewhat eccentric Endecott, the design was a sign of popery and idolatry that the Puritans were obligated to fight at all times.

More moderate residents were not ecstatic at Endecott's directive. The action was deemed indiscreet and possibly incendiary to English pride. The radical was censored and barred from holding office for one year, but the cross remained omitted from local militia flags. In a further concession to orthodox Puritans, the crown ensign was forbidden in all locations except the Castle fort.

In June of 1635, more than a year after the original request for the charter had been made, the home office finally reacted to the sword rattling in Massachusetts. A writ of *quo warranto* was issued by the King's Bench against the original patentees of the Massachusetts Bay Company. Because it was believed that the Court's deputies had no jurisdiction outside of England, notice of the process was not served on local officials in Massachusetts.

Despite the many complaints that had been lodged against Puritan rule, the *quo warranto* was not primarily based on abuses of power. Instead, the action pivoted upon the contention that the charter had been illegal from the beginning or *ab initio*. According to English lawyers, the patent had unlawfully delegated rights to the Company that could not have legitimately passed into private hands.

Corporation members argued vehemently against the writ, but the court found for the crown. The Privy Council once more advised American leaders to surrender the document, but provincials again refused. The official stance was that notice of the hearing had not been served in the colony, and therefore residents had been deprived of the right to reply to charges. For that reason, the court's decision would not be recognized as binding in Massachusetts.

On April 4, 1638, the Lords Commissioners joined the fray by firing off still another command to the recalcitrant Americans. If the patent was not immediately returned, the Lords would "move his Majesty to reassume into his hands the whole plantation."

The Puritans paid no heed to the threat. Royal assumption would be no worse a penalty than the consequences of obeying the court order. The result in both instances would be the loss of the charter. Delay, however, might bring different results. The internal situation in England was growing tumultuous. Both the crown and the Privy Lords were rapidly losing authority as the nation teetered on civil war. The provincials had seen no evidence of punishment for their insubordination. No regional governor or British fleet had appeared despite the refusal to obey a direct order from the King.

On September 6, the General Court framed a reply to the English demands that left little doubt that the third request for the charter would also be rejected. The answer denied that any justification existed for relinquishing the patent and proclaimed that such a drastic action would have dire effects on the plantation. Massachusetts would be exposed to ruin and its citizens branded as "runnigadoes" and outlaws incapable of producing a fit society. In addition, the recall would cast in doubt the veracity of other royal commitments and make the word of the crown suspect.

Perhaps the most incisive thrust was the provincial suggestion that other nations would "speedily embrace" the colonials of New England. The assertion was a thinly veiled threat that if England abused the provinces, Holland, Spain and France stood ready to offer more kindly treatment. The address concluded:

> Lastly, if our patent be taken from us . . . the common people here will conceive that his Majesty hath cast them off, and that hereby, they are freed from their allegiance and subjection, and thereupon, will be ready to confederate themselves under a new government, for their necessary safety and subsistence, which will be of dangerous example to other plantations, and perilous to ourselves of incurring his Majesty's displeasure, which we would by all means avoid.

> Upon these considerations we are bold to renew our humble supplications to your Lordships that we may be suffered to live here in this wilderness, and that this poor plantation, which hath found more favor from God than many others, may not find less favor from your Lordships. . . .

Rebuffed again, unwilling to send the royal fleet to America when the vessels might be required at home, and hesitant to further inflame British Puritans, the Lords of the Privy Council and Foreign Plantations abandoned the effort to recall the Massachusetts charter. The colony had prepared for rebellion, but the victory had come through peaceful, not violent means.

The reluctance of Britain to punish the disobedient colonists was primarily due to preoccupation with domestic emergencies in the mother country. Behavior that might have been deemed rebellious in more passive times was increasingly ignored as the fourth decade of the century approached. Opposing factions in England had moved beyond the point of discord. From the channel to the highlands, competing interests were readying for civil war.

Since the death of Elizabeth, the island nation had undergone profound changes in economics, politics and religion, changes that had not been matched by adjustments in the distribution of power. England half a century after the Virgin Queen, was a vastly different realm than the country that had only narrowly defeated the Spanish Armada. No longer was Britain a dominion in which wealth was concentrated in the hands of a small, landed aristocracy. Trade and overseas expansion had brought a new, commercially-oriented class to the fore.

The shift in emphasis from a rural, agricultural society to an urban, commercial economy had resulted in few political gains for the newly rich. Although many tradesmen boasted riches greater than the King's noble advisers, few were included in policy making positions. As a result, the country faction had emerged as a viable force against the court party.

The two Stuart monarchs, supported by the aristocracy, sought to maintain the status quo in politics by iron-fisted techniques and claims of divine right. Custom and an outmoded system of archaic laws tended to reinforce the hard-line stance, but ever deepening cracks began to appear in the façade.

Despite stringent requirements for voting, representatives of the emerging classes managed to gain significant representation in Commons. Recognition of this strength was not forthcoming from the court that continued to refuse meaningful concessions. Government remained dominated by a handful of loyalist advisors led by George Villiers, the despised Duke of Buckingham. Religion remained Anglican, a faith considered little better than papist by the Puritans and Presbyterians of the commercial classes.

Commons did hold one powerful weapon against the King. For a century, the purse had been acknowledged as the domain of Parliament and dissenters well understood the might of the tool.

Since the middle ages when a large percentage of the nation's wealth was held by the crown, it had been the duty of the reigning monarch to finance government and wage war from royal coffers. Although this system of finance became obsolete after the emergence of England as a major power, no permanent means of revenue allocation was adopted to insure that the crown would have long-range funding capabilities. Instead, Parliament remained content to make short-term appropriations on a piecemeal basis. Commons had no intention of presenting the King with a permanent income so that the monarch might rule "of his own," without the advice of the legislature.

By requiring constant renewal of taxing authority, Commons assured that the King would be forced to call Parliament at reasonable intervals. A major exception to the practice of short term financing was the tonnage and poundage tax traditionally voted for life to each ruler at the beginning of his reign.

Control over sources of revenue had been repeatedly used by Commons to force royal concessions, but the power was not unchallengeable. To combat stingy assemblies and unfriendly Parliaments, the King was empowered to dissolve assemblies and call for new elections in the hope that the voters would return representatives that were more sympathetic to the monarchy. A Parliament favorable to the court could be continued indefinitely with years or even decades passing before new elections were finally ordered.

From the beginning of the seventeenth century, monarchs attempted to avoid dependence upon Parliament by selling huge tracts of royal lands. Much of this property passed to the new country gentry creating a major redistribution of property. To compensate for the loss of revenue and feudal dues from lands thus disposed, the crown was forced to find new fund-raising methods. James I, for example, created the title of Baronet and commanded that all eligible citizens must purchase the distinction. During his twenty-four-year reign, a total of 2,323 such titles were sold at a significant profit to the King. In less successful attempts, the crown sought to impose new and sometimes blatantly illegal duties or customs. The burden of these levies frequently fell heaviest upon the anti-crown factions.

Although signs of vexation had been obvious during the rule of

James I, it was the irretractable behavior of his son Charles that turned discontent into civil war. The second Stuart was a particularly arrogant monarch who had not originally been slated to inherit the throne. He unexpectedly acceded to the line after the death of his elder brother Henry Frederick. Frederick allegedly died after contracting a chill during a tennis match, but it was rumored by Stuart enemies that Charles had dispatched his sibling by poisoning.

From the beginning of Charles' reign in 1625, disquiet mounted on every side. As an absolutist, the King interpreted Parliament's demands for increased power as ludicrous and dangerous. In 1626, he dissolved Parliament because of the body's attempt to impeach Lord Buckingham. The assembly had also irritated the monarch by refusing to vote perpetual tonnage and poundage. The Commons had offered to delegate the authority for only one year at a time.

The assassination of Buckingham removed one area of conflict and in 1629 Parliament was again summoned. Bickering on the King's authority to levy taxes broke out immediately and Charles angrily gave orders that the group be dissolved. His declaration, however, was not automatically obeyed. In an unprecedented move, anti-monarchists physically restrained the speaker until Commons had completed its business. Only then was the official allowed to read the order of dissolution.

For more than a decade, Charles refused to summon Parliament back into session. Instead, he governed completely without the assembly in what was known as the "Eleven Years Tyranny." Only after the outbreak of a Scottish rebellion in 1640, did the King relent. His treasury was empty. The realm's continuance was imperiled. Vast sources of new funds were urgently needed.

The decade of dissolution had brought no significant alterations in the outlook of Commons. The question of Parliamentary supremacy versus crown prerogative remained the dominant and unresolved issue. After just three weeks, the 1640 Commons, known as the "Short Parliament," was dissolved.

Six months later Charles was near destitute. The purse finally proved more powerful than the independence of the crown. Stuart was forced to call elections and suffer while a tide of reform poured forth from the new Commons.

The "Long Parliament" would sit for nearly twenty-three years and survive the King himself. Presbyterians and Puritans held decisive power over the Anglicans, and sensing victory, the dissenters pressed radical changes that severely crippled the sovereign's authority. The King initially accepted the measures, but was finally spurred to action by gossip that the Commons intended to impeach Queen Henrietta Maria, his Catholic consort and the sister of Louis XIII.

Charles refused to tolerate further transgressions. In January of 1642 he personally invaded Commons with a band of soldiers in an attempt to arrest five anti-government leaders. The men had been forewarned and managed to flee, but the breach of Parliamentary rights alienated even moderates in the body. When the King endeavoured to dissolve the group, members ignored the command, maintaining that it was impossible for a monarch to adjourn Commons without prior consent of the body.

The opposing forces garnered men and supplies. In June, Parliament approved a revolutionary document entitled the *"Nineteen Propositions,"* that stripped Charles of virtually all royal powers including control over the courts, army, Privy Council and executive officers. Charles refused to accept the *Propositions* and on October 23, 1642, the first great battle of the English Civil War took place at Edge Hill. Combatants from throughout Britain rushed to join the fray. The precise composition of the belligerents was not absolute, but generally, the King's Cavaliers were Anglican or Catholic nobles from northern and western agricultural areas. Joining these aristocrats were the very poor, who would not benefit significantly from any change, but who were surviving under the existing government.

Arrayed against the monarchists were the Roundheads of Parliament: Puritans and Presbyterians from the commercial and trading cities of the south and east. Small farmers occasionally assisted the Parliamentarians in actions such as the Battle of Bradford when local yeomen armed with scythes fought hand to hand against the Cavaliers for eight hours.

In order to preserve his kingdom, Charles took to the field, leading his troops in battle and overseeing major strategy. Henrietta Maria was not to be outdone. The Queen undertook a vital mission to Holland where she exchanged the royal jewels for arms and troops. Returning to England, she assumed the title of "Her, She Generalissima," and took up the royal standard. In one proceeding, she successfully led

4, 000 foot and horse across the British midlands to reinforce the main Cavalier army.

The tumult that captivated England was not contained by the sea. Discord spread to the New World and became particularly acute in Maryland. The advent was most unfortunate, for in 1643, Leonard Calvert had left the colony to consult with his brother. Giles Brent, owner of a large plantation on Kent Island, had been left in control.

Baltimore, perhaps realizing as a result of Claiborne's rebellion that revolts could be dangerous, had provided strong deterrents to future insurrections. It had been decreed that a woman convicted of treason would suffer death by burning, while a male found guilty of the same crime would be hanged, drawn and quartered. Treason perpetrated by a titled Lord or Lady would result in beheading.

Increased penalties had also been adopted for actions tending to promote rebellion. Conspiring the death of, or attempting violence against, the Proprietor or governor was made a capital crime. Death could also result from conspiring with a declared enemy of the province or rising in arms against the Baltimore rule. Insubordination against the courts demonstrated by striking a law officer, magistrate or witness, would result in the loss of the offender's right hand.

The uneasiness of Chesapeake settlers was magnified in 1644 by news that the Susquehannochs were foraying on the frontier. An added disruption was the old Catholic-Protestant rivalry that had been revived and was being exploited by the anti-proprietary faction. One of the most active troublemakers was Captain Richard Ingle, described variously as a rebel, pirate and a friend of William Claiborne.

Ingle was a tobacco trader who had done business in the colony for at least two years. As a representative of London merchants, Ingle was a staunch supporter of those who had risen up against the King. During a business voyage to St. Mary's in 1643, Ingle had been arrested by Giles Brent for speaking seditiously and treasonously against Charles. While the prisoner was under restraint, Brent with a party of deputies, boarded Ingle's ship the *Reformation* lying peacefully at anchor.

The Marylanders asked Ingle's crew to swear an oath in support of the crown, and when all hands refused, Brent set a guard over the vessel, confiscated the cargo of arms, and nailed a notice of seizure to the mast. With the help of Thomas Cornwallis, a well-placed supporter of

Baltimore and one of the first three Councillors named to assist the Governor, Ingle managed to escape, retake his ship and depart for England. He arrived home declaring that Calvert's representatives had offered the *Reformation's* company bribes to mutiny and turn the ship over to the King's supporters.

Charles had not ignored the activities of Puritan-leaning captains such as Ingle. The wily shippers were succeeding in pouring funds and supplies into the reserves of the Parliamentarians. To halt this danger to the Cavalier efforts, a royal decree was issued that ordered the governors of Virginia and Maryland to seize any ships in Virginia waters that were owned by London merchants or by those in rebellion against the monarchy. One-half of the proceeds of the prizes could be kept by local authorities, and the remaining fifty percent was to be sent to England to support the royal cause.

The directive was not welcomed by Marylanders who were almost totally dependent upon London traders for the export of tobacco and the import of supplies. Baltimore chose to disregard the King's instruction and announced that all shippers would be free to continue trading in the Chesapeake without fear of apprehension.

Ingle was not pacified by the assurance. Instead, he obtained a Parliamentary Letter of Marque, popularly known as a ''thieving letter.'' Such documents had long been issued to private parties in order to stimulate confiscation of enemy ships during wartime. In practice, the letters had become virtual licenses for piracy.

The Captain returned to America in February of 1645, empowered to take all ships and cargo owned by interests who opposed Parliament. After completing a routine trading operation in Virginia, the Captain decided to make use of the letter by launching an attack on Maryland. His sailors, promised a share of the booty, eagerly supported the venture and a force of Virginia mercenaries was recruited to assist in the operation.

On February 24, Ingle arrived off St. Mary's to begin what would be called the ''plundering time,'' or Ingle's Rebellion. The first target of the privateers was the Dutch ship *Speagle,* a trading vessel at anchor with a cargo of sugar, liquor and hats worth 2,338 guilders. Without warning, the boat was captured by a force from the *Reformation* and claimed as a prize. Giles Brent, who happened to be aboard during the raid, was imprisoned.

The party moved on to the capital where the Proprietor's government was expelled and the defensive garrison was reduced. Houses of prominent Catholics were looted and burned before the raiders fanned out to invade plantations farther inland.

Ingle's rebels appeared to follow a set procedure. First, houses were plundered and then set to the torch. Tobacco crops were seized, livestock driven off and servants urged to revolt. Thomas Cornwallis, who had aided Ingle's escape the previous year, was not excluded from the looters' wrath. According to Cornwallis, when the scavengers reached his manor, every possession except his wife's bed was stolen. Not satisfied with appropriating the movable items, the marauders also took the locks from the doors and the glass from the windows.

Ingle attempted to arrest Leonard Calvert as the Governor returned from England, but the Proprietor's brother managed to reach safety in Virginia. Many of the colony's priests were not as fortunate. Those who were captured were clamped into chains and shipped back to Britain.

The anarchy created by the rebellion was welcomed by at least one colonial who had joined the insurgent Puritans. William Claiborne, watching from the old colony, decided that the time was right for reasserting control of his lost plantation. Accompanied by a small force of Virginians, Claiborne invaded Kent Island, organized local residents into an army and took possession of Brent's estate.

Dissatisfaction against Brent was high. In October of 1642, complaints reached Calvert that Brent might attempt to withdraw Kent Island from Baltimore's jurisdiction. Citizens particularly disliked the planter's service as a magistrate. Supposedly, Brent refused to rule on any legal matters put before him, until all debts owed personally to him by any party in the suit were settled in full. Brent was acquitted of misconduct, but as a precaution against future judgments, he transferred title to his property to his sister Margaret.

Claiborne was not content with merely resuming his old trading ground. In the absence of proprietary control, he was able to convince many followers that St. Mary's could be captured. The prospect of an entire colony ruled by William Claiborne apparently struck the Islanders as less than tempting, for on further consideration, the men refused to become involved in an attack on the capital.

For two years near anarchy reigned in Maryland. Bills were not enacted. Courts were closed. Land patents went unrecorded. United defense against the Indians was impossible. Lord Baltimore considered the province lost forever and instructed Leonard Calvert to salvage whatever could be saved and forget the area. The Governor, however, detected a change in attitude was imminent.

Resentment seemed to be building against the raiders who had overthrown the legal government and plunged the colony into chaos. Although many Protestants intensely disliked the Proprietor's Catholic rule, the former administration had been stable and contributed to progress. Further, most Marylanders were not Puritans such as Ingle, but Anglicans who sided with Charles against Parliament. These Church of England members probably decided that once Ingle's men had impoverished the province's Catholics, attention would turn to plundering unfriendly Protestants.

With the help of Virginia Governor William Berkeley, Calvert was able to retake St. Mary's in December of 1646. Viable government was reestablished. The Proprietor was once more in control.

Even after Ingle's men had been successfully expelled, Claiborne remained in control of Kent Island. In April of 1647, Calvert set out to subdue the rebels and Claiborne fled back to Virginia. When Baltimore's rule was reinstated, the Governor issued a pardon for all crimes of "rebellion, sedition and plunder and all other offences whatsoever," that had been committed between February 14, 1644 and April 16, 1647. The sole exception to the amnesty was Richard Ingle.

The joy of Baltimore's supporters was short-lived. Leonard Calvert, the man who had led the immigrants of the *Ark* and *Dove* into the wilderness, who had repeatedly marched at the head of provincial forces against enemies and who had suffered the hardships of the people, died on June 9. He had left the colony safe for the Baltimore line.

Ingle returned to England, his ships loaded with treasures looted from the hated Maryland papists. Giles Brent, aboard one vessel and still a prisoner, suffered a narrow escape as the Channel's cliffs were sighted. According to observers, Ingle urged that Brent be thrown overboard so that no witnesses to the plunder would be available in case legal action was taken. Brent's demise was prevented only by the refusal of the ship's mate to condone the drowning.

Anti-crown forces were in near total control of the English coast, but Ingle found that the Roundheads refused to provide immunity from punishment for piracy. Claims for recompense poured into England from the Chesapeake. Brent and Thomas Copley declared in Admiralty Court that they had been plundered of more than 100 cattle, 20 sheep, 100 hogs, several ships, gold chains, jewelry, guns and large stores of wheat. In addition, twenty-one indentured servants had been made "unuseful." A payment of £4,368 was asked for the losses. Cornwallis joined the pair by entering suit against the Captain for £2,500.

Ingle called the claims "pretended trespasses" and defended his procedures on the grounds that he had only acted to save Maryland Puritans from abuses of government. In a petition to Parliament, the trader suggested that he should be praised for risking his "life and fortune . . . in assisting the well-affected protestants against the tyrannical government and the papists and malignants."

Through what might have been a move to ward off accusations of piracy, Ingle joined with Claiborne in 1647 in an attempt to overturn Baltimore's charter by legal redress. The challenge, like those before it, was denied.

It was perhaps curious that the rights of a Catholic peer from Ireland would be upheld over the complaints of a Puritan trader who had faithfully supported Parliament. The inconsistency was probably due to the confused state of English government. Officials no doubt wished to dispose of the Maryland matter as quickly as possible. Baltimore did hold a patent embossed with the Great Seal, and even the triumphant Puritans may have been reluctant to disregard such formidable authorization without proof of wrong doing. Problems between the Roundheads were already so severe that no new difficulties were needed.

Even before Charles was taken by the Scottish allies of Parliament in 1646, rancor broke out among the victors. The Parliamentarians, controlled mainly by moderate Presbyterians, found themselves opposed by the New Model Army, a force dominated by a variety of Puritan and extremist sects. Discord was increased even further when the King, delivered by the Scots to the Parliamentarians was forcibly taken by the military.

General Oliver Cromwell attempted to frame a workable compromise in which the institution of the monarchy would be retained in the structure of government. Despite Cromwell's popularity and authority, the effort failed.

Charles managed to escape captivity in November of 1647, and from the Isle of Wight, desperately tried to rally his fragmented army so that an invasion of the motherland could be undertaken. The counterrevolution was unsuccessful and the King was captured again.

A crisis in government was approaching. The power of the military was becoming uncheckable. Uprisings sprang up in Wales and Kent. The Scots, declaring that promises of religious freedom had not been fulfilled, also rebelled. Cromwell, realizing that interfactional rivalry could no longer be allowed to continue, joined with those professing that the monarchy could not be tolerated in any form if the goals of the civil war were to be achieved. To drive home his new position, the General decided to eliminate from government, not only royalists, but moderate Presbyterians as well. In an incident known as "Pride's Purge," soldiers under the command of Colonel Thomas Pride stood outside Parliament and refused entry to all but the most zealous friends of the army. More than one hundred members were turned away on the guise that they were supporters of the King. The actual reason was their reluctance to give unchecked power to non-civilian elements.

The remaining M.P.'s, mostly radical Puritans, were allowed to take their places. The ensuing Commons, lampooned as the "Rump Parliament," formed an undistinguished body whose authority was severely curtailed. The only major accomplishment of the Rump was the establishment of a special court to try King Charles.

Little honor was done to English justice by those who pressed charges against the defeated monarch on January 20, 1649. After a week long trial, Charles was found guilty of high treason for conducting war against Parliament. A desperate attempt was made to save the ruler from the executionist's axe. Charles II, the heir apparent, reportedly forwarded to Parliament a blank, signed commission on which any demands that were inscribed would automatically become law. The move was rejected. On January 30, Charles I was beheaded at Whitehall. The monarchy and the House of Lords were officially abolished.

With the removal of the King, nobles and Presbyterians from active participation in government, the way seemed clear for imposition of total Puritan rule. A Free State or Commonwealth based on the Rump and a Council of State composed of forty-one individuals, was established to guide the nation.

Even the radical minority could not maintain a united front. Various sectarians such as the Levellers, Diggers and Independents began quarreling among themselves for a share of the spoils. External dissentions also threatened England's stability. An Irish insurrection was put down unmercifully by the massacre of the entire population of the town of Drogheda. Scottish Covenanters supported Charles II in an effort to retake the throne. Young Stuart's plan was unsuccessful and he was forced to flee into French exile.

A mixed reaction to the change in authority was forthcoming from America. The Massachusetts Bay Puritans, delighted that their religious colleagues had gained control in the Isles, promptly declared themselves a free Commonwealth. Quite a different response was evident in the mid-Atlantic colonies where many cavaliers had fled to avoid punishment.

# Chapter III

# Revolt on the Chesapeake

VIRGINIA IN 1650 was not rent by the internal disharmony that resulted in England after the victory of the New Model Army. During the civil wars, Puritan worship was forbidden in the colony and those who dared to continue the practice were exiled. As a result, the province continued unreservedly Anglican. Defeated royalists became common travellers on the streets of Jamestown.

Popular Governor William Berkeley and the Burgess had no difficulty in coping with the new regime. Both simply refused to recognize that the royal line had been interrupted by Charles I's execution. Commands from Parliament that the assembly acknowledge the Commonwealth's supremacy were ignored. The beheaded monarch's son, Charles II, was proclaimed King and the only legitimate ruler of Virginia.

The twenty-year-old prince did not appear capable of toppling the mighty Roundheads, but Virginia's continued obstinacy was interpreted by Parliament as treason. The provincial assembly, equally critical of the British position, declared that the real traitors to England were those who dared to question the right of the third Stuart to the throne.

The colony's lack of support for the Parliamentary cause had been tolerated during the early days of the civil war when it was feared that the provinces might enter the conflict on the side of the crown. Victory by the Roundheads made such allowances unnecessary. The possibility that pro-monarchy sentiments might disrupt the Atlantic trade and harm the nation's commerical interests no doubt contributed to the increasingly stern position adopted by the new British leaders.

Commons pulled tighter on the loose colonial rein by announcing that the overseas provinces "ought to be subject to such laws, orders and regulations as are, or shall be made by the Parliament of England." In essence, legislative prerogative had replaced royal supremacy.

By the fall of 1650, the government was ready to act against colonies that had not officially recognized the Commonwealth. On October 3, a trading blockade was ordered against the deliquents. The economic sanctions did not impress the Virginians who were content to trade with the more generous European nations such as the Dutch. Instead of bowing to English pressures, the people continued to express loyalty to Charles II.

Parliament reacted by declaring Virginia, as well as Antigua, Bermuda and Barbados, in rebellion. On September 26, 1651, the Council of State was ordered to send an armed force to reduce the errants into submission. An expedition of approximately six hundred men was dispatched together with a civilian commission charged with reorganizing the dissident governments after military conquest had succeeded in deposing the entrenched royalist administrations.

The four Commissioners were empowered to take oaths, pardon repenitent rebels, free servants of the unreconstructed, assure that proper laws were passed, abolish the use of *The Book of Common Prayer* and remove all monarchists who remained in positions of authority. To promote these goals, the men were authorized to use "all acts of hostility," that were considered necessary.

Two of the officials were hardly expected to be impartial in dealing with the colonists. Richard Bennett was a fanatical Puritan leader who had been earlier exiled from Virginia for his religious beliefs. Accompanying Bennett was Commissioner William Claiborne, who had conviently converted to Puritanism.

Bennett and Claiborne might have proved less vindictive if fellow

Commissioners Robert Dennis and Thomas Stagg had survived the ocean passage. Unfortunately, the two moderate appointees were drowned in a shipwreck before the American coast was sighted. Captain Edmund Curtis, head of the military troop, became the third, and a most uninvolved Commissioner.

Governor Berkeley and the assembly had decided to oppose the English fleet bent on vanquishing the old colony. Local resistance was probably strengthened when word arrived that the Commons had approved a navigation act designed to eliminate all foreign trade from American ports. Under the statute, no goods could be imported or exported from any province except in British or American owned vessels, captained and manned by British citizens. If enforced, the new law would end competition between nations trading in America. The provinces would become captive of British commercial interests. Cost of imported goods would escalate and prices paid for tobacco would plummet.

The Virginians' resolve to battle the mother country was overcome when the invasion fleet actually appeared offshore in March of 1652. The ragged defenses of the Jamestown colony were totally inadequate to withstand the cannon balls of the Puritan force. Provincials sadly began negotiations.

The settlement concluded between the Commissioners and the colonists was not a vindictive one. Under terms of the agreement, recognition of the Commonwealth would be considered voluntarily offered rather than militarily forced. All acts of rebellion against the English government were pardoned and citizens wishing to continue support for the King might do so in private. Residents who refused to publicly recognize Parliament as the supreme power in Britain and America were given one year in which to either alter their position or leave the area. Virginia would enjoy the same trading advantages that were provided in England. Berkeley and the royal Council would be dismissed and control of all provincial affairs would pass to the Burgess.

Public compliance with the arrangement was widespread, but the delegation of power which supposedly was to flow to the citizenry was less than had been expected. Richard Bennett was "elected" as Governor and Claiborne was selected as the colony's new Secretary. Ironically, two decades earlier, the trader had accepted appointment to precisely the same office. The first commission, however, had come not from the Burgess, but from the King whom Claiborne had helped to depose.

With Virginia safely ensconced in the Puritan fold, the Commissioners began eyeing other areas that might require subjugation. Maryland was the most obvious target.

The original draft of the Commissioners' instructions specifically included Maryland as a colony to be reduced. Lord Baltimore had been able to eliminate direct mention of the proprietary, but at the last moment, opponents succeeded in inserting a loophole into the directive. In addition to subduing the enumerated provinces, the Commissioners were instructed to assure that all "plantations within the bay of Chesapeake" gave due "obedience" to the Commonwealth. For Claiborne and Bennett, the mere mention of the waterway was sufficient authorization for moving England's forces against the northern territory.

The rebellion that the Commissioners claimed existed at St. Mary's in no way resembled the overt opposition that had defiantly blown forth from Virginia. Instead of revolt by royalists against the Commonwealth, Maryland dissention involved Puritan dissatisfaction with the absentee Catholic government.

Puritans had long been welcomed in Maryland under Baltimore's policy of harboring the religiously persecuted, but the sect did not become numerically significant until Virginia began expelling members of the dissenting faith. In 1649 alone, entire congregations were driven into Maryland. Some received land grants on the Patuxent, but the majority of settlers, about three hundred individuals, chose to plant in a choice spot at the mouth of the Severn River. Here a self-contained community named Providence was established.

Under the leadership of Richard Bennett, the new arrivals served notice that things were not to their liking in Baltimore's dominion. Particularly dismaying was the oath of allegiance required by the Proprietor of all who resided in the colony.

Subscribers to the pledge were forced to concede that Baltimore rather than the King or Parliament was the "Absolute Lord," of the province. Deponents were also made to recognize the peer's "royal jurisdiction," and to swear that they would defend his rights to the last drop of blood. Failure to take the oath was punishable in the first instance by banishment and in the second, by imprisonment.

Oaths were considered of great importance in English custom. The solemn word of a citizen was widely respected and subjects generally believed themselves totally bound to maintain any pledge that was taken. Colonial governments quickly recognized the value of sacred pledges in preventing and uncovering conspiracies against legitimate authority. In Massachusetts, for example, all free men were compelled by law to support the Commonwealth by declaring:

> . . . I will not plot or practice any evil against it, or consent to any
> that shall so do; but will timely discover and reveal the same to lawfull
> authority now here established, for the speedy preventing thereof.

In the confused conditions of the seventeenth century, however, the constant imposition of various pledges of allegiance was most confusing. As soon as one faction gained ascendancy, an oath was imposed. When opposition interests overturned the incumbents, another swearing was required. Even the most intelligent subjects could become bewildered. In a speech before the House of Lords, the Marquis of Wharton begged God's pardon in case any of the promises that he had made had been broken. The Marquis explained that he had sworn so frequently that he could not remember precisely everything he had pledged to do.

Despite irritation concerning the oath, inhibitants of Providence joined the political scene and by 1650 had dispatched representatives to the assembly. Inclusion of Protestants in government was part of a belated move by Baltimore to dilute the concentration of power that had been placed in Catholic hands for two decades. Realizing that "papist" domination would not be tolerated in Puritan England, the Proprietor made several changes aimed at heading off charges of discrimination. Protestant William Stone was named Governor. The acquisition of land by Jesuits was forbidden. An act of religious toleration was passed that provided freedom of conscience to all Christians who accepted the concept of the Trinity. The landmark measure, however, was marred by the proviso that non-believers were entitled to no rights.

By 1650, the policy of Protestant integration was well underway. More than one-half of the assembly were Protestants. Non-Catholics were also being appointed to the Council and to lower level administrative posts.

Baltimore's carefully laid strategy of pacifying the English radicals was upset by the execution of Charles I. News of the regicide arrived in Maryland while Stone was temporarily absent and Catholic Thomas Greene was acting as Governor. Instead of waiting for Stone to return, Greene proclaimed Charles II as the lawful ruler of Britain. The declaration was seized upon by the Proprietor's enemies as proof of treasonous inclinations.

Baltimore attempted to salvage the situation by removing Greene from the Council and announcing that all acts approved by the temporary administration were void. The Proprietor also inferred that Greene's proclamation had been motivated by personal self-interest.

Ironically, at the same time that Parliament was attacking Baltimore for endorsing Charles, the heir apparent was sanctioning the Irish peer for supporting the Puritans. The exiled King revoked the rights of government held by Baltimore, claiming that Lord Cecil: ''doth visibly adhere to the rebels of England, and admit all kinds of schismatics, and sectaries, and other ill-affected persons into the said plantations of Maryland . . .'' On February 16, 1650, young Stuart appointed Sir William Davenant as royal Governor. Fortunately for Baltimore, Davenant's ship was captured by Puritans soon after leaving port. The prisoner, a former poet laureate of England and the godson of William Shakespeare, was saved only through the personal intervention of John Milton, Cromwell's secretary.

During the confusion, William Claiborne renewed his claim to Kent Island, presenting such a threat of imminent rebellion that even the assembly, though heavily dominated by Protestants, did not take kindly to the disruption. All citizens were forbidden to assist Claiborne. The death penalty was set for anyone that disregarded the prohibition.

The assembly was not as supportive of the establishment's interests on the issue of the oath. While much of the original wording was retained, the body removed all references to the Proprietor's royal powers. Amid rumors that the charter would soon be abolished, Maryland's Puritans withdrew from the legislature. The politicians undoubtedly believed that the Commonwealth government would be considerably more effective in limiting the peer's rule, than the representative assembly would be. The conclusion proved correct.

The climate became even more agitated when Bennett and Claiborne arrived in St. Mary's to force obedience to the Commonwealth.

Stone was anxious to compensate for Greene's error, by recognizing Parliament as the rightful authority. He was unwilling, however, to approve the Commissioners' plans for reorganizing the entire provincial government.

Stone firmly refused to agree that legal processes should run in the name of Parliament. According to the Governor's reasoning, the 1632 charter specifically ordered that all writs were to be issued under the Proprietor's authority. To alter a provision passed under the Great Seal was an illegal action that could not be condoned. If even the King had not claimed such power, surely the ineffective Rump would not demand the alteration.

On March 29, Stone was removed from office together with several uncooperative members of the Council. The Commissioners set about establishing an entirely new administration in which Baltimore's interests were completely ignored. The deposed Governor, perhaps hoping to salvage some authority for his lord, reconsidered his earlier stance and agreed to temporarily change the form of the writs. Until the will of Parliament was made known, the Proprietor's name would not be used.

Stone was restored as Governor on June 28, but the post had become little more than a figurehead position. Bennett and Claiborne exercised the real authority, and the pair were anxious to assure that at least one parcel of land would never again feel the proprietory sway. In July, the Commissioners in effect removed Kent Island from Maryland's jurisdiction. The tract was described as privately owned by William Claiborne and as such not subject to regulation from St. Mary's. After twenty years, it seemed that Claiborne had finally secured legal title to the Chesapeake plantation.

The dismemberment of Maryland was impossible for Baltimore to accept. Charging that the Commissioners had acted in excess of their instructions, he brought suit for legal redress and at the same time, issued a pamphlet entitled *The Lord Baltimore's Case. . . .* The broadside was designed as a propaganda instrument to influence public opinion in both Maryland and England.

In his *Case,* Lord Cecil argued that he had expended £ 40,000 in developing the province from virgin land into a profitable asset of England. He had helped to combat the power of Sweden and Holland in the New World and had unselfishly provided shelter to members of all religions. His appointees, Governor Stone and the Council, had cooperated with the Parliamentary representatives and in turn had been poorly used.

Baltimore's pamphlet was to be the opening salvo in a propaganda war that become almost as heated as the political maneuvering taking place behind closed doors. Booklets rebutting the *Case* portrayed the Maryland crisis in a different manner. These brochures accused Baltimore of demanding illegal oaths, harboring Jesuits and selling arms to the Indians. He was further charged with establishing illegal Councils, repressing the interests of Protestants and trafficking with foreign interests to the detriment of English commerce.

In the midst of the pamphlet controversy, political events in England changed the situation. On April 20, 1653, Cromwell expelled the indecisive Rump. A small group of hand-picked favorites was selected to replace the group, but even this "Barebones" or "Nominated" Parliament was unable to deal with the simplest difficulty.

To provide decisive leadership, Cromwell accepted a military-devised proposal called the Instrument of Government. Under the plan, the Commonwealth was replaced by a Protectorate. Cromwell became Lord Protector, a virtually dictatorial post supported by a rubber-stamp Commons and a Council of State. Puritanism replaced the Church of England as the official religion. The army was vested with wide civilian powers such as tax collection. Religious fervor infiltrated government policy at all levels. In an effort to overthrow papist domination in the Caribbean, war was declared on Spain.

Stone, determined not to repeat the miscalculation made by Greene at the time of Charles' execution, immediately proclaimed Cromwell as Lord Protector. Baltimore also acted to take advantage of the change in government. Under the Proprietor's reckoning, Bennett and Claiborne no longer possessed legal power to intervene in Maryland affairs. Their commission had been issued under the Commonwealth, and when that form of rule was abolished, the pair's authorization was also removed. Baltimore instructed Stone to reestablish the proprietary. The oath of fidelity was to be reactivated. The Commissioners were to be ignored. To the consternation of Maryland's Puritans, the Governor complied with the Lord's orders.

Bennett and Claiborne confronted Stone, but were unable to retake control because of the Governor's show of force. The Commissioners temporarily withdrew to muster reinforcements in Virginia.

All hope that the Parliamentary representatives would concede the loss of authority and peacefully leave Maryland ended. As residents flocked to support the Commissioners it became obvious that few in the colony were willing to uphold Baltimore's interests in an armed conflict. Stone realized that he would be unable to retain control. Vastly outnumbered, he surrendered the province without bloodshed.

After removing the Governor and Council from office, the Commissioners on July 22, 1654, established a Puritan council of state to administer the colony. Orders for election of new assemblymen were sent out and all Catholics, as well as Protestants who had supported Stone in the temporary rebellion, were disenfranchised. The resulting legislature was totally dominated by Puritans. The group ramrodded into law a series of religious restrictions which overruled the 1649 act of religious toleration; Catholics were deprived of all protections, forbidden to practice their religion and prohibited from holding office. A strict moral code, consistent with the prudish Puritan ethic, was approved for all citizens. Every Marylander regardless of station was expected to abide by the rigid standards or face stern punishment. Former Councillor William Mitchell, for example, was arrested for a variety of crimes including atheism, adultery, procurring an abortion and fornication.

Catholics were everywhere apprehensive. To eliminate even the most unobtrusive vestiges of "popery", the name of St. Mary's was changed to Mary's. On the frontier, Jesuit missionaries, who had been instrumental in maintaining peace with the Indians, were hunted down by Protestants. One group of priests managed to escape to Virginia, but found the situation little improved. According to one holy man's report, the refugees were forced to live in a "mean hut, low and depressed, not much unlike a cistern or even a tomb."

Baltimore seemed unaware of the military realities. He berated Stone for surrendering the colony and urged that retaliation be taken against the Parliamentary representatives. In January of 1655, the deposed Governor received more useful support when a letter from Cromwell arrived in the province. The Lord Protector condemned Bennett and Claiborne for "disturbing" Baltimore's government and forbade any further usurpation of the Proprietor's prerogatives.

Buoyed by the General's support and Baltimore's urging, Stone garnered an army to put down the Commissioners' government. As part of the strategy, he imprisoned several political opponents, seized the colony's records and confiscated a supply of ammunition. As the loyalist force set out to subdue the Puritan stronghold at Providence, strict instructions were given that the troops should neither plunder enemy houses nor fire the first shot in case a violent confrontation became inevitable.

The opposition at Providence was equally aroused. For several months Captain William Fuller, military commander and Acting Governor under the Commissioners, had been warning that Stone was pressing the Indians to instigate a massacre of the Protestants. The prospect of a full-scale slaughter gave significant motivation to the Puritan defenders.

On March 25, belligerents met in a combined naval and land engagement near the mouth of the Severn. The outcome was devastating for the Proprietor's contingent. One-fourth of Stone's two hundred men were killed or wounded. Less than a dozen participants were able to escape capture. Stone was shot several times, but survived to be taken prisoner. Although the Puritans had promised pardon for all who surrendered, ten leaders were condemned to death. Four were executed immediately, but the remaining six were saved by the pleas of loyalist women and soldiers.

In the aftermath of the battle, Maryland's Catholics were subjected to persecution unseen since the days of Ingle's Rebellion. Estates were confiscated to satisfy the exorbitant prison fees charged to captive soldiers. Heavy fines were placed on those who had opposed the Commissioners in any manner. John Price was sentenced to pay 30,000 pounds of tobacco for supporting Stone. Robert Taylor was fined 1,000 pounds for simply signing a petition against the Protestants.

Care was taken to assure that no word of the battle and ensuing punishments reached England before a reasonable explanation could be prepared by the victors. Mails were stopped. Stone was held incommunicado. The Governor's wife Virlinda, however, managed to smuggle a detailed account of the battle to Baltimore.

As news of the clash filtered into Britain, the propaganda war waxed stronger. The anonymous author of *Virginia and Maryland* . . . likened the Chesapeake colony to a dunghill. In *Babylon's Fall,* Stone and the proprietary force were depicted as "desperate and bloody fellows," who ravaged the Protestants in a "barbarous manner." Baltimore's supporters were described as ruthless oppressors who stole Puritan arms so that no defense could be made against the Indians. The victory at the Severn was seen as God's revenge against evil doers.

Baltimore's defenders also rushed into print. John Hammond in *Leah and Rachel* deplored the "unparalleled inhumanity" with which the Puritans had repaid Baltimore's generosity. John Langford, an old employee of the Calverts who had delivered the first two Indian arrows to Windsor in 1633 wrote that Baltimore had always taken great care to protect every inhabitant in the colony.

Hearings in London were progressing favorably for the Proprietor. Anxious to regain his rights, Baltimore dispatched a Governor's commission to loyalist Josias Fendall. The appointee was arrested before he could challenge for the post, but was released after swearing obedience to the Commissioners. In February of 1657, Fendall broke the pledge by assuming the title of Governor and forming a Calvert-backed administration. Religious tolerance was reintroduced. Loyalist supporters were returned to office. The oath was reimposed.

Fearful of retribution from the Lord Protector, no overt moves were forthcoming against Fendall's regime at St. Mary's. But in Providence, the Puritans refused to relinquish control over the northern territory. For a time, two governments claimed power.

On November 30, 1657, a compromise was reached between the feuding parties. Fendall would be recognized as head of the entire province. Freedom of conscience would be accepted and no retribution would be taken against the Puritans who had overthrown Baltimore's control. Five months later, a newly elected assembly removed all legal restrictions that had been imposed against the Catholics. All acts of rebellion committed by any party since 1649 were officially pardoned. The Puritan revolution had ended in Maryland.

Popular rule was also grinding to a halt in England where Cromwell's gilt was beginning to tarnish. The execution of the King and the mass departure of nobles skilled in government service, had left few individuals in office who were capable of administering the nation's affairs. The Commonwealth and Protectorate had managed to keep England operational only by virtue of the momentum remaining from the royal government. As the end of the decade approached, disintegration of the political and economic sectors became a real possibility. On every side, problems beset the Lord Protector.

The war with Spain, that had generated temporary prosperity, had become an unwelcomed drain on Britain's finances. Taxes had risen enormously. Merchants and manufacturers were dismayed by the declining trade. Cromwell seemed unable to rejuvenate overseas commerce.

Pressure was also being felt in the area of civil liberties. Cromwell, who had initially refused an offer to become king, had eventually moved into Whitehall Palace, assumed the title of "His Majesty," and accepted the institution of a hereditary protectorate. His actions increasingly displayed the same arrogance that had marked the Stuart absolutists.

The possibility that Cromwell would become King Oliver I, was eliminated by the Protector's death on September 3, 1658. The passing brought even further confusion, for Cromwell's son and successor Richard, proved incapable of even limited leadership. The long dormant Commons reasserted its authority, but became embroiled in a new rivalry with the army.

Young Cromwell resigned in May of 1659 in the face of a military coup, prompting revival of the old Rump and a modified Commonwealth. The arrangement was totally unsatisfactory to the people. Apprentices rioted in London and pelted government troops sent to suppress the uprising with shoes and turnip tops. Unrest was everywhere. Commons dissolved itself and a new "Free" Parliament convened. The possibility of restoring the monarchy became an accepted topic of conversation.

Virginians, too, were tiring of non-royal administration. The Commonwealth and Protectorate forms thrust upon the colony had never been popular. Most citizens viewed the arrangements not as democratic utopias, but as abrogations of legitimate authority on which the nation had become great. Three "elected" governors had ruled the province since the Commissioners' arrival in 1652. None had been satisfactory.

It had long been clear that Parliament had never intended that the colony should enjoy total self-determination. From the beginning, all acts of the Burgess were subject to review by London officials. As the years passed, the system became so cumbersome that the assembly was forced to become dominant on its own volition. By 1658, the legislature had so warmed to the idea of citizen supremacy, that the body refused Governor Samuel Mathews' order to dissolve. In no uncertain terms, the Governor was informed that the Burgess, like the Commons, could be suspended only with the members' consent.

When Mathews died in early 1660, the legislature, acting as the supreme power in the colony, summoned back to office Sir William Berkeley, the last royal governor and an unreconstructed supporter of the crown. Berkeley was hesitant to accept the assembly's commission, for he still maintained that the post could legally be filled only through royal appointment. The idea that he would once again lead Virginia was pleasing to Berkeley, a man who had suffered substantial losses since the arrival of the Commissioners. "I should be worthily thought hospital mad," Sir William wrote, "if I would not change poverty for wealth—contempt for honor."

As a compromise, Berkeley consented to accept the post temporarily, until Charles II's wishes in the matter could be determined. To the monarch he explained that the action had been necessary only because the "wolves of scisme" were threatening to tear apart the province. To the Burgess he announced: "You have given me a treasure."

Charles II was officially proclaimed King in Jamestown and because London had become the scene of mass confusion, the rebellious act received little attention. No penalty was forthcoming, for by May of 1660, all England had recognized Stuart as the rightful leader. The Restoration had come.

The prospect of establishing a new rule also swept Maryland where rebels were attempting to overthrow not the interregnum, but the Proprietor. The unlikely head of the 1660 revolt was Josias Fendall, Baltimore's legally appointed governor.

With Fendall's encouragement, the Maryland assembly declared that neither Baltimore's nor the Governor's approval was required for any legislative action to become legal. The dissidents claimed that in all instances, the people's voice through their representatives was sufficient legitimization.

The legislature offered a governor's commission to Fendall, an action somewhat similar to that undertaken by the Virginia Burgess. Fendall agreed to resign his proprietary authorization and accept the assembly's endorsement in a modified Commonwealth arrangement. To assure that their self-proclaimed supremacy would not be upset, the assembly made it a felony for anyone to disturb the newly constituted government.

Baltimore labeled Fendall's defection as "mutiny and sedition," and commissioned his brother-in-law Philip Calvert as Governor. The restored King, a man with little admiration for those who deposed legitimate authority, supported the peer. A royal order was dispatched to Berkeley directing that Philip Calvert was to be assisted in retaking Maryland. The monarch also decreed that citizens in the Chesapeake should help to restore the Proprietor's rights. On November 27, 1660, a pardon for all rebels except Fendall and his colleague John Hatch was proclaimed. The ex-Governor and Hatch sought to entice the population into arms, but the people refused to disobey a direct order from the King. When no groundswell was forthcoming, Fendall surrendered without a struggle.

Though the errant Governor was found guilty of treason, Baltimore was not anxious to alienate the citizenry by vengeful retribution. Instead of execution, Fendall was sentenced to be exiled and his property attaindered by the Proprietor. On appeal to the Governor and Council, even this lenient judgement was reduced. As final punishment, Fendall was ordered to post a peace bond and was forbidden from holding further public office. Hatch was fined.

The Restoration ended William Claiborne's maneuvering. After twenty-seven years of rebellion against Baltimore, the dissident returned to Virginia and settled in New Kent County. In 1677 he petitioned King Charles for an award of £10,000 to compensate for the loss of Kent Island. The feisty trader received no answer. Before the claim could be pressed further, Claiborne had died.

# CHAPTER IV

# Dutch Rule Threatened

C HARLES II, recalled unconditionally to the throne by a population desperate for national stability, entered London on May 29, 1660. The city's streets were strewn with flowers. Church bells pealed continuously. Fountains ran with wine.

The return was a personal triumph for the monarch who had spent many of the exile years in dire poverty. At times, the King's clothes became so ragged that he was mistaken for a thief. Only a £50,000 advance from Parliament enabled the ruler and his entourage to dress themselves in other than pauper fashion.

The England that greeted the King was far different than the nation which Charles had fled in 1651. Perhaps most significant was the change in attitude toward the role of the monarchy. A fundamental alteration had occurred in the outlook of the people during the interregnum. An alienation from the crown had emerged that dismissed the unquestioned homage that had been paid to British kings for centuries.

The execution of Charles I served as a constant reminder that ultimate power lay not in divine right, but in the sovereign citizenry. Delicate problems of defining respective spheres of authority remained, but the recognition of Parliamentary control, particularly in the area of taxation, was firmly established. Although the Commonwealth experiment had failed, capitalist and commercial interests were firmly entrenched in Parliament and these men would not tolerate loss of the self-governing rights for which civil war had been waged.

That Restoration did not mean Parliamentary capitulation was a fact made clear to Charles. Particularly obvious was the reality that the Commons' joyous reception would not be matched by financial generosity. The Restoration Parliament proved as frugal with the purse as had the pre-war assemblies.

Reluctance to approve permanent allowances for the King may not have been entirely due to the desperate state of the national treasury. Moderate representatives wished to observe the conduct of the monarch before granting independence through private income.

Confiscation of royal lands had eliminated many traditional sources of kingly support and royal favorites who had lost millions during the Puritan regime were unable to aid the leader. During the summer of 1660, Charles' position became so straitened that he had difficulty in buying food for his immediate family. Others in the court were near destitute and the Duke of York, brother to Charles and now the heir apparent, was urgently pressed. Describing the situation to Parliament on August 29, Charles explained:

> . . . I [have not] been able to give my brother one shilling since I came into England, nor to keep any table in my house but what I eat myself; and that which troubles me most, is to see many of you come to me at Whitehall, and to think that you must go somewhere else to seek your dinner.

The scramble for funds became frantic. Pleas for royal grants and pensions besieged the court from loyalists desiring rewards for past services. Stuart was exceedingly put to find means of repaying all the claimants and was reduced to satisfying the debts by distributing monopolies such as the right to sell herbs at court or the privilege of scavenging the royal preserves for roots.

The monarch's financial difficulties were typical of the situation into which English men and women of all classes had been cast. The sluggish economy, the collapse of commerce and the high expenditures for the military had bankrupted the nation. At the Restoration, ledgers at the Chancellor of the Exchequer showed cash accounts of only £11 2s 10d.

Citizens of all political persuasions demanded that solutions be found to the country's economic problems, but a return to the past system of large landholdings by the crown and nobility would not be tolerated. Trade seemed to emerge as the surest and quickest road to economic recovery.

Trade became a watchword on which hopes for a better life depended. Trade to provide jobs for thousands of unemployed sailors and dock workers. Trade to bring raw materials from which manufacturers might produce items for export. Trade to create customs fees and end dependence upon foreign suppliers. Through trade, the island nation would recover from the scars of war. Prosperity would heal the wounds between factions. Britain would no longer be forced to fear the military might of other countries.

At the center of the new, commercial network were the American colonies, the lands where nature's bounty had not yet been despoiled. From the hardwood forests of New England would come masts for ships and fuel for foundries. Carolina would provide naval stores, wood ashes, pitch and tar. Crops from the tidewater would supplement the inadequate supply of foodstuffs produced on the depleted soil of England. Fish from northern waters would feed the dissident poor and serve as trading barter. America would be the means by which old England would be rejuvenated.

The reasoning behind the scheme seemed sound. England was saddled with a large, unproductive work force and few natural resources. Conversely, the lack of an adequate labor supply rendered the colonies totally incapable of exploiting the continent's untouched potential.

King and Parliament enthusiastically supported adoption of a comprehensive commercial program. In 1660, a sweeping navigation act was passed that aimed at establishing a monopoly over colonial trade for English carriers and traffickers. The law required that all goods bound for or leaving America must be shipped in English or American bottoms crewed by British citizens. Items included on a list of "enumerated" goods, could be carried only to England, Ireland or other British plantations. Three years later, a further blow was struck to colonial trade with European nations, by passage of the Staple Act. This measure enlarged the list of enumerated items to include virtually every good involved in provincial commerce.

Special provisions were made for administrative handling of difficulties that might arise under the navigation program. A Council for Foreign Plantations was appointed by the King to assure that England's interests would be consistently protected. In his commission establishing the Council, Charles left no doubt as to the importance of the body and the desirability of drawing the provinces under closer British control. He announced:

> . . . [the colonists] have very much enlarged the power, growth and improvements thereof, they being now become a great and numerous people whose plentifull trade and commerce very much imployes and increaseth the navigation and expends the manufactures of our other dominions and exchanges them for commodities of necessary use, and [they] bring a good excess of treasure to our Exchequer for customs and other duties.
>
> In consideration whereof and for divers other causes, us there unto moving; We have judged it meet and necessary that so many remote colonies and governments, so many ways considerable to our crown and dignity and to which we do bear so good an esteem and affection, should now, no longer remain in a loose and scattered, but should be collected and brought under such an uniform inspection and conduct that we may the better apply our royal councells to their future regulation, security and improvement.

The preoccupation with trade that consumed post-restoration England was not completely motivated by economic needs. The new-born age of reason was introducing a different philosophy of life and a spirit of self-determinism that had been absent in the old religious-oriented society. Passiveness to the will of God was dying as a viable mode of conduct. The failure of the Commonwealth and Protectorate had proved that religion was an inadequate tool for solving the secular problems of a nation. Puritans, who had maintained that a paradise would follow establishment of their church state, had been shown in error. The new feeling in England was pragmatic in nature and stressed that advancement came to those who helped themselves.

Commerce was also vitally needed in providing a common goal for the fragmented society. Because cooperation between factions was desperately lacking throughout England, Charles and Parliament sought practical ways to end the resentment over past wrongs that hindered the common effort. The King had been remarkably forgiving in dealing with those who had deposed the Stuart line. Through an Act of

Indemnity and Oblivion, he had pardoned all but a fraction of those who had taken part in the civil war. Only thirteen people had been executed and these were well-known regicides who had personally secured the execution of Charles I.

The new monarch did indulge in one act of private vindication. In December of 1660, the corpses of Cromwell, Thomas Pride and Henry Ireton, the Protector's son-in-law, were disinterred from burial places at Westminster. The decaying bodies were hanged for a day on the public gallows at Tyburn, and then reburied in a common grave.

Efforts to solidify the population were also undertaken by the "Cavalier" or "Pensioner" Parliament that convened in 1661. The legislators called for an investigation into ways of finding and bringing home crown supporters who had been "enslaved" for their loyalty to the Stuarts. Many of the royalists had been forcibly transported to America because of continued opposition to the Puritan regime.

The healing of national wounds was made somewhat simpler by the exodus of hard-core Puritans who left Britain following the Restoration to take up new lives in New England. Secretly hidden among the immigrants were Edward Whalley and his son-in-law William Goffe. Both men had been rabid Cromwellian followers who had signed the death warrant for Charles I. Both had been exempted from the official pardon.

While a massive manhunt was being conducted in England for Whalley and Goffe, the renegades found shelter among American Puritans. Despite a royal order that the regicides be given up, sympathetic New Englanders refused to divulge the outlaws' hiding place.

Difficulties in returning pre-civil war land holdings to cavaliers also placed new emphasis on the American colonies. During the interregnum, huge estates confiscated by the government had been sold at forced auction for a fraction of the land's actual value. Changes in ownership and subdivision of the property had been so prevalent that equitable settlement of claims made after the Restoration was frequently impossible.

Many of the dislanded nobles, unfit by training or inclination to enter the commercial world, were attracted by the idea of establishing fiefdoms on the western continent. American estates would not only provide income, but would cast the cavaliers once more in the role of landed barons.

Charles encouraged such interest, realizing that the colonial land was an effective and inexpensive way of compensating followers who had stood by the royal ensign. The resulting involvement of nobles in American affairs, assured that the provincial region received closer royal attention than would have occurred if the area had remained the domain of middle class traders.

In 1660, British possessions in America were not a neat row of contiguous provinces stretching from Canada to the Caribbean. Rather, the holdings were a conglomeration of isolated settlements separated by undeveloped land and foreign-owned territories.

Nearly a dozen British colonies of various legality were present in New England alone. Some were well populated and tightly structured provinces founded under royal charters, while others had less legitimate origins. On the frontier, squatters often decided among themselves to become a "colony." Basic codes of law, or "plantation covenants" were drawn up in informal discussions to guide conduct in the communities. The very existence of some of these "combinations," was probably unknown in England.

Far to the south were the British possessions of Maryland and Virginia, and an uncolonized tract known as Carolina. The southern settlements were not only exposed to seaborne invasion, but were imperiled by the French and Indians to the west and the Spanish in Florida.

The two concentrations of British territory were separated by a large territory claimed by the Dutch. Holland's presence in New Netherlands and New Sweden not only made unification of England's holdings impossible, but constituted a rival to the mercantilistic expectations in London. The Dutch siphoned off choice Indian goods and offered a home base to foreign vessels preying on English ships. The possibility that a Dutch-French alliance might be formed to eliminate England as a factor in the western hemisphere was a constant danger.

Holland's claim to land north of the Delaware River stemmed from a 1609 voyage by Henry Hudson who explored the region in search of a northwest passage. For years after the voyage, no permanent colonization was attempted, and the vast area remained settled only by Dutch traders in backwoods stations.

In 1621, the newly formed Dutch West India Company received a commercial monopoly and a patent to develop the land. The organization devised a scheme based on a patroon system in which large sections of territory would be granted to wealthy aristocrats who agreed to transport tenants to the colony. Because no provision was made for the eventual ownership of land by workers, the plan attracted few yeomen. Concerted colonization ceased and attention shifted back to trading.

Aided by excellent relations with the Iroquois confederation, the Dutch established a profitable trading empire during the 1630's. Gradually, permanent settlers were attracted to New Netherlands because of expanded commercial opportunities. New Amsterdam took on the character of a thriving cosmopolitan center. Citizens and vessels of many nations frequented the town and unlike the closed ports under English control, the seat of government developed an air of sophistication.

The worldliness and diversity of New Amsterdam lent an unregulated character to the entire province. Contemporary visitors noted that residents quarrelled incessantly and that drunkenness was common. The rancor may have been partially due to the authoritarian structure of the colonial administration. Near total powers were vested in an appointed Director-General who could be removed only by a Dutch-based oversight committee known as the Amsterdam Chamber. No provision was made for a representative assembly, and citizen appeals against arbitrary decisions often took years to resolve.

Despite the internal conflicts, New Netherlands grew prosperous, mirroring Holland's emergence as one of the world's mightiest trading states. Exploiting England's turmoil during the civil wars, Dutch traders roamed almost unhampered on the high seas. Markets for goods out of New Amsterdam were limitless.

In 1643, the success of New Netherlands began to dim. A major factor was the disastrous leadership of Director-General William Kieft. The official committed many blunders, but his most damaging action was the instigation of a massacre in February of 1643, in which more than 600 peaceful Indians were slain. The incident sparked a two year Indian war which left New Netherlanders shaken and apprehensive. This error, coupled with general misconduct, resulted in the recall of Kieft and the 1647 appointment of Peter Stuyvesant as Director-General.

Stuyvesant, known as "old silver leg," because his artificial limb was decorated with sparkling metal, was an unpopular, but respected official. The soldier relied upon dictatorial powers to bring order to the colony, but even Stuyvesant discovered that one of the province's most pressing problems was beyond internal control.

All along the eastern border, Puritans were pressing into Dutch lands. Effectively cut off from expansion to the north by the French presence in Canada, the New Englanders were quick to take advantage of the sparsely settled and poorly defended outposts of Holland. Out of Hartford and New Haven came westward moving pioneers with little regard for foreign territorial claims. A similar encroachment took place on Long Island, where Puritans hoped to establish bases for trading with the southern colonies and the Indies. Holland's prior stake on the island was given little consideration by the English.

In September of 1647, one Andrew Forrester appeared in the area announcing that henceforth he would serve as Governor of Long Island. Forrester urged that the local English settlers should expel the Dutch, but before the inhabitants could be rallied into revolt, the newcomer was arrested. New Amsterdam officials dispatched Forrester to Holland for trial, but the Scotsman managed to escape from detention when his vessel put into England for repairs.

Although decisive action had thwarted the 1647 agitation, Stuyvesant realized he would be unable to halt more extensive incursions. Perhaps fearful that defense by his dilapidated army would result in the loss of the entire colony, the Director-General agreed to submit the disputed boundaries to arbitration. The resulting judgement, ratified in the Hartford Treaty of 1650, was not favorable to the Dutch. The Connecticut boundary was drawn just ten miles from the Hudson. All of Long Island east of Oyster Bay was also dispensed to the English.

Stuyvesant may not have been the entirely innocent victim of Puritan greed. It is possible that the Director-General was conspiring with William Coddington, a Massachusetts Bay exile, in a land grab design involving Rhode Island. Coddington, who had established a "democracie" on Narragansett Bay, was suspected of attempting to use the Dutch in order to overturn Roger Williams' control in the area.

The Treaty of Hartford brought temporary peace on the mainland, but its effects on Long Island were far from soothing. Five primarily English inhabited towns were located within Dutch jurisdiction and the threat of rebellion from the aliens created mounting anxiety in New Amsterdam.

In 1653, John Underhill was arrested for fomenting revolt in the

Puritan villages of Flushing and Hempstead. Underhill appeared to be entirely incapable of living under any organized government. He had previously been expelled from both Massachusetts Bay and from New Hampshire because of undisciplined behavior. Underhill found Long Island equally restricting. The dissident issued a public manifesto accusing Stuyvesant of repressing the British through illegal taxation, unlawful imprisonment, invalid seizure of land and conspiring to murder British residents. A prison term did not discourage Underhill. After being released from jail, he returned to Long Island, raised the Parliamentary flag and continued to call for revolution against the Dutch. His announcement that an independent "English Union" had been founded on the Island proved too much for the patient Hollanders. The erring Puritan was ordered to depart from the area immediately.

Providence Plantations proved receptive to the Englishman's plans to free Long Island. From local leaders, he was able to secure a Letter of Marque authorizing privateering against Dutch shipping. War had broken out between Holland and England and Underhill was anxious to take full advantage of the financial opportunities presented by the conflict.

Like Richard Ingle in Maryland, Underhill refused to admit that the letter pertained only to confiscations at sea. Instead of patrolling Long Island Sound in search of enemy vessels, he sailed up the Connecticut River and captured Fort Good Hope, a derelict blockhouse that had been abandoned by the Dutch many years earlier.

Announcing that the territory surrounding the installation was his by right of war prize, the adventurer began selling titles to unsuspecting Puritans.

Two years after Underhill's attempted rebellion, George Baxter made a similar foray into Long Island by declaring that a "Republic of England" existed at Gravesend. For his mutinous activities, Baxter was imprisoned by the Dutch. In 1657 James Grover also attempted to stir the area into rebellion, but he too was arrested.

Threats to Holland's control were accelerated as a result of the Restoration and England's commercial expansion. The territory on the Hudson was becoming almost irrestible to the British. Profits from Indian trading were enormous. The highly developed colony had already experienced the initial, non-productive period of settlement and seemed capable of returning financial rewards without further monetary investment. Strategically, New Amsterdam was a superb base from which the English might launch attacks on the Canadian French. Its rich and undeveloped farm lands could satisfy the New England Puritans' clamour for additional growing room.

Conquest of New Netherlands did not appear to present difficulties. The penurious West India Company had left the area poorly equipped for defense. According to Stuyvesant's evaluation, New Amsterdam's major fort was "more a molehill than a fortress, without gates, the walls and bastions trodden under foot by men and cattle." More important, there were evidences of growing internal dissatisfaction. The lack of a representative assembly so rankled citizens that an informal convention had been organized to request right of approval over taxation and legislation. Stuyvesant refused to even consider the proposal. Announcing that he was responsible only to God and the West India Company, the Director-General disbanded the meeting. A brief revolt by a semi-independent council known as the Board of Nine Men had been instantly quashed when Stuyvesant ordered the arrest of chief rabble-rouser Adriaen Van der Donck.

One of the most interested observers of the Dutch situation was John Scott, an adventurer whose arrival in America had been neither auspicious nor voluntary. Like other royalists, young John's family had suffered as a result of anti-Parliamentary activities. After Scott's father, a Cavalier officer, was killed in the service of the King, John found a more passive method for combating the Roundheads. At Turnham Green, he managed to impede the Commonwealth force by cutting the bridles and girths of a calvary troop. In punishment, the youthful saboteur was shipped to Massachusetts as an indentured servant.

Scott remained in the colony after his period of forced labor had ended. The provinces were vastly more promising than confused England, particularly for one unaverse to bending the law for private gain.

The ex-bondsman ventured from Massachusetts Bay to Long Island and began selling titles for land he supposedly had purchased from the Indians. The fraudulent transfers were frowned upon not only by the English who had designs on the territory, but by the Dutch who held rights of the soil.

After the Restoration, Scott returned to England and launched a

program aimed at stirring up resentment over the supposed enslavement by the Dutch of British colonists on Long Island. Loudly and
frequently he complained that no born Englishman should be forced to
endure the indignities to which the Puritans in New Netherlands were
subject. His efforts were not intended as an unselfish, humanitarian
endeavor, for Scott hoped that he would be able to take control of the
territory if the Dutch were expelled.

Like thousands of other loyalists, Scott formally petitioned the
crown for rewards past due. His pleas to Charles described the daring
maneuver at Turnham Green and the resulting servitude that had been
imposed because of his unswerving allegiance to the Stuarts. Scott
stated that despite the humbling punishment, he had been able to
acquire one-third of all Long Island. In recognition for his suffering on
behalf of the monarchy, Scott requested an appointment as the territory's head of government.

Scott's tale of Dutch horrors succeeded in arousing English enthusiasm for conquest of New Netherlands, but the interest was not channeled in the direction he had wished. James, Duke of York, became so
convinced that glowing possibilities for profit existed in New Netherlands, that he requested title of the land for himself. In a contest with
the Duke, John Scott was bound to lose.

Even as he returned from England in the fall of 1663, Scott was
evidently aware that plans for a British invasion of the area were underway. He was not willing, however, to wait for the fleet's arrival.
Perhaps hoping to secure the region before the Duke could receive a
charter, Scott accepted a military commission from Connecticut authorities. Under the arrangement, Scott led two hundred armed men
onto the island so that the English towns could be annexed to Connecticut. The expedition was not pleasant to those in the combat area.
Observers noted that Scott and his soldiers plundered and assaulted citizens who were reluctant to acknowledge the foreign authority. Supposedly, the leader inelegantly threatened to stick his rapier ''in the
guts'' of anyone who refused to relinquish fidelity to Holland.

The heavy handed methods were successful. On December 14,
Scott notified Puritan officials that the Long Island English had at last
overthrown the ''cruel and rapatious'' Dutch.

Whatever joy that resulted on the mainland as a result of the rebellion's success was soon ended. By February, events had taken a new
turn. The English communities had indeed been willing to depose rule

from Holland, but residents displayed no eagerness to submit to control by Connecticut. Scott announced that the liberated villages had rejected the idea of annexation and had instead established an independent republic. He had accepted their gracious offer to be President of the state.

Scott and his force showed little compassion for the Dutch who resided in the newly declared colony. Homes of Hollanders were looted and families forced from the land so that Englishmen might take control of cultivated fields. To solidify his control and deter a Dutch counterattack, the President revealed that an English fleet was secretly being made ready for the conquest of all New Netherlands. It is unlikely that the disclosure was looked upon kindly in London.

Stuyvesant, outnumbered six to one on Long Island, involved on the mainland with a war with the Esopus Indians and probably fearful that a convoy might already be en route, chose not to act against the insurgents. Company officials ordered the Director-General to attack, but the Dutchmen were not as generous with troops and money as with advice. After Scott threatened to march on New Amsterdam, Stuyvesant and the President of Long Island agreed to halt all combat for one year, or until the land rights could be settled by higher powers.

Within months the truce was broken. Scott was imprisoned by Connecticut authorities on a multitude of charges including perjury, blasphemy, forgery, calumny, treachery, sedition, usurpation and defamation of the King. In June, Governor John Winthrop at the head of a Puritan troop, invaded Long Island and brought the area under Connecticut rule.

Winthrop's hopes for annexation were to be as futile as Scott's. On March 12, a patent granting to the Duke of York all land between Connecticut and the Delaware Rivers passed the Great Seal. York wasted no time in securing the domain. Under the guise of the Second Dutch War, Colonel Richard Nicolls was commissioned as Deputy Governor and placed in charge of a joint naval-land force. On August 18, Nicolls arrived off Manhattan and called upon Stuyvesant to surrender. The Dutchman hesitated, but reconsidered when Nicolls mustered four hundred redcoats and a large company of volunteers from Long Island and Massachusetts. The capital seemed on the verge of mass rioting. On August 27, the Director-General resigned control. The English colors were hoisted over the Hudson.

The elimination of Holland no doubt cheered many in the colony who had grown weary of arbitrary, corporation rule. Like the Virginia Company's failure forty years earlier, absentee ownership by commercial interests had proved ineffective for managing a complex governmental structure.

Disappointment ran high in Connecticut where officials were forced to withdraw all claims in light of the Duke's charter. During the confusion, John Scott managed to escape from jail and returned to Long Island. According to reports, he reconstituted a small armed force and resumed the plunder of Dutch citizens. Disappointed in his efforts to secure a major role in government, he returned to the old practice of selling invalid land titles.

Stuyvesant's surrender of New Netherlands did not signal the end of operations against the Dutch. In September, two frigates were dispatched to the Delaware River to subdue New Sweden, an area on which the entire colonization hopes of the Scandinavian nation had once rested.

In March of 1638, a small band of Swedes and Finns under Peter Minuit sailed up the Delaware to found a community dubbed Ft. Christina. Minuit, the man who had originally purchased Manhattan Island for New Netherlands, had left Holland to organize the Swedish South Company, the promoter of the Delaware venture. The financiers attempted to paint an attractive picture of the New World, but popular response did not materialize. Conditions in the homeland were far more congenial than in England or France and few Swedes were interested in American immigration. The reputation of Delaware as a land less than ideal was reinforced when the Swedish government began sentencing errant soldiers to two years in exile at New Sweden as punishment for crimes.

Despite three supply voyages within a five year period, the population of New Sweden showed little increase. When Governor Johan Printz arrived to take control in February of 1643, the entire population was less than one hundred individuals.

Printz, who weighed an estimated four hundred pounds, was a bizarre and unstable character. He reportedly consumed a minimum of three alcoholic drinks at every meal and measured precisely 5'6" high and 6'5" around.

The new executive instigated a despotic reign designed to tighten the laxity that marked the colony and to assure maximun financial return to corporate backers. As an indication of the faith that the Governor placed in military authority, he brought with him twenty-four privates, a corporal, sergeant, lieutenant, drummer, trumpeter and provost. Also included in the company was a hangman and a barber who also served as a surgeon.

Printz proved to be a violent man who repressed any opinion considered not in the best interests of New Sweden. Foreigners were not welcomed and anyone refusing to take an oath of allegiance was immediately exiled. Under his tyrannical rule, orthodox standards of conduct were not always observed. Interrogation of supects, for example, featured some of the less attractive aspects of the Spanish Inquisition. As the Governor watched approvingly, his servants tossed suspects about the official's offices until confessions were obtained.

Though unprofitable, the Swedish settlement acted as a magnet for other European powers. Holland, eyeing the Scandinavian monopoly on Indian trade, reactivated a previously abandoned fort in the area. In 1641, an English contingent of approximately sixty settlers established an outpost at Ferken's Kil, almost within view of Fort Christina.

The British, under the direction of George Lamberton, were financed by New Haven Puritans who intended not only to trade, but to permanently colonize the river. The move was the first English encroachment on the territory since the early 1630's when Sir Edmund Plowden had used dubious authorization in an attempt to establish the Earldom of Eriwonick.

Both the Swedes and the Dutch were alienated by the Puritans. Printz called the intruders "evil" and resented their attempts to interfere with trade. Stuyvesant threatened to settle any difficulties that might arise with bloodshed.

Lamberton was believed to have been the instigator of considerable unrest that swept the Delaware and was accused of involvement in a plot to bribe Indians to murder the Swedes and Dutch. Continuing conflicts and the lack of significant progress discouraged the English and their settlement was soon abandoned.

Relations between the remaining outposts did not improve after the departure of the New Englanders. Printz was accused of entering into a conspiracy with the Indians similar to that supposedly planned by Lamberton.

Despite Printz's almost fanatical efforts, the success of New Sweden was made virtually impossible by the neglect shown on the part of the parent company. When Governor Johan Rising arrived in May of 1654, the colony received its first word in more than six years from the promoters. Many residents had become so discouraged that they had moved to Maryland or Virginia.

Rising had little opportunity to reverse the downward spiral, for in September of 1655, Dutch troops under Stuyvesant captured Ft. Christina. Unlike the French, English and Spanish, the Swedes had been unable to secure a permanent foothold in the New World.

Life under Dutch control was not a significant improvement over that of the neglectful Swedish South Company. The local population, disheartened by disease, famine and a lack of direction, continued to emigrate southward into English lands. Morale became so depressed, that when the Duke of York's ships arrived in 1664, the population unhesitatingly agreed to surrender.

In the confusion, however, misunderstanding by English officers resulted in an unnecessary and unexpected attack on the disarmed community. Surprised citizens watched helplessly as British troops plundered the town, killed several colonists that had capitulated and apprehended the small contingent of Dutch soldiers. This unpromising beginning set a pattern of resentment that would come to fruition four years later.

The English allowed local officials to remain at their posts, but final disposition of all important matters was made by the Duke's Governor and Council in New York. No major disturbances marked the initial years of transition, but the old attachments had not been obliterated. The lesson became glaringly obvious in August of 1669 when a corps of disgruntled colonists joined in an effort to throw off English authority.

Leader of the rebellion was a shadowy figure known as Marcus Jacobs or Long Finne. Jacobs claimed to be the son of Count Connigsmarke, a Swedish General and confidant of King Charles of Sweden. With little forewarning, Jacobs began mustering the Swedes, Finns and Dutch to arms. Internal revolt was essential, he explained, because a Swedish expedition was preparing to invade the area and retake the lost colony.

Evidently locals were expected to assist in the battle by either forming a fifth column or by gaining sufficient strength to expel the English from the Delaware Valley before the friendly ships arrived. Although Swedish rule had ended twenty-four years before, and little interest had been shown in the province while the motherland retained possession, Jacobs was able to convince many residents that the insurrection could succeed.

One of the most avid revolters was Henry Coleman, a farmer who officials noted had: "left his habitation, cattle and corn without any care taken for them to run after," the rebel leader. The British were particularly concerned that Jacobs and Coleman would use their knowledge of Indian languages to enlist local tribes in the revolt.

On August 2, New York Governor Francis Lovelace ordered the arrest of both men. By September 14, the Council at Manhattan was notified that Jacobs had been taken. Apprehended along with him, were several lesser conspirators including Armgart Printz, daughter of the ex-Swedish Governor. Lovelace was surprised and disappointed by her involvement in the rebellion. Armgart's participation was scored by the official as "high ingratitude for all those indulgences and favours she hath received from those in authority over her."

Despite the arrests, many in the Delaware community remained apprehensive that insurgents still at large would continue to press the revolt. Lovelace shared the concern and dispatched orders that Jacobs should be put in chains and that firm measures should be instigated to discourage others from joining the rebellion. Lovelace informed his subordinates:

> . . . I do recommend unto you now, [you] must rather respect the stopping of the spreading of the contagion that it grow not further, then by any way of amputating or cutting off any member to make the cure more perfect.
>
> . . .
>
> For those of the first magnitude concerned with [Jacobs], you may either secure them by imprisonment or by taking such caution for them to answer which shall be alledged and proved against them. For the rest of the poor deluded sort, I think the advice of their own countrymen is not to be despised; who knowing their temper well, prescribe a method for keeping them in order which is: severity and laying such taxes on them as may not give them liberty to entertain any other thought, but how to discharge them.

Lovelace also suggested that the lesser offenders should be put to work repairing public installations. The seeming compassionate approach to dealing with rebels was in curious contrast to the Governor's bureaucratic report that several pleas received from the prisoners would be ignored because the petitions had not come through official channels.

By October 18, the situation was sufficiently stable that Lovelace and the New York Council were ready to make disposition of the matter. Jacobs was found guilty of perpetrating rebellion, a crime punishable by death. Execution of the ringleader, however, presented a dilemma to the judges who feared that if one traitor was hanged, then all involved in the insurrection should receive equal punishment. Deciding that most of the rebels were "simple and ignorant" people who had unwittingly been drawn into committing a capital crime, the Council refused to endorse mass executions.

Thus Jacobs' sentence of death was reduced to a public whipping and branding on the face with the letter "R," a lasting symbol of conviction for rebellion. After being marked, the leader would be sold as a servant in a remote area of the British West Indies. Chief accomplices in the insurrection were sentenced to forfeit one-half of their worldly goods to the King. Lower level followers received more minor penalties.

Before his deportation could be arranged, Jacobs attempted to escape from jail in the company of an Indian sentenced to die for the rape of a settler woman. The insurrectionist was transferred to Manhattan and on January 28, Lovelace issued a warrant to the Captain of the *Fort Albany,* a vessel bound for the West Indies. The order read:

> These are to impower you when you shall have brought the said Marcus Jacobs, alias Long Finne, to the Barbadoes, that you cause him to be sold for a servant to the best advantage for the space of four years, or the usual time servants are there sold at, and that you make return of the produce to this port, deducting the charges of his passage and other necessary expenses about him. And for so doing, this shall be your warrant.

With the expulsion of the Dutch, England's North America colonies became contiguous, but the settlements were far from united. The absence of roads, difficulties in communications and radical differences in philosophies separated the British possessions as surely as had the Dutch communities.

Apart from a common subservience to the crown, the territories operated as semi-independent republics. Each was concerned almost totally with local issues and little attention was paid to the problems of neighboring colonies. Uniformity of government was unknown; the form, spirit and power of individual administrations varied according to local custom.

The confusing maze of institutions made comprehensive oversight from London impossible. It was clear that maximum benefits to the mother country would accrue only if effective means of uniform control were established.

Activities by the crown and Parliament in the early 1660's indicated that the provinces would quickly be welded into a manageable administrative unit. Pressures from commercial interests had prompted formation of the Council for Foreign Plantations, approval of the navigation acts, expulsion of the Dutch and a new patent to develop the Carolina territory. For the first time, cohesive control seemed an achievable goal.

Yet after the initial burst of enthusiasm, British attention was diverted from the colonies. As in the period of the civil wars, the needs of England required almost total concentration at home. Americans were again left alone to conduct their affairs without outside intervention. The result of this freedom was development of governmental forms in which self-determination played an increasingly vital role.

Events that forced the mother country to turn inward began soon after the Restoration with the realization that Charles could not provide immediate solutions to long-standing problems. Dissatisfaction with the monarch's efforts was perhaps inevitable in light of the unrealistic expectations that had surrounded his return to the throne.

Minor misunderstandings escalated into major political conflicts. Natural calamities, seen by religious fanatics as acts of a vengeful God, seemed destined to bring down the nation.

Because political opposition might have been construed as treasonous in the unsettled post-restoration period, public opposition to the King was channeled into disgust over Charles' unconcealed dalliances with the ladies of the court. Although the King worked long hours on national issues, his unbridled cavorting brought complaints that Charles' interest in government had become secondary to the pursuit of immoral pleasures.

The King's revels in various bedchambers of London became open scandals that were blatantly obnoxious to the prudish Puritans. By 1662, it was alleged that Stuart was no longer in charge of government, but had abdicated control to his Catholic mother Henrietta Maria. Reportedly, the demands of his favorite mistress, Lady Castlemaine, left the King with little time for state business.

More serious disruptions to the national peace came from elements who were not intimidated by potential sanctions for political dissent. Attempted rebellions were made by the Quakers at Yorkshire and by the Fifth Monarchy Saints, a radical sect that believed the end of the world was imminent. Rebels in Ireland and Scotland also took to the streets.

In 1665, a tumultuous natural disaster befell the country when the Great Plague swept through London. For centuries, the disease had been more dreaded than the most prolonged war. The illness had left a trail of death even greater than the most barbaric army and its toll on Britain was calamitous.

An estimated 68,000 of London's 460,000 citizens died. Death carts rolled unabated through the city. Normal activities ground to a halt as the infected were quarantined and the untouched refused to venture from their homes. Thousands of residents fled to the countryside in an attempt to escape, but the illness followed. All England seemed at a standstill, unable to fight the internal enemy that preoccupied all thoughts.

Within a year the plague had done its worst and began to subside. But even as the death rates decreased, a new horror appeared. On September 2, 1666, a small fire in Pudding Lane blazed out of control. Fanned by a "Belgium wind" from the lowlands, the fire fed on wooden structures in the crowded city. For four days the blaze swept unopposed through major sections of London. Charles and James rode tirelessly through the smoky thoroughfares directing firefighters. The fleet, in port because no funds could be raised to finance its sailing, was threatened.

Before the conflagration was brought under control, more than 13,000 houses were burned together with uncounted shops, warehouses and guild halls. Convicts escaped from Newgate and Fleet Street prisons. St. Paul's cathedral and eighty-three other churches were destroyed. More than £200,000 of books and presses were lost at Stationers' Hall alone. Half the population was left homeless.

Residents had not recovered from the disastrous effects of the Great Fire when foreign domination loomed as a distinct possibility. In June of 1667, Dutch forces, taking advantage of England's weakened state, sailed inland, up the Thames to strike at the fleet. The King's flagship, the *Royal Charles,* was taken. England, unable to mount a counterattack, was forced to accept less than favorable terms to end the Second Dutch War.

As the result of tensions created by the plague, fire and war, religion reemerged as a divisive factor breeding hatred and fear. Unlike the Anglican-Puritan conflict that had helped to precipitate the civil wars, the new rivalry pitted Catholic against Protestant.

Most Anglicans and dissenters firmly believed that a giant Catholic conspiracy had been formed to eliminate Protestants and their faith. Even as the Great Fire burned, streets were filled with gossip that the blaze had been kindled by papists who raced about the city heaving "fire balls" into wooden structures. Supposedly, thousands of foreign Catholics were poised to strike from the sea. The tales of arson were so widely accepted that Charles was forced to summon the people of London to a gathering at Moorfields. Here he announced that the fire was an act of God, not a villainous plot.

The King's reassurance did not convince everyone in the capital. When a meteor flashed over the city in May of 1668, Samuel Pepys recorded in his diary that citizens interpreted the event as a sign that Catholics were readying for another fire. This time Protestants would be slain in mass executions.

Despite Charles' continued pledges of loyalty to the Protestant cause, the King was generally thought to be under the complete influence of Catholic-leaning advisers who valued the interests of the Church above those of the nation. Among the most distrusted confidants was the "CABAL," an acronym for the Lords Clifford, Ashley, Buckingham, Arlington and Lauderdale.

The influence of romanist government upon Stuart was also eyed with suspicion and distaste. The King's Portuguese wife, Queen Catherine of Braganza, openly practiced Catholicism with her faithful retinue. Charles' sister Minette was married to the Duke of Orléans, the brother of Louis XIV.

In 1670, fears that the King would subvert his nation's interests to those of Catholic countries were partially vindicated by the signing of secret agreements between Charles and Louis. Known as the "Dover

Plot'' these compacts provided that the English monarch would receive £150,000 annually from the French. The funds would enable Charles to govern without calling the unfavorable Parliament, promote the Catholic faith and begin still another war with Protestant Holland, France's long-term rival on the continent. Charles also agreed to make no alliances without the specific approval of the French leader.

The disturbances in England were reflected in the low priority given to overseas territories. The Council for Foreign Plantations worked intermittently and without adequate staff. The group disintegrated into an instrument of little importance. Instead of centralized control in a single administrative unit, supervision of colonial affairs became dispersed among many agencies.

England's long period of internal dissension was not destined to continue indefinitely. As the years passed, memories of the plague and Great Fire dimmed. By 1675, optimism was again returning to England. It was time to reconsider the American situation. In still another reorganization, provincial problems were made the responsibility of twenty-four distinguished Englishmen known as the Lords of Trade. The group, formed as a standing committee of the Privy Council, was faced with an immediate emergency. The most significant threat of colonial rebellion that had yet confronted England, was emerging on the horizon in Virginia.

# CHAPTER V

# Bacon Takes Virginia

THE YEARS BETWEEN 1660 and 1675 had been difficult ones for Virginia as well as for England. Natural calamities, political discord, economic trials and changes in the social structure altered the attitudes of many colonists. Loyalty to the monarchy, a deep-seated emotion that had impelled the Virginians to risk invasion by Parliamentary forces, had not been rewarded. Instead of gratuities, the Restoration had brought a series of affronts that shook the rock hard allegiance that had bound the province to the crown. By the mid-1670's, Virginia was no longer the obedient jewel of the British empire, but an alienated hotbed of discontent.

One of the most irksome problems involved the long-standing practice of "transporting" undesirables into the province as punishment for crimes. Since the earliest days of settlement, America had served as a dumping ground for the unwanted of England.

In what was perhaps the first Royal Proclamation dealing with the New World, James I had ordered on September 17, 1603, the speedy execution of plans to dispatch "rogues, vagabonds, idle and dissolute persons" from Britain to the colonies. The removal was desperately needed, according to the monarch, to eliminate the menace caused by "incorrigible or dangerous" persons who "swarmed and abounded everywhere."

The desirability of sparsely inhabited Virginia as a place of exile was abundantly clear. Some Englishmen such as the poet John Donne, hoped that the area would serve "not only [as] a spleen to drain ill humours of the body, but a liver to breed good blood." Such rehabilitative advantages were generally ignored by the majority of Britishers who wished merely to insure safety at home.

On December 23, 1617, James perpetuated the system of transportation by ordering that England's "most notorious and lewd" citizens be ferreted out and sent either to war or to Virginia. Presumably both choices were equally unpleasant. In 1632, the province's General Court made a lame attempt to cleanse Jamestown of undesirables. The entrance of two "maids" who had become pregnant during the trans-Atlantic voyage was forbidden, but the jurists were less successful in halting the influx of felons.

Because the harsh English code prescribed death for at least three hundred crimes of varying severity, many of the "criminals" forced to America were not hardened offenders, but harmless, erring citizens. A large percentage of the exiled prisoners no doubt welcomed the opportunity to escape jail and begin a new life. Less delighted at the ordered immigration were captive soldiers banished because of participation in war or rebellion. To these proud men, whose only crime had been attachment to the losing side or a political controversy, transportation and forced servitude was perhaps particularly dreadful.

After the Restoration, unrepentant Cromwellian soldiers were exiled to America in significant numbers and their presence in Virginia was believed by locals to constitute a considerable threat. In September of 1663, fears were confirmed when a widespread conspiracy was uncovered in York, Middlesex and Gloucester counties.

The rebellion was a joint effort between black slaves and indentured soldiers who agreed to rise up and murder their masters. It is unlikely that the insurgents envisioned capturing total control of Virginia. A more likely possibility is that the men, on gaining freedom, intended to escape westward and found a new, outlaw nation on the frontier.

The revolt was scheduled to begin on September 13, but as the conspirators prepared for action, a Gloucester servant named Birkenhead turned informant. Governor Berkeley reacted to the warning by calling out the local militia. The show of official force prompted most of the plotters to flee or disavow knowledge of the uprising. Four plotters were executed for their attempted rebellion. Birkenhead received a reward and was freed from his indenture.

Despite continued complaints from Virginia and the obvious threat created by the deportees, transportation of the "Newgate Birds" was not stopped. On April 20, 1670, the Virginia General Court moved to solve the problem by forbidding the introduction of additional "desperate villians sent hither from the prisons of England." Although public safety was cited as the prime motive, the reputation of the colony was also deemed at stake. According to the Court, the province was increasingly viewed as a "place only fit to receive such base and lewd people" as were fleeing the British gallows.

America continued to be perceived in some circles as a land inhabited by society's dregs. Forced transportation thrived until the mid-eighteenth century. After the 1746 defeat of the Scots at Culloden Moor, British victors ordered that one out of every twenty captured soldiers should be executed. Lots were drawn to determine which unfortunate prisoners would be marked for death. The remaining nineteen soldiers were shipped to the colonies as indentured servants.

The General Court's action in barring felons must have been prompted by overwhelming public apprehension, for in labor-starved Virginia, workers of almost any physical or mental condition were desperately needed to tend the tobacco fields. Unlike corn or livestock, items that could be produced with relatively little direct labor, tobacco cultivation was a delicate and constant process involving continual care.

By the mid-1660's, Virginia's economy was totally dependent upon tobacco, but the leaf that had earlier insured the survival of the fledging colony had resulted in costs as well as benefits. Among the most pressing problems was the effect of the weed on land availability.

The sweet scented Virginia varieties of tobacco leached the soil of potash and nitrogen. After only a few years, farms were left "spoiled" or unfit for further use. New fields were in constant demand and the countryside that had once seemed limitless was increasingly taken up by planters or speculators. Further pressures were created by the burgeoning population which rose more than one hundred and fifty percent between 1649 and 1670.

Decreases in the availability of land contributed to mounting stratification of the formerly fluid society. Small farmers found it difficult to expand their holdings. Indentured servants no longer automatically assumed that material betterment would follow their release from bondage. The beginnings of a landed aristocracy emerged as channels for social and economic mobility closed. Class lines hardened.

Both the rich and the poor, however, were affected by restrictive mercantilistic policies adopted in England. In 1673, Parliament passed the Plantation Duty Act, a measure that proved even more harmful than the navigation and staple statutes. Under the new bill, customs were to be levied on all enumerated items leaving colonial ports for any destination save England. By pre-taxing goods in intra-colonial commerce, London officials not only hoped to increase revenue, but to halt smuggling and trade with foreign nations. The customs on tobacco was set at one penny per pound.

The elimination of European trade forced Virginians to either accept low tobacco prices offered by English merchants, or risk imprisonment by smuggling to non-British ports. The lack of competition sent crop prices plummeting, while the costs of imported merchandise soared to new levels. In order to produce more income, farmers planted additional acreage, but the increased supply only lowered profits even further. Each small reduction in price, or increase in freight rates was critical to colonial farmers, who netted only about fifty shillings per year on their harvests. Inflation boomed on the Chesapeake as frustrated planters watched helplessly while control over the economy passed into English hands. Colonial secretary Thomas Ludwell announced that the yeomen were so desperate that "mutiny and confusion" might break out at any moment.

Paradoxically, Virginia's economy was verging on ruin at precisely the same time that the province's importance to Britain was becoming near overwhelming. Critics of the restrictive trade policies insisted that the mother country was more dependent upon America, than America was on England. By 1670, duties from the tobacco colonies alone, constituted one-third of all English customs.

Environmental and political calamities also beset the hard working colonists. In 1666, Virginia's entire tobacco harvest was left to rot when the plague made it impossible for the London merchant fleet to leave home port. Conditions did not improve the following year. In April of 1667, a hailstorm ravaged the colony with missiles said to have been as large as turkey eggs. Early crops were destroyed and

livestock killed in significant numbers. Soon after the summer planting, a forty day rain washed the fields clean. On August 27, a hurricane known as the "Great Gust" caused flooding that destroyed virtually every place of habitation in the colony.

The disasters of 1667 were not over. Holland, bringing the Second
Dutch War home to England's American possessions, dispatched a
fleet up the James. A twenty ship convoy, fully loaded and ready to
put out, was destroyed and a British frigate on escort duty was captured.

In 1673, the Dutch, at war with England for the third time in
twenty years, attacked again from the sea. Virginians were unable to
mount an effective defense because farmers, suspecting that rebellion
by slaves and servants was imminent, were unwilling to leave their
homes defenseless for even a brief period. In another tragedy, a cattle
epidemic destroyed one-half of the colony's livestock and settlers attempted to save the remaining animals by using grain stockpiled for
human consumption. Remnants of the cattle survived, but the people's
food supply was exhausted in the process. Famine became a reality.

Amid the natural and economic disasters, a new anxiety confronted
Virginians. Concern stemmed from resumption of royal land grants to
favored courtiers. It seemed likely, that the entire concept of private
ownership was being placed in jeopardy.

In 1669, four English patentees, including Governor Berkeley's
brother Lord John, resurrected a twenty-year-old land grant made by
Charles during the interregnum. The patent bestowed upon the Englishmen all lands between the Potomac and the Rappahannock Rivers, an area of more than five million acres. The gift was shocking to
Virginians, for much of the land had been under cultivation for decades and was considered privately owned by local inhabitants. The
uproar ensuing from the old colony, prompted British officials to
modify the original terms of the deed. Land rights by existing residents would be recognized if eleven years back quitrents were paid to
the new owners.

Reaction to the Rappahannock grant had not stopped reverberating
when the King deeded away the rest of the colony to Thomas, Lord
Culpeper and Henry, Lord Arlington. Under the February 25, 1673
patent, the two men would hold rights to the province for thirty-one
years. Their position would be that of Lords Proprietors, similar to

Baltimore and the Duke of York. Fears arose among the population that civil liberties would be abolished, the Burgess dismantled and long term inhabitants put under the sway of grasping English lords anxious only to collect quitrent and fees.

The assembly dispatched agents to London to fight the grant and secure a royal charter that would guarantee that the ancient rights of Britishers, considered inalienable in Virginia for fifty years, would not be abolished. A poll of fifty pounds of tobacco per person was approved to finance the representatives who were able to reduce the proprietary claims to quitrents and escheats in exchange for a one-half penny per pound fee on all exported tobacco.

In the tense days of 1675, even the Burgess had become a topic of dispute. The assembly was no longer honored as a conduit for popular complaints, but viewed by many as the tool of the royal Governor. Sir William Berkeley had found the Restoration Burgess so agreeable that he had continued the body for nearly thirteen years without calling new elections. Because of the extension, citizens had been unable to remove legislators who did not respond to local needs. The number of such men was significant, for few Burgess dared to openly oppose the dictates of the Governor. In practice, law-making had become a function of the administration rather than the legislature.

Further limitations were placed on the ability of the population to control government in 1670 when voting requirements were tightened. All tenants and freemen of modest means were disenfranchised together with marginal farmers owning less than the minimum personal and real property required by law.

Adding to the Burgess' unpopularity were the exorbitant costs necessary to conduct each session. Total expenditures for the 1675 meeting were 539,390 pounds of tobacco, a staggering amount to local planters whose annual production was approximately 1,200 pounds. An additional 24,000 pounds of tobacco was levied to pay for a twenty-four man bodyguard retained by Berkeley.

Although ill feelings ran high among all classes, unrest was most apparent among marginal farm families. These men and women, who composed a majority of settlers, felt economic hardships first and strongest. Unable to accumulate savings, small farmers could not withstand even a single year of low prices or inadequate crops. The Virginia poll, a regressive form of revenue collection under which all citizens paid identical taxes, was an ever present burden.

Equally troubling to small farmers, were the irregularities of corrupt local officials. Public funds were expended without open accountability. Tax receipts disappeared without explanation. Urgent programs went unfunded. Allegations of embezzlement extended to the highest levels where large sums of public monies were reportedly taken for the private use of the Governor's friends.

Defense expenditures were particularly vulnerable to abuse and fraud. It was generally suspected that most of the taxes levied for construction of forts were misappropriated. The few garrisons that were built generally proved substandard. During heavy rains for example, the sturdy looking blockhouses of brick, stone and wood, collapsed to reveal flimsy foundations of mud.

Monies for maintenance of installations disappeared before repairs could be made. Guns rusted into ruin. Castle duties, a medieval means of raising supplies for defense, were subject to intense fraud. Under this system, merchant captains supposedly left in each port a supply of shot and powder for the common stores. In Nansemond, residents complained that the collectors of the castle duties were refusing to accept military supplies and instead were ordering captains to make payments in tradeable items. These goods were then sold by the collectors for personal profit. Port garrisons were left with insufficient arsenals.

Misappropriation of military funds was of utmost concern, for in Virginia society, defense was a constant preoccupation. Even residents in the long-settled tidewater area were not immune from seacoast invasion or Indian attack. On the frontier, the issue of adequate protection reached near obsessive levels.

Defense in the provinces was not the responsibility of a well-trained, standing army, but the assignment of the common people. Every able-bodied, white male was required to possess and keep in good order, a gun, shot and powder. By law he was compelled to muster periodically for training and report for military duty when so ordered. Virginia's women constituted a strong second line of defense. When their males were absent or injured, the province's females were expected to take up arms to defend the colony's farms and villages.

Virginians had been spared a total Indian uprising for three decades, but recollections of a 1644 massacre still wrought fear in the hearts of older residents. During the earlier war, tribes attacked south of the James and more than five hundred whites had been slain. Towns and crops were burned in a swath of devastation. There had been no warning in 1644, but some claimed to have seen an ominous sign. Just before the attack, a giant flock of pigeons filled the sky in a sudden flight. The colony had been saved from destruction only after Governor Berkeley assumed command of the military and personally captured Oppecancanough, the master Indian strategist.

Upon close inspection, the much feared warrior did not present a countenance of terror, but appeared to spectators as only a pathetic old man. Historian William Beverley wrote that the Indian:

> . . . was not able to walk alone, but was carried about by his men wherever he had a mind to move. His flesh was all macerated, his sinews slackened, and his eye-lids became so heavy, that he could not see, but as they were lifted up by his servants.

Oppecancanough was not forced to bear the curiosity of the whites for long. While in prison, the Chief was shot in the back by one of his captors.

Local whites benefited from the 1646 treaty that ended the uprising. Defeated and severely weakened, native tribes relinquished all land between the York and the James. They also agreed to acknowledge the English King as sovereign over all Virginia. As a sign of tribute, the Indians vowed to pay twenty beaver skins to the colony "at the going away of the geese yearly."

Changes in official policy accompanied the victory and the concept of coexistence between English and Indian was replaced by a system of complete separation. Friendly tribes were placed on reservations and required to send Indian children as hostages to white communities. It was understood that if difficulties were encountered because of Indian aggression, retribution would be taken on the children. In addition, strict laws on native travel were enacted and it was declared that if a white was slain by an Indian, warriors of the village nearest to the murder would be automatically punished for the crime although no evidence might be presented against them.

The reservation strategy did not hold back the land hungry whites. When native populations became depleted by small pox, venereal diseases and tuberculosis, planters became even more exploitative. White "land Lopers" unhesitatingly grazed their livestock on territory reserved for Indians, rationalizing the encroachment by claiming that rights had been acquired through purchase of territory from the tribes.

Even Sir William Berkeley, perhaps the most avid preserver of Indian liberties, sent explorations into tribal territory. In the early 1670's, it was still believed that a passage to the South Seas lay close by, and the Governor hoped to find the strait so that the local economy could be diversified.

Berkeley's protection of friendly tribes drew considerable criticism from frontiersmen who believed that all Indians were treacherous. To these backwoodsmen, the harboring of any native was a perilous undertaking.

Apprehensions of the hard-liners deepened in 1675 when large numbers of Susquehannoch suddenly appeared on the frontier. For many years, Maryland had protected the Chesapeake Bay tribe, and allowed its members to live in relative peace within Baltimore's jurisdiction. Contrary to colonial practice, the Proprietor's deputies had given guns to the Susquehannoch and urged the warriors to protect the province from unfriendly Indians such as the warlike Senecas.

The careful balance of power was upset in 1674 when Baltimore concluded a peace with the Senecas. As a result of the treaty, the Susquehannochs were left without English support and were decisively defeated by the Iroquois nation. Survivors fled southward into the Potomac River area above Great Falls. Homeless, defenseless and without food, the Susquehannoch began to forage. The desperate search for sustenance expanded beyond Maryland's boundaries to include Virginia territory across the river.

Omens were not promising in the old colony during the spring of 1675. A great comet appeared in the sky "streaming like a horsetail westward." Even stranger was an infestation of locusts that emerged from holes in the ground. For perhaps a month, the noisy insects ate tree leaves and then disappeared as unexpectedly as they had arrived. In a third mysterious happening, armies of squirrels descended from trees. Finally, an enormous flock of pigeons blackened the sky. Such a sight had not been seen for years. Not since 1644.

The disquiet was broken in July, when the Potomac River plantation of Thomas Mathew was invaded by Indians. Before wounded overseer Robert Hen died from wounds suffered in the attack, he accused the unruly Doeg tribe of the deed.

The raid had not been unprovoked. Mathew had previously taken trading goods from the Doegs and refused to pay. The Indians had reacted by sending a party to confiscate hogs equal to the debt. In repelling the party, the planter had killed several braves, and it was to avenge these slayings, that the tribe had attacked Hen.

Reasons behind the killing were of little concern to whites in the Potomac area. Vengeance was seen as the only response and within days it was forthcoming. A party of armed colonials crossed the river into Maryland, attacked a Doeg settlement and killed eleven members of the tribe. Minutes after the confrontation, a second camp was discovered. Without warning, whites opened fire and cut down even more warriors before it was learned that the encampment was not Doeg, but friendly Susquehannoch.

Maryland officials were furious at both the invasion of their province and the murder of the innocent Susquehannoch. Unlike Virginia where Indian hatred was accepted, considerable effort had been made in the Proprietor's territory to maintain coexistence. An element of anti-Indian feeling did exist among the frontiersmen, but the bias had been checked by the success of governmental policies.

Berkeley was also angered by the incident and ordered Colonel John Washington to investigate the episode so that guilty parties might be brought to justice. Instead of obeying the Governor's instructions, Washington contacted low-level militiamen in Maryland and requested assistance in forming a punitive expedition. Major Thomas Truman agreed to raise two hundred and fifty Marylanders for a march on a Piscataway fort across from Mount Vernon. Here the fearful Susquehannoch had taken refuge.

On September 26, the 1,000-man combined force reached the Potomac installation. In an attempt to avoid bloodshed, five chiefs of the Susquehannoch emerged from the fort under a flag of truce. Truman, angered by the Indians' refusal to admit responsibility for frontier raids ordered the emissaries to be killed. Though many of the pioneers were shocked at the violation of the truce, the executions were carried out and a siege was thrown up in an attempt to starve the remaining one hundred men, women and children into submission.

Even the popularly elected assembly at St. Mary's was appalled by Truman's action, a crime that placed the entire colony in danger. The militiaman was impeached by the lower house and fined for the slayings. The upper house, representing more conservative interests, maintained that the punishment was insufficient.

A saddened Berkeley also took the side of the dead warriors. The Governor declared: "If they had killed my grandfather and my grandmother, my father and mother, and all my friends, yet if they had come to treat of peace, they ought to have gone in peace."

The Piscataway siege was broken after seven weeks when the Susquehannoch managed to escape under the cover of night. Disgruntled militiamen plundered the fort and returned home. The Susquehannoch crossed the Potomac and began raiding in Virginia with a vengeance.

During January of 1676, Indians struck with deadly retribution along the heads of Virginia's major rivers. Berkeley ordered a counterattack under the leadership of Sir Henry Chicheley, a cavalier who had fled to the colony after the English civil wars. At the last moment, however, the expedition was cancelled. Although the tribal raids were continuing, the alerted militiamen were instructed to return home. The volunteers were astounded by the disbanding. The Governor's refusal to act in revenge for the Mathew's raid had caused extensive resentment. The January cancellation seemed entirely unjustified.

Berkeley had evidently chosen not to make public the reasons that prompted the sudden reversal in policy. A peace offer had been tendered by the Indians who suggested that tribal honor had been satisfied by the killing of ten whites for every chief slain at Piscataway. The red men were ready to parley.

A truce proved impossible. The Indian chiefs were unable to control the small raiding parties roaming unsupervised on the frontier. The killings of both whites and reds continued.

Additional kindling was added when word reached the Chesapeake that a massive Indian rebellion had broken out in New England. The colonies of the North were engaged in a total struggle known as King Philip's War. Thousands of belligerents were being slain. Refugees were streaming into cities with gory tales of horror and death.

To Virginians the news was terrifying. The unrest of the Susquehannoch was no longer viewed as an isolated, local uprising. Instead, many settlers concluded that a conspiracy existed among all eastern tribes. From Maine to Carolina, the red men had joined in a concerted, coordinated scheme to push the English back into the sea.

Berkeley attempted to control the growing panic by relying upon a "stronghold defense." He ordered frontier residents to leave their farms and congregate at the most well-fortified plantations. The suggestion was unacceptable to pioneers who feared they would return home to find crops burnt, livestock slain and cabins destroyed. Apprehensive that friendly tribes might be drawn into the action, Sir William arranged for food to be shipped to the reservations. The move enraged small farmers who believed that no Indian could be truly neutral.

In early March, the Burgess convened to consider the situation, but those expecting the group to take corrective action were bitterly disappointed. The assembly continued to rubber-stamp Berkeley's suggestions. Although an estimated three hundred colonists had already been killed, the legislators refused to recommend official military action. Instead, the group passed several innocuous measures aimed at treating the symptoms rather than the cause of the war. Pacified tribes were ordered to send more hostages. The trading of ammunition and guns with warriors was made a capital offense. A bounty of one coat was voted to each friendly Indian who brought in the head of an enemy. In what was perhaps their most unrealistic undertaking, the Burgess requested help from the King.

The prospect of waiting more than a year for troops to arrive from Britain was not reassuring to settlers facing immediate annihilation. Even more infuriating was the legislative endorsement of Sir William's defensive strategy.

Under the Governor's plan, ten forts would be constructed, primarily along the headwaters of provincial rivers. About three hundred and seventy-five men would be garrisoned in the posts while an additional one hundred and twenty-five rangers served as a mounted patrol between the blockhouses. No soldier would be authorized to fire unless fired upon and the enemy could not be pursued unless specific approval was secured from the Governor in Jamestown. Funds for the entire system would be raised by a heavy new tax. Satisfied that their business had been concluded satisfactorily, the Burgess adjourned, suggesting that residents observe a two-day fast and pray for divine intervention.

Frontiersmen interpreted the defensive tactics as a preposterous betrayal. The invaders could hardly be expected to march conveniently under the fort's guns when sneak raids had proved so effective. It was only a remote possibility that the mounted rangers would be able to find, much less destroy, small parties of woods-wise red men. In the long term, the line of forts would no doubt freeze westward expansion at the river heads, and drive land costs even higher. With few exceptions, Berkeley's program was dismissed by small farmers as a blatant sacrifice of frontier lands so that eastern interests could be protected.

In April, a throng of several hundred western planters gathered at Jordan's Point at the intersection of the James and the Appomattox. The meeting was in response to rumors that Indians were preparing to begin a major invasion that would sound the death knell for whites on the frontier. Believing that Berkeley would ignore the peril, the colonists had decided to move on their own. In a rousing display of mass democracy, Nathaniel Bacon, Jr., a member of the Governor's Council, was chosen to lead the force. According to British commissioners who later investigated the incident, the "election" of Bacon was neither spontaneous nor undertaken in complete sobriety. The official report suggested that the most important elements in the entire affair were the planters' fear, Bacon's ambition and a large quantity of rum.

Nathaniel Bacon, a farmer whose own land had been attacked, had arrived in the colony less than two years earlier. The personable young man quickly made friends in high circles, perhaps through the entree of Lady Berkeley, Bacon's distant cousin. His acceptance and subsequent appointment to the Council, were particularly unusual in light of the dubious circumstances surrounding Bacon's immigration.

The new leader of the frontiersmen had been born in England in 1647, the only son of a country gentleman of prosperous if not lavish means. After attending Cambridge and studying law, Bacon became involved with Elizabeth Duke, daughter of Sir Edward Duke.

Sir Edward heartily disliked the suitor and sought to discourage a permanent commitment by his daughter by rewriting his will so that Elizabeth would be disinherited if she married Bacon. The couple ignored the stipulation and promptly eloped. Duke refused to speak with his wayward offspring and maintained the silence until his death a year later. Bacon and his bride contested the will, but the provisions were upheld by the Lord Chancellor who condemned the wedding as a "presumptuous disobedience." The Duke's legal heir was more forgiving and consented to a financial settlement.

Elizabeth's funds, coupled with a stipend from Bacon's father, proved inadequate to maintain the high style of living that the couple chose to assume. In what was probably an effort to finance the good life, Bacon became involved in a sordid arrangement involving criminal fraud. The accusation was a serious one that could have meant imprisonment, but Squire Bacon was able to still public complaints by dispatching his son and daughter-in-law to Virginia.

America was a land of opportunity for the prodigal who received a final stake of £1,800 from his father. The money allowed Bacon to purchase a large plantation at Curles Neck on the James about forty miles up river from the capital. Joining with neighbor William Byrd, Bacon also organized an Indian trading venture that promised to return enormous profits. Berkeley approved of the partnership and awarded a license to the pair. To Bacon he revealed: ''Gentlemen of your quality come very rarely into this country.'' The Governor soon had cause to regret the complementary evaluation.

Sir William had also come to America with high hopes. In 1642, thirty-six-year-old Berkeley became Governor of the colony, a post from which he gained the affection of the people. During his early years, the Oxford-educated official worked tirelessly for the interests of Virginia. Special attention was given to the needs of the poor and marginal citizens. In a radical departure from tradition, Berkeley attempted to restructure the tax system so that each resident would pay according to means rather than by poll.

He personally risked death at the head of colonial forces during the 1644 Indian war and stood against Parliament after the death of Charles I, relenting only when the destruction of his beloved Virginia seemed likely. In appreciation for his sacrifices, the assembly awarded Sir William two houses and an orchard. When he fell upon hard financial times, the Burgess approved a special stipend.

Protection of the colony's interests remained Berkeley's major concern after the Restoration. He attempted to diversify the economy by promoting flax cultivation, ship building and a silk industry. Unlike most royal appointees, Berkeley was outspoken against crown policies that were detrimental to provincial interests. He fought against the navigation acts and went before the royal court to defend America's opposition to the measures. In a direct condemnation of British leaders, Sir William rudely implied that London's merchants had made servants out of every Virginian.

In addition to respect, Berkeley found wealth in the province. By 1676, he held title to five houses in Jamestown, and a thriving plantation at Greenspring. Despite large personal expenditures in government services, he officially had been able to accumulate a herd of four hundred cattle and sixty horses. In addition to profits from farming, he received a large income from the issuance of licenses to Indian traders. The monopoly to Bacon and Byrd, for example, was expected to net Sir William eight hundred pounds of beaver skins the first year, and six hundred pounds each year thereafter.

Berkeley's early liberal attitudes hardened with the passage of time. His abhorrence to undisciplined masses developed into mistrust of popular opinion. "I thank God," Sir William wrote of Virginia, "There are no free schools or printing, and I hope we shall not have these . . . for learning has brought disobedience and heresy and sects into the world, and printing has divulged them, and libels against the best government."

Both the Burgess and the General Court were used by the Governor to suppress the disobedience that seemed to grow stronger. Even routine complaints against government actions rankled Sir William into threats of sedition. By 1675, the love of many for the executive had been replaced by suspicion. Everywhere the common people felt alienated by Berkeley, a man they believed refused to risk his trading income by suppressing the Indians on the frontier.

The wariness of the men gathered at Jordan's Point was heightened when Berkeley issued a harsh denunciation of the meeting. According to Sir William, unauthorized actions against the Indians was grossly illegal and teetered on rebellion.

Bacon did not allow his band of followers to become dissuaded by the Governor's rebuke. Instead, the de facto "General" labeled the official as "negligent and wicked, treacherous and incapable." Bacon also promised to personally finance any expedition undertaken by the farmers against the enemy.

Lady Frances Berkeley was annoyed at the abuse being heaped upon her husband. In a personal declaration, the young woman announced that Bacon was so deeply in debt that he was unable to support his own wife and child, much less pay for a costly war. "I do accuse him of a worse crime than poverty," she wrote. "I do accuse him of ingratitude, and that of a deep dye, to return the favorable amity of the Governor with casting all kinds of aspersions upon his courage and conduct in the government of this colony." The outspoken Lady Berkeley was soon dispatched to England by her husband to present the administration's view of the situation to high ranking officials.

On May 3, Sir William marched out with three hundred supporters to inspect the western forts and confront the farmers at Jordan's Point. He had delayed too long. By the time the loyalists reached the campground, Bacon and the western planters had moved southward toward the Roanoke River where a large band of Susquehannoch were said to be bivouacking.

After arriving at the Roanoke, the backwoodsmen who had clamoured so loudly for action, were less than enthusiastic for battle. Bacon was able to keep order by recruiting mercenaries from the local Occaneechee tribe, a small band who agreed to attack the Susquehannoch in exchange for captives and booty. Their willingness to serve as surrogates was peculiar, for the Occaneechee were known as peaceful traders. Their experiment in violence was successful. The Susquehannoch were totally routed.

But the Indian victors were destined to receive more than a share of the spoils. Immediately after the battle, Bacon accused the tribe of refusing to supply food to the hungry backwoodsmen. The pioneers attacked the exhausted warriors and set fire to the Indian village. Men, women and children who ran from the burning huts were shot on sight. The groans of the victims were so loud that not even the Virginians' shouts could cover the sound. Only a handful of the one hundred Occaneechee escaped the slaughter. An anonymous Baconite involved in the battle later wrote: "in the heat of the fight we regarded not the advantage of prisoners . . . but burnt and destroyed all. . . ." The rebel army, heavily laden with skins and pelts which the Occaneechee had collected for trade, turned back eastward.

Procedures devised by Bacon during the Roanoke expedition became the accepted mode of operation for the extra-legal army. During the remainder of 1676, many Indian men and women would be killed by the force, but few victims would be from enemy tribes. Only friendly, passive groups would be attacked. Most vulnerable were those living in villages rich in furs and corn, and located close enough to be attractive to white settlement.

Bacon arrived home a near savior to the small farmer. Not only had scores of Indians been killed, but the frontiersmen had escaped harm and reaped significant monetary profits. Berkeley was not ecstatic. In early May he declared that the illegal march constituted rebellion, but promised pardon for all but three leaders who agreed to desist. Bacon was once of those exempted.

On the Governor's orders, the hero of Roanoke was removed from the Council, but in a more conciliatory gesture, Sir William dissolved the old Burgess and called for elections in which all freemen would be eligible to vote. He declared that the new members would be instructed to consider all grievances submitted by the people and investigate allegations of official misconduct. If the legislature found even the slightest abuse had occurred on his part, Sir William promised to offer his immediate resignation.

Few accepted Berkeley's pardon, for total attention was now being lavished on the people's general. Elizabeth Bacon noted that the population was so enamored of her husband, that "they would not leave him alone."

That the Roanoke expedition had intensified rather than lessened the war was a fact apparently unrecognized by the citizenry. Friendly and neutral tribes, learning of the Occaneechee's fate, showed a decided reluctance to assist the English. In some cases, formerly peaceful tribes joined the Susquehannoch. The shift in allegiances was disappointing to Sir William, who had labored for years to find a way in which red and white might live together. On May 15, he notified a militia officer: "I believe all the Indians, our neighbors, are engaged with the Susquehannoch, and therefore, I desire you to spare none that has the name of an Indian, for they are now all our enemies."

Berkeley continued overtures to Bacon, but the young dissident refused to discuss surrender. Encouraged by growing support from wealthy planters and eastern farmers, Bacon informed Sir William that peace could be reestablished only when the Governor consented to the demands of the war faction.

Berkeley refused to accept the dictate. On May 29 he issued a *Declaration and Remonstrance* branding Bacon as a dangerous traitor who had repeatedly refused pardon. Less than a week later, Sir William secretly notified London: ". . . I am so over weaned with riding into all parts of the country to stop this violent rebellion that I am not able to support myself at this age six months longer and therefore on my knees I beg his sacred majesty would send a more vigorous Governor." On the frontier, voters elected the declared rebel as a member of the new House of Burgess.

Bacon stole into Jamestown on the night of June 6 to reconnoiter the situation and determine if he should attempt to take the assembly seat. After a surreptitious meeting with capital intimates headed by ex-Carolina Governor William Drummond, the insurgent decided to return home. Escape was impossible. En route, Bacon was captured and returned to Jamestown to stand trial.

Word of the arrest brought hundreds of frontiersmen into the village. The unruly throng unbalanced Berkeley and made the official reluctant to extract the full penalty of the law. A compromise was devised that allowed both the law-maker and the law-breaker to save face.

On June 9, in a public display of repentence, Bacon fell to his knees before the Governor and begged pardon for rebellion and mutiny. He swore to abide by all statutes and pledged his entire estate as a good behavior bond. Sir William accepted the apology and issued a general pardon. Bacon was readmitted to the Council.

With peace restored, the Burgess convened in anticipation of a landmark session that would bring significant changes in both law and government. The new representatives were far different from the conservatives who had sat in the Restoration body. Most assumed that an early order of business would be consideration of grievances submitted by the small farmers.

Berkeley, however, reneged on his public promises and enjoined the group from debating any domestic matter until an Indian policy had been formulated. The situation was further complicated by the executive's refusal to accept any plan that involved offensive tactics. As a result, the Burgess was unable to produce a strategy that differed from the previous design of fortress defense. Days dragged on without progress. Issues such as taxation, illegal fees, abuses by officeholders and navigation policies received no significant attention.

Amid rumors that Berkeley was planning to have him assassinated, Bacon left Jamestown and returned to the frontier to reassemble the citizen army. Recruitment boomed as a result of the belief that Sir William had intentionally deceived the people with false vows in order to halt the momentum that had been building against the Indians. Ironically, the ire of the planters was no longer directed against the red men, but had shifted in focus to the Governor. When the reconstituted force moved out to do battle, the men did not head west, but turned east toward the capital. On June 23, the rebels occupied Jamestown.

An estimated six hundred frontiersmen held guns on the Burgess,

Council and Governor while Bacon demanded that a commission be issued for immediate military action against the Indians. Berkeley, who had been unable to rally sufficient strength to defend the community, refused to sign the document. Members of the assembly showed less concern with the moral obligations of upholding crown authority. According to Secretary Ludwell, the body was paralyzed by "fear of having their throats cut by Bacon, or their scalps taken by the Indians." When the assembly joined in pressing Berkeley to concede, the Governor at last relented. He not only signed a commission for Bacon, but approved blank authorizations for any lieutenants that the rebel might wish to appoint.

The capitulation did not end Bacon's demands. Berkeley was ordered to pardon all insurgents, justify the rebellion to the King and prohibit certain loyalists from holding office. In addition, the Governor, Council and Burgess were all directed to recant any previous criticism of the insurrection that might have been sent to England.

Although Bacon seemed totally concerned with securing protection against punishment, the Burgess was more committed to solving the grievances that had caused the revolt. Freed from Berkeley's arbitrary hand, the assembly enacted reforms that provided remedies for the oppressed small farmer. Changes were made in requirements for officeholdings. County courts were given new authority. Fees were regulated and the vote was returned to propertyless freemen. Indian trade was regulated and the tax-exempt status of government officials was removed. Finally, all "treasons, misprison of treasons, murders, fellonies, offences, crimes, contempts and misdemeanors" committed since March 1 were pardoned by the group. In all, twenty new statutes were approved before the body adjourned on June 25.

Bacon also left Jamestown. Informed that an Indian party was less than forty miles away, the planter and his followers evacuated the village, but did not march on the invaders. Instead of engaging the red men, the rebels meandered through the Virginia countryside confiscating supplies from plantations owned by the Governor's supporters. From Gloucester County came reports that the army had confiscated all available guns and horses. Local residents, rendered defenseless against Indian attack, had also been warned that if opposition was made against the seizures, Bacon's men would return to ruin the country. When the Gloucestermen asked the Governor if Bacon's commission was indeed legal, the official replied that the document was no more legitimate than if "a thief should take my purse and make me owne I gave it [to] him freely."

With the insurgents occupied beyond the reach of Jamestown, Berkeley withdrew the commission and declared Bacon and all who followed him to be traitors. Militiamen from adjoining counties were summoned, but although 1,200 answered the call, few agreed to move against the popular army. The Governor's deceptions had brought even the eastern farmers to the side of the insurgents. No longer was Bacon's movement a frontier-based fight against the Indians. The Rebellion had become a broad action to redress arbitrary government.

Trappings of permanency began to emerge. Without overt opposition, the popularists gained control of all but a small portion of the colony. Berkeley was forced to flee Jamestown and cross the Bay to the eastern shore where pockets of loyalists remained committed to the crown. From Accomack, the Governor and a small group of faithful watched as Bacon solidified his authority over the province.

On July 30, Bacon issued a *Manifesto Concerning the Troubles in Virginia,* and a *Declaration of the People.* The documents reiterated the abuses of government that had reportedly driven the people to arms. All who had not officially joined the insurgents were ordered to do so within four days or face punishment. Nineteen individuals were singled out as "wicked and pernitious councellors" who had abetted Berkeley in "traiterously" governing the people. Included on the list was William Claiborne.

To enforce the manifesto, armed parties were dispatched against the plantations of known royalist supporters. Neutrality was not to be permitted to anyone. Seventy of the colony's most prominent men were called to a conference at Middle Plantation, later known as Williamsburg, to discuss formation of a new government. Each of the attendees was instructed to swear that he would actively work against Berkeley and would fight royal troops that the King might send to put down the rebellion. According to witnesses, the latter stipulation stunned the participants.

Active resistance to the crown was considered the highest treason in the seventeenth century. The delegates refused to even consider opposing the King's forces despite Bacon's attempts to rationalize the pledge. According to the rebel, Charles would dispatch troops only because Berkeley had provided the monarch with false information. When the true facts became known, the redcoats would be recalled and Berkeley would be punished. Despite the nimbled-tongued explanation and the presence of a citizen army of 1,300 foot and horse, the men continued to reject the oath.

In the midst of the impasse, circumstance again intervened to make Bacon's position appear acceptable. A messenger burst into the conference announcing that Tindall's Fort on the York, supposedly the strongest garrison in the colony, was in danger of falling to the Indians. The disaster had occurred because Berkeley had secretly taken the fort's guns and ammunition for his own use. Because of the official's selfishness, the heavily populated eastern region now lay at the mercy of the savages.

The conferees were thrown into consternation. Bacon pressed even harder for approval of the pledge. Such a complete endorsement was essential, he claimed, if he was to save the colony from destruction. Thomas Mathew witnessed the scene at Middle Plantation and was amazed at the dissident's ability to sway the opinion of seemingly intelligent men. The Virginian later recalled that the conferees' minds became "flexible" by Bacon's "cuning and subtillety," and that the oath "became now more smooth and glib, to be swallowed even by those who had the greatest repugnancy against it."

On August 3, the entire conference swore to fight against the English troops.

Bacon's actual plans were far more radical than his public reassurances. Just days later, the planter reportedly discussed with intimates, the possibility of joining with dissatisfied elements in Maryland and North Carolina to permanently secede from British rule. Presumably, the outcome of such a withdrawal would be an alliance with Spain or France and the creation of an independent state under the leadership of Nathaniel Bacon.

Less grandiose, but more in need of immediate attention, was the progress of an expedition that Bacon had dispatched into the Dragon Swamp to subdue unfriendly Indians said to be supporting the Susquehannoch. Characteristically, the citizen army had been unable to locate even a single warrior, and the force's one major engagement had involved the killing of Indian women and children.

For the first time, desertions became a problem. Felled by swamp sickness and disgusted at the lack of productive accomplishments, men simply drifted away. Hoping to reestablish public support with a new victory, Bacon lead the remaining force in a surprise raid on the friendly Pamunkey. The powerful Queen of the tribe had given strict orders that her people were not to fire on the whites. Although the Indians showed no resistance, the frontiersmen pressed the attack until the entire tribe had been killed or taken prisoner. Following the one-sided battle, the army proudly marched back to English territory, parading captives and displaying a rich booty.

Less successful was an amphibious landing on the eastern shore, where loyalists under Philip Ludwell had been able to seize the entire invasion fleet. In exchange for a pardon and immunity from taxes for twenty-one years, many of the rebel prisoners joined forces with the Governor. Believing that the pendulum of public opinion had begun to swing away from Bacon, Sir William crossed the Chesapeake with a substantial army and navy. On September 8 he succeeded in retaking Jamestown.

Less than one hundred and fifty men remained in Bacon's ranks after the Dragon Swamp venture, but the Governor's return, the fear of punishment and the display of the Pamunkey treasures swelled the rebel force. By September 13, six hundred insurgents had encircled the heavily fortified walls of the capital. The rebels began digging in for a seige, equipping themselves for the long wait by taking supplies from nearby plantations.

To forestall any challenge before their defenses could be completed, Bacon directed that the wives of prominent loyalists, including his own cousin, should be placed atop the unfinished parapets. The captured Pamunkey were added to the decoys and behind this human wall of protection, the rebels worked feverishly to complete the seige line.

Inside Jamestown fort, Berkeley's troops were becoming restless. One limited charge was made, but the Governor's force quickly retreated when Bacon's men began firing. Unable to return the volleys and seemingly outnumbered, the loyalists began discussing mutiny.

Berkeley sought to reinforce his army by announcing that all indentured servants and black slaves who enlisted in the King's cause would be rewarded with freedom. The Jamestown defenders, no doubt horrified at the specter of thousands of bondsmen running free, pressed even harder for surrender. On the evening of September 18, it became apparent that retreat was the only solution. Berkeley and a small cadre left the fortress and sailed again for the eastern shore.

The evacuation was ill-timed. Colonel Giles Brent had managed to gather nearly one thousand men and was marching cross country to reinforce the loyalists in the capital. When word of Berkeley's withdrawal arrived, Brent's troops dispersed in fear of retaliation by Bacon's company. Sir William's retreat also discouraged defection of lukewarm Baconites who might have been persuaded to support the crown. Moderates were becoming progressively disenchanted with the dissident movement. The rebellion had gone much farther than most had anticipated and few positive accomplishments had been forthcoming. Hostile Indians still menaced the frontier and instead of directing their efforts towards the west, the rebels seemed totally engaged in looting eastern farms.

On September 19, Jamestown was set to the torch on Bacon's order so that Sir William would be unable to use the seat of government as a rallying point. Martial law was declared. Berkeley was branded as a traitor. Reparations were levied against those on the eastern shore who harbored the fugitive. All citizens in the colony were ordered to take the oath to fight against British troops.

At Gloucester, provincials balked at acknowledging Bacon as virtual dictator and claimed they would never consent to take up arms against the crown. Bacon ordered neutrals imprisoned and farms plundered. One settler who attempted to leave the rebel camp in disgust was executed as a deserter. So harsh did the reign of terror become, that even the rugged Gloucestermen approved the pledge. There was no doubt that the first of his Majesty's colonies was seceding from English control.

On October 26, however, a dramatic reversal swiftly ended the threat. Nathaniel Bacon died unexpectedly. Death was attributed to the bloody flux, probably contracted in the Dragon Swamp, and to "Lousey Disease," a condition in which the victim's body is totally covered with lice. No doubt few opponents were surprised by the repulsive manner in which the insurgent died, for it was commonly believed that traitors were particularly susceptible to death by loathsome illness.

Bacon was buried in secrecy so that royal officials could not disinter the corpse for public display. Charles II's treatment of Cromwell and his associates after the Restoration was evidently still current in the minds of the provincials.

The rebellion immediately began to collapse. Only the charismatic force of Bacon's personality and the terror imposed by his rabid lieutenants had prompted the majority of Virginians to remain in the movement. As soon as the leader's reassurance disappeared, doubts as to the legitimacy and propriety of the cause became overwhelming.

Bacon's successor Joseph Ingram was unable to control the undisciplined army. Elements drifted from farm to farm taking whatever was desired. Berkeley did not allow the revolters time to recoup from disarray. In early November, loyalists under Robert Beverley landed in York and found little opposition even from dissident strongholds. The communal bounds between provincials of both persuasions reappeared as the followers of each side attempted to end the conflict without bloodshed.

The announcement that all but the top leadership of the rebellion would be pardoned outright was a strong incentive to surrender. Equally inspiring was the news that a British force was expected to arrive at any moment. Nowhere was there an indication that the redcoats would be confronted by those who had taken the treasonous oath. Berkeley applied further pressure by forbidding the newly arrived tobacco fleet from trading in areas that had not yet returned to crown control.

The Governor, however, had no inclination to deal as leniently with those who had led the rebellion, as he had promised to treat those who had merely followed behind. In mid-November, Baconite lieutenant Thomas Hansford was convicted by court martial and sentenced to hang. When Hansford protested that he should be shot as a soldier, he was informed that he had lived as a traitor and would die as befitted the crime. Thomas Chieseman, also a Bacon intimate, was condemned despite his wife's pleas that she be killed instead. By Lydia Chieseman's testimony, Thomas joined the rebellion only because of her incessant nagging. Without that incentive, he would have remained neutral. The henpecked husband did escape the noose, but only by dying in prison before the execution could be arranged.

William Drummond temporarily escaped capture by hiding in Chickahominy Swamp, but even the marsh was penetrable by the

Governor's lawmen. Drummond was apprehended, forced to walk five miles in heavy chains and condemned after a thirty-minute trial in which he was not allowed to present a defense.

Instead of chancing such questionnable justice, at least four other high ranking officers made their way into the wilderness and were never again heard from.

Sir William's vengeance multiplied when he returned to Greenspring and discovered that everything of value had been destroyed or stolen. The Governor, forced to borrow a bed on which to sleep, instructed county sheriffs to begin confiscating goods from rebel estates and not to stop until every item taken from his plantation had been replaced. Berkeley estimated his losses £8,000 and claimed that not a grain of corn or a single cow had been left by the insurgent looters.

The administration's most avid supporters, the Greenspring Faction, no doubt contributed to the increasingly severe retribution taken against former insurrectionists. Members of the Faction had been the special targets of rebels and like the Governor, most had suffered extreme financial losses. Each day their anger became greater. So severe did the reaction become that even those speaking or writing in favor of the popular movement were subject to branding, flogging and the pillory. Such punishments would not have been approved in England.

The first reports of the Virginia unrest had reached Britain in April of 1676, but because merchant shipping from the colony was curtailed, additional information arrived only sporadically. English officials were concerned with the potential threat to royal authority, but also deemed critical was the disastrous effects that rebellion might cause on the economy of the home isles. Abhorrence to citizen uprisings was near universal in councils, but many national leaders no doubt recognized that the colonial protest was rooted in legitimate grievances. Allegations of inferior administration were not new to the advisers.

It was indeed important that rebels against the crown be punished, but it was of practical necessity that the province should be bound together as quickly as possible so that normal trade might be established. Widespread recriminations would merely prolong the resentments and impede the speedy conclusion of the episode. Revenge as punishment was rejected and a conciliatory policy was adopted toward all but one of the rebels.

Twelve hundred redcoats were assigned to stifle the rebellion. Dispatched with the contingent were three Commissioners charged with investigating the causes and conduct of the insurrection: Sir John Berry, Francis Moryson and Colonel Herbert Jeffreys. Jeffreys, commander of the troops, was appointed to replace Berkeley until a permanent governor could be appointed. Sir William was ordered to return to England as quickly as possible, and to complete the normalization; the King on October 27, 1676, issued a royal proclamation dealing with the rebellion. The document stated that all who had taken part in the movement were deemed guilty of high treason, but added that anyone who voluntarily swore allegiance to the crown would be pardoned, forgiven and freed from "all punishments and forfeitures."

In January, 1677, Commissioners Berry and Moryson arrived in Virginia to a chilly reception. Both men became immediately embroiled in quarreling with Berkeley, who ignored their authorization, declined their advice and refused to publish the King's pardon. Instead of making the crown's amnesty known, the Governor insisted on issuing his own version, a pardon that exempted scores of rebels that Sir William felt were unworthy of forgiveness. None, however, were specifically mentioned. Because no citizen could be certain that he was eligible for pardon, many hesitated to come forward and swear to uphold the established government.

The Commissioners' task of investigating charges of maladministration was made almost impossible by the Governor's vengeful attitude. Throughout the colony, dissatisfied provincials were unwilling to submit criticism of an official who still held legal control over their life. Already twenty-three individuals had been hanged, more than Charles II had condemned for the death of his father and the loss of the empire. Recriminations had become so severe, that many former revolters discussed the possibility of leaving Virginia and establishing a new state on the frontier.

Despite the Commissioners' insistence that confiscation of property before legal trial was an infringement on English liberties, Sir William continued to seize estates of suspected insurrectionists. The Governor rationalized his actions by insisting that the measures were no different from the royally endorsed plundering of Roundheads, that had taken place during the English civil wars.

Jeffreys arrived on February 11, with troops ready to do battle against the rebels. The massive arsenal accompanying the force included one hundred barrels of gunpowder, 1,000 muskets, 1,000 bandoleers, seven hundred carbines and crates of hand grenades. Jeffreys soon discovered that the need for military intervention had passed and that more than arms were required to subdue Sir William.

The Governor refused to recognize Jeffrey's appointment as Acting Governor and ignored the King's instructions to return to England. In a further display of obstinacy he refused to give an accounting of confiscated property or halt the trials of accused rebels. Only after strong pressure was exerted by the Britishers, did he agree to publish Charles' general pardon, but the Governor and assembly continued to add names to the exempted list in violation of the King's wishes. Sarah Grendon, for example, found herself branded as a chief "encourager" of the rebellion and guilty of high treason for supplying powder to the popular army.

The Governor's belligerent attitude was soundly supported by the new Burgess that was heavily anti-Baconite. The 1677 legislature repealed the progressive reforms enacted by the previous assembly and praised Berkeley as a worthy official who had always taken care to recognize the problems of even the "meanest or poorest man or woman." The fearful population remained unwilling to contradict such glowing pronouncements.

Frustration over the lack of progress began to tell on the Commissioners. In early April, Moryson claimed that the situation "makes us all fools and shortly [will] bring us to cuddy cuddy." Jeffreys, grown disgusted with the Governor's refusal to leave, publicly announced that Sir William had been called home.

Notice of Berkeley's reluctance to turn over the administration had also reached England. Charles notified Jeffreys to deport the official on the next boat leaving Virginia for England. The King also commanded that his royal pardon be applied without exception.

Only grudgingly did Berkeley leave the colony that he had served for nearly thirty-six years. Circumstances had indeed changed since the Restoration when the Burgess had begged the honored official to resume the governorship and Sir William had written the King, that a royal frown was more to be feared than the "swords or tortures" of the enemy.

One of Jeffreys' first duties as the interim head of the province was the settlement of the Indian situation. Instead of bowing to extremists who demanded that the natives captured during the rebellion be sold as slaves, Jeffreys announced that most were friendly and were therefore free to return home. On May 29, ten tribes entered into a treaty with the English. Under terms of the pact, each group was given valid title to reservation lands and additional frontier territory if needed. In return, the Indians swore fidelity to Charles and agreed to inform the colonists in case other tribes planned to attack the province. As an act of allegiance, each nation vowed to pay the reigning Governor an annual quitrent of three arrows and twenty beaver skins.

The Susquehannoch were not among the parties to the treaty. Pushed out by the rebellion and once again landless, the remnants of the tribe went north and were absorbed by the Iroquois. Berkeley arrived in England during June, demanding compensation for the losses he supposedly sustained in the rebellion. He also pled for a hearing in which his name could be cleared, but before action could be taken on either request, he died of natural causes.

The official's reputation was not to be cleansed posthumously. Commissioners Berry and Moryson returned to Britain declaring that the executive and his Greenspring Faction had been the major "disturbers and obstructors" of the peace. Particularly obnoxious to the crown were reports that Berkeley had embezzled tobacco customs by changing the King's arrow to his own mark.

Sarah, widow of William Drummond, joined in criticizing the ex-Governor. The pioneer woman stated that although her husband had not taken up arms, he had been disgracefully hanged as a revolter. She and her five children had been driven from their home and left with no means of support. The King agreed that the Drummonds had been unjustly penalized and ordered restoration of all property that could be identified.

On January 18, 1678, Charles declared all confiscations and repressive actions of the 1677 Burgess to be contrary to the royal pardon. The Lords of Trade followed the monarch's lead by ordering restitution for property taken after January 16, 1677.

For a brief period, quiet marked life in Virginia. The British redcoats became restless from continued inactivity. One exciting moment came when several soldiers ate poisonous Jimson weed in a salad. According to witnesses, the hallucinogen "converted them into idiots, who amused themselves with blowing feathers into the air or sat and made mouths at each other for nearly a fortnight. . . ."

The mood was not so jovial when the soldiers were told that their pay was to be drastically reduced. Colonials feared that the military men's resentment would become so great that a rebellion might erupt. To prohibit the soldiers from capturing the arsenal imported to put down Bacon's rebellion, the magazine was distributed among the people. In this strange turn, the weapons intended to subdue the citizens of Virginia, were given to the population to protect themselves against the crown's forces.

Governor Jeffreys died in 1678, long before the scars of the insurrection could be healed. Thomas, Lord Culpeper, named as the Colonel's replacement, allied himself with the Greenspring Faction and did nothing to promote reconciliation.

The aftermath of Bacon's Rebellion left a permanent mark on the citizens of the old colony. Grievances remained unresolved. The loyalist faction that had taken huge amounts of goods from the people went unpunished. Taxes were not reduced and the King as well as Parliament refused to make trade concessions. The Virginians, once the most loyal of the monarch's subjects, increasingly saw the English as adversaries rather than fellow countrymen.

Both opponents and friends made a thorough search for Bacon's bones, but individuals privy to the secret hiding place remained silent. No trace was ever found of the body, but the rebel's spirit of defiance could be seen in villages and plantations throughout the colony.

# CHAPTER VI

# *Trouble in Carolina*

VIRGINIANS FLEEING the excesses of arbitrary rule tended to reject the far Appalachians as a destination and instead, turned south to the immense Carolina territory. But rather than finding peaceful sanctuary, the immigrants discovered the new country was as tumultuous as the Jamestown colony. Revolution seemed imminent.

Albemarle, the coastal area bordering on Virginia, was known in 1675, as a retreat for citizens of disreputable character. Virginia Governor Thomas Culpeper called the area the "refuge of our renegades," a backwater where pirates and smugglers might go unmolested.

Though squatters from other colonies had been arriving since the early 1650's, no significant immigration from England had taken place. From the mountains to the eastern shore, Albemarle was marked by a frontier mentality in which touches of civility had little place.

The lack of development was curious, for to the first European explorers, Carolina had seemed perhaps the most promising section of North America. Continual attempts had been made to exploit the area's possibilities, but each endeavor had ended in failure.

In 1524, Giovanni da Verrazzano sailed past the outer banks and sighted a great body of water beyond the dunes near Hatteras. The

114

If any maid or single woman have a desire to go over, they will think themselves in the golden age, when men paid a dowry for their wives; for if they be but civil and under 50 years of age, some honest man or other will purchase them for their wives.

It would have been difficult to actually locate the droves of "honest" men, whom the anonymous writers suggested were eagerly awaiting the arrival of brides. Like large investors, even small farmers displayed no inclination to embrace the northern section of Carolina.

Although the Proprietors no doubt hoped for some intra-colonization to soften the uncivilized image of the territory, few incentives were made to encourage such movement. The Carolina lords, anxious to reap immediate profits, set annual quitrents at one-half penny per acre a year payable in coin. The fee was exorbitant, particularly when compared to Virginia rates of a farthing per hundred, payable in commodities. In a belated effort to make the colony more attractive, new settlers were exempted from paying taxes for one year and a five year moratorium was declared on collection of debts contracted in other colonies.

Appointment of a governor and six "fitting persons" to serve as a council was left to the discretion of William Berkeley who oversaw the Proprietors' interests from Jamestown. In October of 1664, Berkeley selected William Drummond to fill the post, but after three years, the Scotch immigrant was removed after a disagreement with Sir William. A decade later, Drummond would be executed on Berkeley's order for participating in Bacon's Rebellion.

Albemarle's small population was rent by constant political discord. Drummond's successor Samuel Stephens was threatened by sword-welding dissidents who disagreed with official policy. Internal rivalries became so disruptive that the Proprietors considered appointing more than one governor so that each faction might have its own legitimate leader.

The people's aggressiveness against symbols of authority reflected a basic resentment of any outside intervention in provincial affairs. For years, Carolineans had lived without established government and the imposition of absentee rule would not have been welcomed under the most favorable circumstances.

Unrest was also fanned by the settler's realization that the land they had struggled to develop might be taken away at any moment. Squatters who had simply drifted into the colony and begun farming had no pretense to legal title. Some colonists claimed land rights based on Indian purchase or dubious deeds issued by Virginia interests. None could match the royal patent held by the eight English lords.

Animosity increased in 1669 when the Proprietors issued a pompous document intended as the ultimate authority for all law in the province. The declaration, written by proprietary secretary John Locke, was named *The Fundamental Constitutions of Carolina,* or the "Grand Model." According to the lords, the Constitutions were "unalterable" and not to be debated by the people.

Locke would become England's foremost political theorist, and a severe critic of arbitrary government, but in the Carolina model he had produced an almost medieval-type structure pathetically out of touch with reality. The *Constitutions* regulated virtually every aspect of daily life and placed residents under a near dictatorship based on tutelage.

Under the plan, lands would be divided into signories, baronies and manors. Each would be governed by a hereditary lord of the appropriate rank, who enjoyed sweeping powers similar to those exercised by ancient barons. Quasi-administration functions would be lodged in a complicated series of eight supreme courts and other judicial bodies under the direction of the colony's Admiral, High Steward, Chief Justice, Chamberlain, Chancellor and Treasurer. A Palatine Court, composed of deputies appointed by each Proprietor, was included to administer general matters.

To the several hundred residents that composed the entire population of Carolina, the *Fundamental Constitutions* must have been bewildering indeed. Many clauses appeared totally irrelevant. The Chamberlain's Court, for example, was solemnly given jurisdiction over matters of heraldry, protocol, pedigree and ceremony as well as the power to "regulate all fashions, habits, badges, games and sports." The High Steward was charged with prohibiting the "infection of the common air or water," in the nearly untouched province.

Equally unrealistic was the creation of a Grand Council composed of the fifty highest ranking noblemen in the colony. Supposedly, Council members would recommend laws to a Parliament that in turn was restricted to planters owning more than five hundred acres. Participation in government by smaller farmers was severely limited for Carolina was envisioned as a land of extremes. Few citizens would fall into the area between the very rich aristocracy and the poor tenants, bound to the soil as virtual serfs and believed unequipped mentally to take part in government. Carolineans with less than fifty acres could not vote. Those with less than two hundred could not serve on juries.

Although the *Constitutions* endorsed black slavery, the document was remarkably progressive in allowing freedom of religion, but even this tolerance was tempered with strict regulation. If as many as seven people agreed upon a religion, they were ordered to form a church and give the belief a name "to distinguish it from others."

The *Constitutions* was decidedly pre-Elizabethan in character. A more suitable or inept instrument of seventeenth century colonial administration could hardly have been imagined. Even before efforts were made to implement the plan, the document was an anachronism.

Peter Carteret, named Governor of Albemarle in March of 1670, found locals highly aroused against not only the *Constitutions* but by what was deemed general misrule by the Proprietors. Arms and ammunition to fight the Indians had not been forthcoming. Quitrents had been raised without consultation with the people and some believed that the increases would go as high as six pence per acre. Colonists suspected that the ever increasing fees were part of a plot by the lords to drive established residents from their lands.

The economic situation was little better than the political scene. Droughts and hurricanes destroyed much of the tobacco and corn crop, making survival a perilous uncertainty. Carteret sympathized with the Carolineans and wrote of the area:

> . . . it hath pleased God of his providence, to inflict such a general calamity upon the inhabitants of these countreys, that for several years, they had not enjoyed the fruits of their labor, which causes them generally to groan under the burden of poverty and many times famine. . . .

The Governor became so distressed by deteriorating conditions that he left Albemarle in 1672, to argue the province's viewpoints before the Proprietors in London. Settler John Jenkins was appointed to act as Governor in Carteret's absence.

The European trip was not marked by success. Instead of agreeing to lift the increasing tax burden and provide legitimate channels for hearing grievances, the Proprietors berated Carteret for his lack of success in producing profits. The Governor's complaints, like the mounting grumbles from the colony, were ignored.

Yet even the lords had come to realize that strict interpretation of the *Constitutions* was impossible. Not only had wealthy buyers failed to appear, but the increasing hostility from small settlers made it obvious that only through military means could the feudal-type government be forced upon the people. Unwilling to incur such an expense, the Proprietors modified the original blueprint. The *Constitutions* would remain technically in effect, but a more workable system involving an appointed governor, a council and a representative assembly would be put into operation.

In allowing for a popular legislature, the Proprietors had only slightly modified their earlier reluctance to recognize the importance of citizen participation in government. The continuing distrust of popular ideas shown by the lords stemmed from personal experiences with the excesses of mass rule during the civil war and interregnum. Whatever the cause, the practical result of the owners' inflexibility was the emergence of two distinctive political factions. Most numerous were the anti-proprietary groups composed of old line settlers who had entered the colony before the 1663 charter. More recent arrivals and official appointees made up the Proprietary party. Nowhere were the differences between interests more pronounced than in economics.

Unlike the Chesapeake colonies where deep navigable rivers ran far inland, Carolina's northern coast was entirely blocked by shifting sandbars subject to powerful currents from the nearby Gulf Stream. In Maryland and Virginia, ocean-going vessels could sail inland and load tobacco directly from the wharfs of remote plantations for non-stop transit to England. In Carolina, however, access to even coastal villages was blocked to all but small boats with draft keels. Direct overseas trade was impossible.

Initially, farmers attempted to take their harvests of corn and tobacco overland to Virginia ports. The trek was long, time consuming and dangerous. Farmers who successfully completed the trip were at the mercy of old colony shippers who offered only minimum prices, knowing that the southerners could not go elsewhere.

A more viable alternative emerged when New England's crafty traders sensed that profits were to be made in Albemarle. The Yankee traffickers, long experienced in the coastal trade, were easily able to pass over the sandbars in their shallow draft vessels. Unfortunately, transportation costs were high, cargo space was limited and the shipments had to be reloaded into larger vessels in New England ports for the trans-Atlantic voyage.

Carolinians received far less for their crops than farmers in neighboring colonies, but the New Englanders were able to recoup the added expenses by shipping goods directly to Holland, Spain and France. In the European ports, prices paid for tobacco far exceeded those of London. Such direct transportation, of course, was in violation of the navigation acts, but the lack of inspectors in Carolina and the active cooperation of local residents made the smuggling a low-risk proposition.

Parliament's approval of the Plantation Duty Act in 1673 threatened to upset the comfortable arrangement. Prepayment of customs on items clearing one colonial port for another would remove the profit margin that had initially attracted the New England traders. Strict enforcement of the measure would be disastrous for Albemarle residents.

Instead of protesting the duties that would so damage the interests of their subjects, the Proprietors lauded the Parliamentary action. For some time, the Carolina lords had attempted to convince citizens to diversify their crops by planting ginger, indigo and sugar cane. The Proprietors no doubt hoped that the new duties would force residents to begin cultivation of non-enumerated items and thus end the dependence upon tobacco that had made the area a captive of market fluctuations.

Nervousness concerning the security of their patent may have also prompted the lords to press forward with the Plantation Duty. Rumors in England suggested that the King was preparing to move against Baltimore's Maryland charter and reorganize the lucrative colony under the crown. If Charles' attempt were successful, other areas would certainly come under scrutiny. Carolina was among the most vulnerable. Refusal to enforce the navigation acts would undeniably constitute grounds for vacating the 1663 patent under *quo warranto*. The Proprietors had no intention of voluntarily presenting the monarch with due cause.

British authorities demanded immediate compliance with the 1673 act and Charles sent personal warrants to each provincial governor ordering the appointment of Collectors of Tax and Surveyors of Customs. The officials would be responsible for assuring fees were properly paid and forwarded to Britain.

John Jenkins, still acting as Governor in Carteret's absence was among those who strongly opposed the duty. As head of the anti-proprietary faction, Jenkins originally ignored the bill, but was persuaded by English pressure to appoint the two revenue officers. Timothy Biggs was named as Surveyor, while Valentine Byrd was selected as Collector.

In addition to his good standing in the anti-proprietary movement, Byrd's primary qualification for office was his avowed intention of collecting no customs at all. As further insurance that intra-colonial commerce would not be harmed, the General Assembly specified that the duty, if levied at all, would not be a penny per pound as required by law, but one farthing. Even the reduced levy was not collected on countless numbers of tobacco hogsheads that were exported under the guise of bait for the New England fishing fleet.

The casual attitude of Jenkins and Byrd was deplored by proprietary supporters such as Assembly Speaker Thomas Eastchurch and apothocary Thomas Miller. Jenkins, backed by the prestige of wealthy planter and Attorney General George Durant, attempted to stifle the opposition by jailing Miller for "treasonous" utterances.

According to witnesses, Miller's seditions covered a wide range of blasphemies. Among the indiscretions supposedly spoken by the suspect were accusations that the King was an immoral man who constantly had his hand in a "whore's plackett," charges that the Proprietors were "fools and sotts," the Cavaliers rogues and that the sacraments of the Church of England were useless. Miller was also credited with expressing delight when told that the Duke of York had been killed. To worsen the insult, he had reportedly expressed the hope that other high level officials would follow the heir apparent's example.

Eastchurch and the proprietary faction reacted aggressively to Miller's imprisonment. Jenkins was ousted from office and jailed. Similar moves were made against other anti-proprietary critics, some of whom were forced to flee the colony with a price on their heads.

Eastchurch, believing the situation in Carolina was under control, left for England together with Miller who had been released from jail. The purpose of the trip, was to convince the lords that citizens who displayed loyalty to the establishment should be given control in the province. George Durant set out to present the opposing faction's defense.

With the jailing or departure of the old guard, new forces emerged among the dissidents. One of the most prominent was John Culpeper, a kinsman and perhaps the brother of Lady Frances Berkeley. Culpeper had arrived in Charleston from Barbados in 1671 to serve as the province's Surveyor-General. At the time, attack from the Spanish seemed imminent and unrest was high. Culpeper sought to exploit the disquietude and became involved in a conspiracy to rouse the masses against the government. The insurrection was not successful and the Surveyor-General fled the city for the more permissive atmosphere of Albermarle.

Turmoil appeared to be a magnet for Culpeper. The Englishman was known to have been in Jamestown at the height of Bacon's Rebellion but whether he served as a participant or an observer is not clear. He may have discussed Albemarle's unsettled state with the Virginia rebel and given encouragement to the notion that the southern colony would be amenable to joining in a secession from English rule.

As the unrest mounted in Carolina, Eastchurch and Miller continued lobbying in England. The men's appearances were so effective that on November 21, 1676 Eastchurch was named Governor of the province and Miller received the potentially lucrative post as Collector. The accused slanderer was also selected to serve as Deputy-in-residence for Lord Shaftesbury.

Though he had earlier seemed most anxious to take control of Carolina, Eastchurch was soon waylaid by more important and pressing matters. On the return voyage from Britain, the Governor became preoccupied on the island of Nevis, by a wealthy and available woman. Eastchurch decided to remain in the Indies. Miller continued on to Albemarle so that collection of the Plantation Duties could begin. To help in overcoming reluctance by local citizens, Eastchurch named Miller as President of the colonial Council.

Popular dislike of Miller resurfaced in the summer of 1677 when the Collector returned aboard a speedy revenue vessel. Even more alarming than Miller's obvious intention to rigidly enforce the duty, was his announcement that he would head the colony until Eastchurch could arrive. Despite widespread complaints that the assumption of power was not legitimate, residents accepted the usurpation without violent opposition.

As Miller consolidated his hold on the province, Albemarle's unhappy settlers began complying with the offensive new customs. The

Collector and his deputies were determined that no smugglers would escape their net. The crackdown was strikingly productive and within five months an estimated £8,000 in customs were collected. Unfortunately for the Carolineans, Miller did not confine his iron-fisted methods to the area of tax collection.

In a note of reality, the self-proclaimed "Governor" established an expensive corps of body guards. Agencies of government became instruments to still persistent complainants. Prominent members of the anti-proprietary faction were summoned into court, fined and forced to post good behavior bonds. In some instances, those who refused to acknowledge the Collector's authority were declared outlaws.

The piecemeal silencing of objectors evidently proved too cumbersome for Miller. In a drive to sweep dissidents out of office, the official called new assembly elections. It was ordered that citizens who had been convicted in court were ineligible to hold office. Because virtually every member of the opposing faction had at one time been summoned, the list of anti-Miller candidates was not extensive. The Governor, however, took no chances. To assure that his slate would be elected, Miller also stipulated that balloting would no longer be anonymous or by voice vote. Instead, citizens were commanded to cast written ballots on which their names would be inscribed.

Carolinians disregarded the restrictions and voted viva voce for anti-proprietary candidates. Miller reacted by disallowing all such selections and installing his own followers in the assembly. The usurpation of power was not openly contested, but the patience of the citizenry was rapidly being exhausted. Within months, toleration of Miller's capriciousness was sorely tested by an episode involving the ship *Carolina*.

On December 1, Captain Zachariah Gillam, skipper of the trading vessel *Carolina,* put into port at Albemarle. Aboard was George Durant who was returning home after discussions with the Proprietors. In the ship's hold was a cargo of London goods, cutlasses, guns and ammunition.

Gillam left the boat soon after docking to present his ship's papers to Miller. Instead of routinely processing the entry, Miller demanded payment of Plantation Duties on a load of tobacco which Gillam had supposedly smuggled from the province a year earlier. Though Gillam explained that legal customs on the cargo had been paid in England,

Miller refused to accept the explanation. The trader was arrested. The *Carolina* and its crew were ordered to be placed under guard. In a personal act of retribution, the Governor boarded the ship to arrest Durant on charges of treason.

The ship's confiscation and Gillam's apprehension were not tolerable to the *Carolina*'s crew. The angry mariners rebelled and seized Miller. Within hours, word of the official's detention reached farms in the backcountry. Planters flocked to the port where arms and ammunition were being taken from the vessel and distributed to the public. The rebellion had begun.

Leaders of the impromptu revolt realized that it would be difficult to justify long-term imprisonment of a proprietary appointee. In order to safeguard rebel interests and attract other dissidents to the insurrection, a *Remonstrance* was hastily composed, probably by John Culpeper. The document asserted that Miller had defrauded the King of 130,000 pounds of tobacco and imposed "many injuries, mischiefs and grievances" upon the people. Unless quick action by all the population was taken, the manifesto declared that the colony would surely fall into "inevitable ruins."

The *Remonstrance*'s call to action succeeded in igniting the long-thwarted population. Proprietary deputies were captured with great enthusiasm. John Nixon was clamped into irons on charges of treason. Timothy Biggs was unceremoniously apprehended by what he described as a "seditious, factious and rebellious rabble mustered in arms."

As establishment figures were jailed or intimidated into silence, the rebels began forming a new government. An eighteen member assembly, dominated by insurgents, was elected and quickly chose John Jenkins as Governor, George Durant as Attorney General and John Culpeper as Collector.

An untimely threat to the new regime occurred when Thomas Eastchurch arrived in Jamestown from Nevis. On December 22, the proprietary Governor ordered that all rebels lay down their arms and return ousted officers to power. He was reluctant, however, to confront the insurgents on Carolina soil. Instead of setting out for Albemarle, Eastchurch remained in Virginia and directed that a delegation be sent to Jamestown to explain why the uprising had taken place. The insurgents reacted by taking up positions along the province's northern border. In desperation, the Carolina Governor began recruiting Virginia mercenaries, but in the midst of the effort, Eastchurch contracted a severe fever and died in the old colony during February of 1678.

English reaction to the insurrection was vastly more subdued than the excitement generated by Bacon's Rebellion. Troops were not ordered out. Angry reprisals and denunciations were not forthcoming. The Proprietors seemed reluctant even to admit that the overthrow had taken place. The passiveness did not indicate that the rebellion was considered proper by the lords, but instead mirrored the owners' growing fear of a crown takeover. To acknowledge the success of an uprising would be to admit that administrative control had been lost. Such a recognition might prompt a legal move by the King to have the Carolina charter annulled.

The pact of silence maintained by the lords was soon imperilled by the arrival of Timothy Biggs, the ex-Surveyor of Customs who had escaped jail and crossed the Atlantic to denounce the American rebels. It had been rumored that the Surveyor's fellow Quakers were planning a counter-strike against the insurgent government. In order to quiet Biggs' cries for reprisals, the Proprietors shuttled the complainant back to Albemarle where he immediately clashed again with Culpeper, left his post and returned to London.

Other attempts by the lords to settle the provincial unrest were equally disappointing. A mediator empowered to hear citizen grievances was arrested before leaving England for an entirely unrelated matter. Seth Sothell, a Proprietor who had bought Edward Hyde's share of the patent, was named as Governor, but the appointee was captured during the Atlantic crossing by Turkish pirates and taken to Algiers to await ransoming.

In an attempt to reestablish a semblance of control, the lords appointed John Harvey as temporary Governor of Carolina. Unfortunately, Harvey died within six months, long before stable leadership could be secured. The provincial Council reinstated John Jenkins and the Proprietors appeared to acquiesce.

For more than two years, the popularly-elected administration provided relatively capable and orderly rule in Albemarle, an accomplishment that had not been forthcoming under more legitimately installed governments. During the period, no retribution was taken in England.

To the insurgents, it seemed safe to dispatch an agent to Britain so that an explanation could be made into circumstances involved in the 1676 rebellion. John Culpeper was selected for the task.

The assumption that all had been forgiven was erroneous. When Culpeper arrived in England during November of 1678, he was arrested on a charge of embezzling at least £3,000 from the King's customs. The complainant was Culpeper's old adversary Timothy Biggs.

For a time it seemed that the accusations could be settled amicably and that Culpeper would be free to return home. The arrival of Thomas Miller, however, provoked serious charges that even the nervous Proprietors could not whitewash. Miller, who had escaped from Carolina jail, alleged that Culpeper and Gillam were guilty of high treason in connection with the revolt. The Lords Commissioners of Plantations, although conceding that Miller was "given to drink," agreed with the charge and notified the King: ". . . we are fully satisfied that the said John Culpeper hath, by diverse seditious practices, abetted and encouraged a rebellion in that province." Gillam was able to prove his innocence, but Culpeper was ordered to stand trial before the King's Bench.

The 1680 hearings brought a surprise to Miller and other advocates of firm colonial rule. Instead of supporting the allegations, the Proprietors, under the leadership of Shaftesbury, Craven and Colleton, announced to the court that the insurgents in Carolina were not rebels, but innocent victims of unbearable abuses perpetrated by Miller. It was impossible, they claimed, that rebellion had occurred. Eastchurch's absence had left the province without any legally constituted authority. In defiance of English tradition, Miller had usurped governmental powers and subjected peaceful citizens to harmful illegalities. His removal, the election of an assembly, and the selection of new officials by the people, had been done correctly under provisions of the *Constitutions*.

The glowing description of Culpeper as a wronged hero was accepted by the King's Bench. Arrangements were made for repayment of customs lost during the insurrection; the defendant was released and allowed to return home.

The provisional government ruled in northern Carolina until 1683 when Seth Sothell, fresh from an African prison, at last arrived in the colony. Sothell was an obnoxious man, incapable of sustaining the fragile bond of cooperation that had developed between the Proprietors and the people as a partial result of the rebellion. The new Governor quickly managed to surpass the excesses of Thomas Miller. Reportedly, he conspired with pirates, misappropriated property of critics such as George Durant, imprisoned suspects without trial, accepted bribes, attempted to influence the courts and generally ruled without respect for individual rights.

In May of 1689, insurgents once more rose up in the area, this time under the leadership of Thomas Pollack. Sothell was arrested and tried on more than a dozen charges. Following a verdict of guilty, the Governor was banished for one year and forever enjoined from holding office. The people's action brought no condemnation from London. The lords had long been suspicious of Sothell's accounting of revenues and quitrents.

Sothell, however, was not daunted by the setback. The Englishman was an enterprising individual who possessed a valuable talent for surmounting adversity. After being deposed in Albemarle, Sothell headed south for Charleston, buoyed by a provision in the *Constitutions* that Proprietors in residence on Carolina soil were automatically vested with supreme powers of government.

The southern settlements of Carolina boasted a gentility unknown in the north, for the deep water port on the Ashley River provided a window on the world. The affluence brought by trade and great plantations, was in marked contrast to the straitened economy in Albemarle. But the fertile land and navigable rivers were not the only attraction for colonists. According to rumors, rich lodes of metal lay in the region. In 1682, Thomas Ashe wrote:

> . . . it's supposed and generally believed, that the Apalatean Mountains . . . yields ore of gold and silver, that the Spaniards in their running searches of this country, saw it, but had not time to open them, or at least, for the present were unwilling to make any farther discovery till their mines of Peru and Mexico were exhausted, or as others, that they were politically fearful that if the riches of the country should be exposed, it would be an allure to encourage a foreign invader. . . .

Unlike other English colonies on the mainland, a large percentage of those in South Carolina were immigrants from Barbados, an overpopulated island dependent upon slave labor and the sugar industry.

Unlike the independent squatters in Albemarle, the Barbadians were accustomed to strong central government. Arbitrariness was deemed essential to maintain order in slave holding societies such as the British West Indies.

In their new colonial homes around Goose Creek, the aggressive Barbadians were remarkably successful in building fortunes based on merchandizing and farming. However, the islanders were in constant conflict with both the Proprietors and the backwoodsmen who immigrated to South Carolina from other American possessions or directly from England. In 1672, the domineering Goose Creekers had deposed legally appointed Governor Joseph West and installed islander Sir John Yeamans as head of the colony. Two years later, however, West was able to retake the office.

Fundamental differences in attitudes and needs underlay the planter-pioneer rivalry. The Goose Creekers with their large land holdings supported a labor system based on Indian slavery. The suggestion horrified backwoods settlers whose small farms were the first to feel tribal retribution. Similarly, the easterners constantly pressed for war against the Spanish in Florida. By such hostilities, the Barbadians hoped to keep coastal defenses strong and eventually open up southern land for speculative purposes. To the inland pioneers, war with the Spanish was an unnecessary drain on provincial revenues and uselessly exposed the colony to possible capture.

James Colleton, brother of the Proprietor, took up duties as Governor in November, 1686, and proved unwilling to bow to the Goose Creekers' demands. Instead, he set about enforcing the expressed wishes of the Proprietors, most of whom were in opposition to the interests of the islanders. Colleton forbade trafficking with the Indians without governmental approval, attempted to collect back quitrents and tried to eliminate native slavery. He further attempted to curtail traffic between Goose Creekers and pirates, but most offensive to the islanders was the Governor's refusal to invade Florida. The official's stance was based on the claim that only the King might authorize war with a foreign nation.

Despite his evident capabilities in administration, Colleton, like so many other foreign appointees, lacked a basic understanding of the importance of independence in a frontier society. He seized and opened the public mails, imprisoned opponents on dubious charges and insisted on strict adherence to the unworkable *Constitutions*. The mounting press of unfavorable decisions at last became too great to be tolerated by the population.

In early 1690, an aroused mob of citizens arrested Colleton's secretary of state and seized the provincial records. Colleton reacted by declaring martial law and summoning the militia. The assembly blocked the Governor's maneuver by labeling the call to arms as illegal.

As the crisis mounted, Seth Sothell arrived in Charleston fresh from his Albemarle trial. The deposed official immediately formed an alliance with the Goose Creekers and announced that he was assuming control of the government under the authority of the *Constitutions*. An added impetus was a petition signed by five hundred Barbadians who supposedly pled with Sothell to assume the reins of administration.

Colleton ignored Sothell's legal justification and readied the militia. The Governor's forces, however, were greatly outnumbered and in October, Sothell was installed in office without opposition. Proprietary officials holding commissions from Colleton were replaced and a new assembly, dominated by Goose Creekers, banished the old Governor from the province on pain of a £5,000 fine.

The change of government did not quiet the political discord. On June 10, Virginia Governor Francis Nicholson notified the Board of Trade: "I hear that at South Carolina, one Mr. [Sothell] who was banished by the mob out of North Carolina, now heads them there, so they are in great disorder."

Confusion had indeed been the harvest of the overthrow, for Sothell proved to be no more capable of honest conduct in the south than he had in the north. Complaints concerning his unorthodox administration came forth not only from elements loyal to Colleton, but from the Goose Creekers as well. When the Proprietors instructed Sothell to return home and answer for misconduct, he merely ignored the directive.

The Barbadians, who had enabled Sothell to gain power, were most harmed by the resulting regime. The new Governor demanded a large portion of all fines and fees collected in the province, and regulated Indian trade even more strictly than had Colleton. Instead of promoting land speculation, expansion virtually ceased for, during the new Governor's entire rule, only three grants were approved and two of these were issued in Sothell's own name. To the dismay of the intensely monarchist Goose Creek merchants, it was rumored that Sothell planned to withdraw South Carolina from the jurisdiction of England.

By the spring of 1692, Sothell's power base was almost totally eroded. With popular support at drastically low levels, the official was confronted with the arrival of Philip Ludwell, a Virginian who displayed a proprietary commission as Governor. Ironically, Sothell found himself in a position similar to that which had earlier confronted Colleton.

Sothell reacted in much the same manner. He refused to voluntarily give way and announced that the established government would fight the interloper. Sothell attempted to rally support, but found that even the most loyal backers had deserted to Ludwell. Unable to mount an effective challenge, he grudgingly relinquished control.

The debacle of Sothell's governorship convinced the Proprietors that the *Constitutions* were entirely impractical for use in America. Never again would the unrealistic document be seriously pressed as a practical scheme of governing the colony.

CHAPTER VII

# *Riot or Rebellion?*

DIFFERENCES in government, religion, society and geography tended to isolate the communities of the lower colonies, but from Maryland to South Carolina, all provincials shared a common dependence upon the weed tobacco. The reliance was not one of personal addiction, but of economic necessity, for cultivation of the tender crop consumed the waking hours of most farmers and their wives. Individuals not directly involved in production, found employment in related fields such as coopering or shipping. Even artisans in seemingly unrelated crafts depended upon tobacco to produce the monies spent by customers.

Tobacco served as the principal source of income for almost every colonial in the south and the mid-Atlantic. In the absence of specie, the crop became a medium of exchange. Court fines were levied in "lb. tob:" pounds of tobacco. Land prices were quoted in hogsheads rather than pounds sterling. Ministerial prayers concentrated not only on the salvation of souls, but on pleas for sufficient rain and sun to produce fertile crops.

Tobacco determined in large measure the major directions in which Southern society moved during the seventeenth and eighteenth centuries. The need for a vast and continuous labor supply laid the basis for the system of indentured servitude under which hundreds of thousands of Europeans came to America during the first century of settlement. This vast influx assured that England's outposts would be sufficiently manned so that enemy attacks might be staved off. The extensive use of bonded servants also contributed to the development of a democratic spirit in the tobacco colonies. The more than one hundred thousand bondsmen and women who became free in the seventeenth century South, served as a powerful deterrent to the development of a class-oriented culture.

Not all of the effects of the tobacco-dependent society were desirable. When voluntary bondage proved an inadequate source of low-cost labor, planters unhesitatingly enslaved Africans to insure that the crop would be turned out. Wars resulting from Indian displacement could also be partially attributed to the weed. The rapid spoilage of land that resulted from tobacco created a premature demand for physical expansion that would not have occurred if more traditional crops had been grown.

The constant political dissension that marked life in Virginia, Maryland and the Carolinas was directly related to the dependence upon a single crop. The lack of counterbalancing sources of income made the entire colonial economy subject almost entirely to the dictates of the London tobacco market. Resentments between the provinces and England that might have remained dormant in a more diversified structure, ballooned into heated extremes over even minor adjustments.

From the first introduction of the leaf, the demand in England for tobacco seemed insatiable. The weed was considered not only important for medicinal purposes, but as a status symbol among the privileged, despite James I's admonition that smoking was "loathesome to the eye, hateful to the nose, harmful to the brain and dangerous to the lungs." Users developed a series of tricks dubbed with popular names such as the whiffle, the Cuban ebolition, the euripus and the gulpe. Enthusiasm was more blunted in Puritan New England where cultivation was prohibited in many areas. In Connecticut, smoking was forbidden by anyone under twenty years of age or not already addicted. Completely banned was the use of tobacco in places where fires might break out, such as in fields, woods and barnyards.

To satisfy the cravings of Old World residents, Americans worked long hours in hot fields, often destroying their health as well as their soil. As the seventeenth century progressed, the increasing colonial population was able to produce ever larger harvests, partially through application of advanced methods of cultivation. Soon the weed was no longer a luxury reserved for the wealthy, but a commodity available to all.

In years of good harvests, the supply of American leaf far outstripped the English demand. Barred by the navigation acts from legally selling to European markets, farmers were faced with drastically falling prices and rising freight rates. To compensate for reduced income per pound, planters laid in additional acreage or planted two crops per season. When prices dipped even lower because of overproduction, farmers again increased their acres under cultivation in an effort to gain a subsistence income. By 1679, the glut had become so great that 10,000 hogsheads of Virginia tobacco were left in the province because the English merchant fleet was unable to accommodate the entire harvest. A year later the yield was even larger.

The relationship between supply and demand was known during the seventeenth century and regulation of tobacco planting was among the first topics considered by Virginia's Burgess. As early as 1633, the assembly had attempted to limit the number of plants each producer might set out, and in 1666, the body called for a total cessation of cultivation for one year. It was hoped that during the hiatus, stores in England would become exhausted and prices for the crop would soar.

Cessation meant extreme hardships for small farmers who had little to sustain themselves from one harvest to the next. In supporting the assembly's call for non-planting, provincial yeomen had made a serious sacrifice that would expose their families to a possible substandard existence.

The Virginia action, however, would be totally ineffective unless similar restraint was shown by fellow producers in Maryland. Although the Chesapeake farmers were willing to join in the cessation Lord Baltimore was not. Instead, the Proprietor doomed the entire effort by refusing to approve legislation endorsing Maryland participation.

Fifteen years later, Virginia Governor Thomas Culpeper was no more impressed with public demands for cessation than Baltimore had been. Culpeper, acting in the tense days following Bacon's Rebellion, was determined to take a firm stand against any dictates put forth by the population. His refusal to support the movement toward cessation was consistent with his record of advocating England's, rather than Virginia's interests whenever possible. Since his arrival in the spring of 1680, Culpeper had shown no hesitance in overriding policies beneficial to the colony. Most noteworthy was the Governor's conduct in a shady scheme involving "light" pieces of eight, coins in which the metal content was below officially accepted standards.

Culpeper had imported a considerable amount of lighted coin to meet the payroll of redcoats sent to quash Bacon's Rebellion. In an arbitrary pronouncement, the Governor declared that the coins, traditionally valued at five shillings, would henceforth be worth six. The upward evaluation netted the Englishman a profit of twenty percent on every transaction. Locals soon discovered that their goods and property had been decreased by the same amount.

Opposition eased as the coins passed into general circulation and became useful in paying customs and other official assessments. Culpeper, realizing that the revenues were being remitted in cheap coin, promptly revalued the tender to previous levels. For a second time, citizens were victimized by the Governor's financial manipulation.

After just three months in office, Culpeper left Virginia for a temporary visit in England. Sir Henry Chicheley, the old Cavalier, was named as Acting Governor and the Burgess was prorogued until January of 1682 when Lord Thomas was expected to return. Strict orders were given that under no circumstances were the representatives to be called into session in the official's absence. The prohibition was doubtless to insure that an unchecked assembly did not revive grievances that had underlain Bacon's insurrection.

During the Governor's furlough, economic conditions continued to deteriorate. Bumper crops pushed tobacco prices to dangerously low levels. London warehouses became so glutted that merchants began dumping stocks on European markets. Sales slumped in Holland, Spain and France. Even smuggling was eliminated as a recourse for Chesapeake planters. The alarmed Virginia Council notified English officials that the colonial situation was desperate. According to their account, citizens were "extremely poor," and unable to secure even necessities. Cessation seemed to be the only plausible solution.

The commissioners of customs would not consider even one season's respite, purportedly because a temporary halt would stimulate tobacco planting in rival nations. Such competition would impair the preferred advantage that London shippers and traders had established in the world market.

Equally disheartening was the refusal of English leaders to alter the basis on which tobacco duties were collected. Under law, tobacco was taxed at a set fee per pound, regardless of the going market price. Planters wished to change the inflexible arrangement so that customs would fluctuate according to the selling price. Instead of positively approaching the issues of cessation and customs, the English lords chose to answer the American complaints by dispatching flax and hemp seeds to Virginia, along with instructions that the items should be planted as alternative crops.

The ramifications of the staggering economy could not be ignored indefinitely. The Lords of Trade and Plantations acknowledged that the depressive conditions might result in outrages similar to those that had brought about Bacon's de facto government. In October of 1681, the Lords noted: ". . . tis feared [poverty] may induce the servants to plunder the stores of the planters and the ships arriving there and to commit other outrages and disorders as in the late rebellion."

Charles Scarborough sounded an even more foreboding note from the old colony. "The whole body is sick and the whole heart is faint," Scarborough wrote, "from the sole of the foot, even unto the head there is no soundness in it."

Ill tempers had been partially held in check by public confidence that the Burgess would find positive ways in which to deal with the issues. A disappointment occurred when Culpeper did not return in time to summon the session set for January of 1682. As spring approached, Sir Henry Chicheley became convinced that the Governor's arrival was imminent. No doubt in order to eliminate undue delays, the Cavalier announced that a Burgess would convene in mid-April. By that time, Lord Thomas would have returned and the question of cessation could be considered.

As the delegates rode toward the capital, hope was high among the population that ways could be found to arrest the general economic decline. However, hours before the representatives were scheduled to take their seats, instructions arrived from the King: Culpeper had not yet departed England and under no circumstances was a Burgess to meet without him. In a second crushing announcement, the crown revealed that the redcoats would no longer be maintained at English expense. The colonists would be totally responsible for the troops' maintenance.

The messages stunned the colonists. Without a general agreement the spring planting must go on as usual. It would be still another year before cessation could be undertaken. Obviously, the straited economy could not absorb the expenses of unused and unwanted soldiers whose dissatisfaction already menaced the safety of the province.

Despite the King's prohibition, the Burgess met for four days. Irate oratories filled the pages of the official journal and members insisted that the discord should be printed and distributed throughout the colony. One of the most unbridled and outspoken Burgesses was Colonel Robert Beverley, a planter who had been the trusted Lieutenant of Sir William Berkeley during Bacon's Rebellion. After the revolt, Beverley became disillusioned with crown rule and transfered his loyalties to the popular faction. It was not until April 27 that Chicheley managed to successfully prorogue the assembly. The date of the next session was set for November 10.

Four days after the legislators were dismissed, disgruntled farmers and their wives in Gloucester County decided to settle the matter of cessation without official intervention. After destroying their own fields, mobs of Virginians fanned out through the county, slashing the crops of more reluctant neighbors.

Learning of the disorders, Chicheley forbade further "riotous and tumultuous gatherings," but the ban had no effect. Sir Henry found himself confronted with a serious dilemma. The possibility of arming the redcoats to put down the mobs was not a pleasing one. According to the Acting Governor, the troops were more apt to mutiny than to obey his orders. The only remaining alternative was to call out the militia and hope that the home guard would not rebel when ordered to move against fellow citizens who were attempting to end the despicable situation that faced all in the colony.

Chicheley's decision to use local men proved the correct one. The militia moved into Gloucester County, ordering the plant cutters to desist. Under the show of force, the movement did decelerate, but destruction of the tobacco did not completely halt. When militiamen guarded the fields during the day, cutters took up night operations. When leading planters were arrested, their wives began slashing the crops. Within a week, the plants on two hundred planations had been destroyed in Gloucester County alone. Despite the presence of mounted guards kept in constant motion, the cutting mania spread. Parties of insurgents sprang up throughout Middlesex, York and New Kent counties.

Arrests of the ringleaders continued. Robert Beverley was considered so dangerous an instigator that he was apprehended and placed incommunicado aboard a visiting English frigate. Even those accused of "uttering words" of encouragement to the demonstrators were ordered jailed. Lord Baltimore, fearful that the cutters might cross the Potomac, stationed Maryland's foot and horse brigade at the river's edge.

By June, the situation was quieting. Thousands of hogsheads had been destroyed. Chicheley helped in restoring order by offering a general pardon to all who returned home. The amnesty was possible only because Sir Henry had defined the disturbances as riot, a crime pardonable by provincial governors.

During the early summer, small fines and minor punishments were meted out to those who had been arrested. John Suckler, one of the most "notorious" plant cutters, was pardoned on the condition that he build a bridge across Dragon Swamp and maintain the structure for twenty-one years. It was perhaps more than coincidence that one of the major beneficiaries of the bridge was Sir Henry Chicheley, whose plantation lay near the swamp.

Other prisoners, mindful of the harsh recriminations that occurred after Bacon's Rebellion, chose not to trust the good will of the courts. John Haley, for example though "well loaded with irons," managed to break through a wall of the James City jail and make good his escape while the keeper was at dinner.

Long after the majority of planters had desisted, isolated incidents continued. On August 12, the royal Council was forced to declare those who persisted were in open rebellion.

Despite crown instructions that he return to Virginia as quickly as possible, Culpeper did not arrive back in the province until December 16. The plant cutting episode had faded from prominency, but the Governor chose to resurrect the incident. At a special Council meeting on January 10, 1683, Culpeper announced that he had reversed Chicheley's earlier policy. Instead of riot, the planter cutters were to be punished under statutes dealing with rebellion and high treason. Despite the Acting Governor's pardon, the full measure of the law would be exacted on the leaders.

Culpeper's position was based on English law that made depriving the King of revenues a treasonous offense. Although customs had not been physically taken during the rebellion, the effect of cutting an estimated ten thousand hogsheads was to reduce the royal duties by a significant amount. To reinforce his contention, Culpeper cited precedents dating from the days of Elizabeth that showed the intent to deprive was as serious a crime as the actual performance.

Warrants were issued for the apprehension of four principal cutters: Sommersett Davies, Bartholomew Austin, Richard Baily and one Goodman Cocklin. Insufficient evidence was found against Robert Beverley, but the Burgess secretary did not escape unscathed. He was forbidden from holding further office, barred from employment as a lawyer and denounced for "rudeness and saucyness."

The death of Sir Henry Chicheley on February 5 perhaps compensated Culpeper for the battle lost with Beverley. The Governor showed little grief at the passing of the loyalist who had once been imprisoned in the tower of London for allegiance to the Stuart line. Instead of regrets, Lord Thomas wrote the Chicheley's death "hath eased this place from all future maladministrations."

On March 13, a grand jury indicted the four defendants and in formal trial, all but Cocklin were found guilty. Austin and Davies were executed, while Richard Baily, a young and repentent cutter, was reprieved until pardon could be begged of Charles.

Culpeper apparently decided that two hangings were a sufficient deterrent to future rebellions, for on May 22, the official issued a pardon that exempted only seven leaders of the movement.

Lord Thomas, realizing that pardon for rebellion was not within his official powers, went to extended lengths to rationalize the action. To the Lords of Trade he explained that the amnesty was essential if "peace and quiet" were to be maintained in Virginia. All other means of punishment had been discarded as impractical: fining was impossible for most of the cutters were "scarce . . . worth a farthing." Imprisonment was unsatisfactory according to Culpeper, because "there are in effect no prisons, but what are so easily broken that I count it a miracle the four I committeed did not escape." He continued "I am sure I was in pain all the while and would scarcely sleep for fear thereof." Finally, mass hanging was not feasible because most of the cutters were merely followers who did not deserve to die for a mistake in judgment.

Unknown to the plant cutters, the entire rebellion had been unnecessary. On June 17, 1682, before word of the revolt reached England, the Lords of Trade had agreed to a cessation. Culpeper, believing that the chastened Virginians no longer constituted a threat to the peace, did not publicly announce the Lords' decision. Instead, he returned the commission and notified the officials:

> . . . finding that I could keep the peace and quiet without it, and that the last Assembly busyed itself in other matters, I took advantage thereof, and never discovered it to any one person whatever either there or here, on the contrary, I so encouraged the planting [of] tobacco this year (as thinking it the greatest service I could possibly do) . . . I am confident the customs next year from them will be 50,000 lb. more than ever heretofore in any one year, instead of falling as much if I had done otherwise.

It was obvious that Culpeper's handling of the rebellion did nothing to improve citizen morale or economic stability. Tensions did ease temporarily, but the cause of the relaxation was not action by the Governor, but rising prices on the English tobacco market. The calm only reflected a lessening of the symptoms. The basic problem of a one crop economy remained unsolved.

The rebellion did help to alter certain public attitudes toward wholesale violence as a means for producing change. For nearly eight decades, Virginia had been rifled with rebelliousness. Members of the Burgess were growing increasingly intolerant of the periodic upheavals. In April of 1684, the assembly enacted a strict anti-riot law that branded plant cutters as "evil and ill-disposed persons." Under terms of the measure, eight or more people gathering to destroy plants or pull down fences so that animals might do so, could be apprehended as traitors to England. Punishment for the crime was death by hanging. Such a clear prohibition was required, the assembly announced, so that no Virginian would be: "seduced by the specious pretenses of any persons, that such tumultuous and mutinous assemblies . . . are but riot and tresspasses. . . ."

The distinction between riot and rebellion was important not only in the South. As the last of the plant cutters were being subdued in the old colony, a small group of protesters were rising in arms in New Hampshire. Their bellicosity did not appear to present a serious danger, but to Edward Cranfield, the province's new royal governor, the disturbances were unmistakable rebellion against the crown.

Rights to the territory north of Massachusetts Bay were awarded in 1623 to John Mason, one of the original financiers of New England settlement. Unlike the Puritan enclaves, Mason's plot did not immediately attract permanent residents. For several years, New Hampshire's provincials were a conglomeration of itinerant trappers, fishermen, squatters and religious dissidents escaping from persecution by the saints.

Only gradually did the development accelerate. Timber resources stimulated lumbering and immigrants seeking permanent homestead began to arrive. Because formally constituted governments were largely unknown in the remote area, citizens resorted to plantation covenants or combinations to provide the stability that was needed.

After a questionable "annexation," in 1641, New Hampshire was ruled by Massachusetts Bay, but in September of 1679 the arrangement ended. A commission was issued in England authorizing appointment of a royal governor to serve solely in the northern province. New Hampshire had become an official, independent colony under control of the crown.

The change in status was welcomed by the founder's grandson, Robert Mason, an heir who still claimed rights of the soil. As long as the area had been tied to powerful Massachusetts Bay, Mason had little success in collecting fees and quitrents. Hopefully, the elimination of the Puritans would end the difficulty.

Declaring himself "Lord Protector," Mason recruited a corps of agents to assist in fee collection. The deputies' tactics were far from subtle and proved offensive to New Hampshirites who were unaccustomed to proprietary infringements. Residents were threatened with the loss of their property unless back quitrents were paid immediately. Use of common ground was prohibited and citizens were barred from cutting firewood on unclaimed land.

Mason had grossly overestimated his power and was soon summoned to appear before the provincial Council on charges of "usurpation over his Majesty's authority." Sensing the hostile mood of the population,. the Proprietor beat a quick exit and managed to escape back to England before a warrant could be served. Safely at home, he concluded that it was improbable that great riches could be forthcoming from the American inheritance.

The pessimistic outlook was not shared by Edward Cranfield, a Britisher who had been appointed as Governor. Cranfield saw in the colonies an opportunity to accumulate a vast fortune and the New Hampshire post was merely the first step in the process. To begin his venture, the new Governor leased Mason's rights for a period of twenty-one years at £150 annually for the first seven years. The payment was merely a fraction of what the official calculated could be collected in quitrents alone.

Less than a week after his arrival in October of 1682, Cranfield made the first in a series of moves intended to leave no doubt as to where governing power lay. Two popular councillors, known for their long opposition to Mason, were dismissed. In another action, Cranfield recommended that constraints be put upon the Puritan clergy, a rival power group that he believed was endeavoring to disturb the peace.

The Governor's main attention, however, seemed to be centered on Massachusetts Bay where the charter was once more under attack from the King. The success of *quo warranto* action was essential to Cranfield's plans, for the Englishman fully expected to be named as the Bay colony's first royal governor. The post would be a lucrative one.

To insure that royal oversight came to Massachusetts as quickly as possible, Cranfield worked secretly to promote misunderstanding between the Puritans and the English. In a particularly blatant intrigue, Cranfield convinced Bay officials that a bribe of £2,000 should be offered to the King on the condition that the charter revocation be halted.

As Cranfield expected, the clumsy attempt ended in disaster for the colonists and the Puritans were soon the object of derision in court circles. Joseph Dudley, Massachusetts agent in England, was furious that his delicate negotiations had been upset by the bumbling of those in America. Dudley warned Massachusetts Governor Simon Bradstreet, that Cranfield was a dangerous man whose intentions were not as friendly as they might appear. Dudley explained to Bradstreet:

> Truely, sir, if you was here to see how we are ridiculed by our best friends at court for the sham Cranfield hath put upon you, it would

grieve you. I will assure you, whatever letters he hath shown you, his Majesty last night told my friend, that he had represented us as disloyal rogues.

The New Hampshire Governor had indeed slandered the saints. In private correspondence to London, Cranfield insisted that the Puritans were encouraging revolt among the people and would never submit to Charles' Catholic successor. He forewarned that instead of acknowledging rule by James, the colony would "fall off," from the empire and perhaps form an alliance with England's enemies. To prevent the secession, Cranfield suggested that the British send troops to suppress the mutiny and place all "militia, castles and forts into the hands of loyal and honest gentlemen." Presumably, one of the most loyal was Cranfield himself.

Internal difficulties intruded on Cranfield's maneuverings and the Governor was forced to turn his attention back to New Hampshire. Funds for operating government were nearly exhausted and to secure additional financing, an assembly was summoned. Cranfield's suggestions for legislative appropriations were rejected by the body, a move that prompted the Englishman to veto several popularly approved bills. Instead of seeking a compromise, the angry Governor dismissed the assembly on January 20, 1683.

Prorogument, an accepted practice in Britain, was alien in New England where the rights of popular assemblies were cherished as near indisputable. That a royal official would presume to suppress legislative deliberations was considered a shocking and reprehensible act. One of the most alarmed by the suspension was Edward Gove, an assemblyman who reacted by urging dissatisfied citizens in Hampton and Exeter to join a hasty, unorganized protest aimed at unseating the Governor.

Shouting the battle cry "liberty and reformation," Gove marched through the New Hampshire foothills, demanding that his fellow countrymen take up their muskets in revolt. The uprising was surprisingly unsuccessful. Citizens tended to ignore the entire affair, and by the assemblyman's own count, only sixteen or seventeen men felt compelled to join the movement.

Cranfield reacted harshly to the episode. Gove and his entire army, which had been reduced by attrition to eight individuals, were arrested and indicted for high treason. The force was then bound over for a February 15 trial before a special court of Oyer and Terminer.

The Governor's severe response to such a minor threat was undoubtedly related to the Massachusetts charter difficulties. An uncontrolled breach of the peace in New Hampshire would reflect poorly on Cranfield's administrative ability, but firm, decisive handling of the dissidents would stand in favorable contrast to the chaotic conditions in the Bay.

For precisely the opposite reasons, Massachusetts officials desperately wished to halt the proceedings against Gove. The Puritans no doubt feared that if the incident were magnified, London officials would view all of New England as an undisciplined, ungovernable territory that required closer British rule. In an effort to downgrade the political connotations of Gove's rebellion, the Puritans attempted to prove that the insurgent was merely suffering from severe mental illness. The rebel's kinswoman Hannah Gove, supported the diminished capacity defense, by swearing:

> He fell into his crime by reason of a distemper of lunacy or some such like, which he hath been subject to by times from his youth, and yet is until now, as his mother was before him.

From prison, Gove aided the effort by composing a rambling, incoherent letter to the justices of the court. In the correspondence, Gove prophesied that God was closely observing the proceedings in New Hampshire, and that if justice was not done, then divine retribution would be extracted. Comparing himself to Old Testament saviors, Gove concluded: "If ever New-England had need of a Solomon or David or Moses, Caleb or Joshua, it is now. My tears are in my eyes. I can hardly see."

The pathetic appeal made little impression on the court. Gove's followers, found guilty of abetting treason, received mercy, but it was decided that the ringleader would receive the full penalty prescribed for traitors to England. He was sentenced to be hanged, cut down while alive and then disemboweled. His entrails were then to be burned before his eyes, his head removed and his body quartered. Various parts of the corpse would be put on public display in locations designated by the King.

The execution was delayed, probably because of Gove's appeal for royal clemency, but Cranfield remained in terror of the felon. Although the rebel was bound by heavy irons five feet long, the Governor notified colonial Secretary Sir Leoline Jenkins:

I cannot, with safety to myself or the peace of the country, keep him longer in custody; for besides the great and daily charge of guards upon him, I have cause to fear that the soldiers in time may be remiss or overpowered and so he be set at liberty . . . If Gove escape the sentence of the law, there is an end of his Majesty's business in New England.

In an extraordinary action, Gove was transported to England and placed in irons at the Tower. The depiction of the prisoner as a dangerous rather than a pitiful character was not obliterated from official minds. Tower Lieutenant Thomas Cheek was concerned that insufficient funds would be available to finance the close surveillance required for such a mutineer. On June 7, Cheek wrote Jenkins: "The fellow is poor, and I desire to know what the King will allow him for maintenance. I keep [two guards] . . . one to lie in his chamber, and one never to be out of his sight."

Four days later, Gove begged Massachusetts official Edward Randolph for help in securing a pardon and raising money to satisfy the jail fees. Gove claimed to have been entirely unaware that his actions in the New Hampshire countryside constituted treason. Similar disturbances had taken place for fourteen years, the rebel claimed, and "no notice at all" had been taken.

Higher authorities were deaf to Gove's requests for pardon, but no one seemed willing to authorize his execution. For three years the provincial remained in the Tower, seeking release through a variety of defenses. He credited his rebellious conduct to drunkenness, "distemper of mind" and lack of sleep for twelve nights before the insurrection.

In 1686, the royal pardon at last was granted. Gove returned to New Hampshire but lived only a short time before succumbing to what he announced was a slow acting poison his jailors had surreptitiously fed to him.

The possibility that future conspiracies might erupt did not deter Cranfield from continuing to disregard citizen rights and sensibilities. However, it was rumored that the shaken official organized a force of "spies and pimps" to watch for any hint of unrest among the population.

In February of 1683, Cranfield launched a major effort at private fund-raising by directing all landholders to obtain from Mason leases for their property. The applications would be a tacit admission that the

Lord Proprietor did hold rights of the soils and that quitrents could be justifiably imposed. Because of the lease agreement between Cranfield and Mason, the rents would go directly to the Governor.

When the great majority of homesteaders ignored the official's command, Cranfield instigated lawsuits to force compliance. At the same time, the Cranfield-Mason faction, which had gained control of the Council, began packing juries and replacing provincial officers with hand-picked appointees. As a result, court judgments consistently went against the landholders who were further penalized by exorbitant fines and court costs.

Cranfield also stepped up a campaign against the clergy. Puritan ministers, whom the official called "half-witted philosophers" and disseminators of "rebellious principles," were marked for special attention. For example, the Governor decreed that the Puritan holy men were obligated to administer Anglican sacraments to anyone who requested the service. When popular Reverend Joshua Moodey refused to comply, he was sentenced to six months imprisonment.

By 1684, Cranfield had effectively eliminated the assembly as a viable part of government. With the help of Mason, who had been appointed Chancellor, Cranfield ruled with few visible limitations. His independence extended beyond the boundaries of New Hampshire, for when the Lords of Trade ordered the Governor to convene an assembly, he refused to do so, announcing that the people were of such a rebellious temperament that it would not be safe.

Despite the growing despotism, residents were unwilling to forcibly overthrow the King's representative. Apprehension created by Gove's punishment may have significantly contributed to the reluctance. Instead of launching a rebellion, citizens chose to raise private funds so that an agent could be sent to England to petition for removal of the Governor. When Cranfield learned of the design, he imprisoned for nine months a guard who had escorted the representative to Boston.

Ultimately, it was not the official's attack on property rights, or the invasion of church prerogatives that lead to violent protests. The final incitement was an outgrowth of Cranfield's attempts to impose taxes without the people's approval.

Lack of a sitting assembly created complicated, but not impossible problems of financing government. When existing authorization for taxation lapsed, Cranfield remained unwilling to summon the assembly. Instead, he devised a scheme under which fees would be approved not with legislative consent, but with the approval of the Council. The subservient advisers complied with the Governor's request that new assessments be imposed.

Residents of New Hampshire were not as eager to approve the illegal solution as the Council had been. Throughout the province, citizens refused to pay taxes on the grounds that their representatives had not authorized the levies. Cranfield put collection into the hands of sheriffs and constables and when the boycott continued, he directed that property of the delinquents should be seized, to be sold at auction. Those who would not willingly relinquish the items would be jailed.

On December 29, 1684, club-wielding citizens at Exeter attacked a sheriff attempting to enforce the Governor's decree. At Hampton, a lawman was beaten and forced out of town with a rope about his neck. When a local judge ordered leaders of the riots brought into court, both the jurist and the lawman were set upon. Mason called out the militia, but not a single man appeared.

Action was also underway in England where the Lords of Trade were presented with a list of twelve grievances against Cranfield. In addition to illegally usurping powers of the legislature, the Governor was accused of establishing unjust courts, capriciously imprisoning citizens, interfering with religious freedom and establishing unnecessary fees. The weight of evidence against the Governor was too great to be ignored. The Lords withdrew Cranfield's commission and reassigned the official to the post of customs collector in Barbados.

Few changes in administration were evident after Deputy Governor Walter Barefoote temporarily replaced Cranfield. Sheriffs were instructed to continue serving warrants against tax evaders, but the resentments of the people had not altered. When lawmen attempted to enter a Puritan meeting at Dover, one young woman became so irate that she knocked a collector to the floor with her Bible. Barefoote claimed to have lost a tooth and sustained two broken bones during an altercation with angry assemblyman Thomas Wiggin. Mason, involved in the same fracas, was thrown bodily into a roaring fireplace.

Tensions between colonists and royal appointees were becoming commonplace throughout America. Gone were the days when provincials, proud of their heritage as transplanted Britishers, obeyed government orders as a matter of faith. It had become increasingly obvious that British authorities did not automatically act in the best interests of the provincials. The arbitrariness displayed by Culpeper in Virginia and by Cranfield in New Hampshire seemed part of a calculated system of control approved by London.

A decided change took place in official British attitudes after organization of the powerful Board of Trade. Gradually, Charles, occupied with domestic tribulations, relinquished administration of the American possessions. Members of the Board, most of whom were connected with commercial enterprises depending upon foreign trade, had few reservations in recommending that the heterogenous settlements of the west should be drawn under the full control of the crown.

Administrative uniformity and coordination of policy became watchwords against which the actions of provincials were measured. It soon became clear to the Board, that colonial assemblies presented the most glaring barrier to cohesive government.

For nearly fifty years, inadequate supervision by the crown had enabled legislatures to assume increasing power. In many colonies, assemblies enjoyed revenue and law-making authority that far exceeded what was deemed tolerable in England. Of particular significance were legislative gains incurred at the expense of gubernatorial authority.

Americans had come to view their assemblies in the same manner in which Englishmen revered Parliament. Both constituencies believed the representatives met by fundamental right under ancient and uncontestable privileges that could not be diminished by executive decree.

The Board of Trade did not share this philosophy, but held that legislatures, like every other instrument of colonial government, existed only by grace of the King. The institutions had been granted to the people, and could be taken away without explanation. At the heart of this royalist interpretation, was the belief that colonists should not be treated as Britishers living on foreign soil. Rights of Englishmen did not necessarily extend to the ends of the earth. Americans were dependents of the crown, subject to extensive control by the King and Privy Council. It was questionable if they were even protected by the Magna Carta.

The suggestion that colonials were not equal to residents of England was preposterous to many Americans. Just as the struggle between royal prerogative and Parliamentary supremacy had characterized Britain during the 1640's, so did the question of royal control versus inherent citizen rights mark the Anglo-American scene in the 1670's and 1680's.

Those in the home office wasted no time in ideological debates, but embarked upon programs to reassert control by strengthening colonial governors. At the same time that crown appointees were rising in importance, it was hoped that power would flow out of the popular assemblies.

Soon after Bacon's Rebellion, it was declared that Poyning's Law would be put into effect in the old colony. This statute, devised in 1494 to subjugate the Irish Parliament, declared that assemblies could not initiate legislation. The sole function of these groups was to provide pro forma approval of measures submitted by the King. Virginians would not tolerate emasculation of the honored Burgess. The law was ignored and quickly faded from discussion.

The Lords of Trade were more successful in imposing other limitations on American assemblies. It was unquestionably established that the legislatures had no right to pass bills that impaired crown revenue or to reapprove measures that had been disallowed in England. "Suspending" clauses were required so that assemblies could no longer avoid royal vetoes by passing temporary regulations.

Perhaps the most effective limitation on popular government was the forced recognition of a governor's power to prorogue or dissolve legislatures. With this weapon, executives were able to halt discussion or passage of measures that were unfavorable to English interests.

The authority to remove advisers from royal Councils was also bestowed on governors. Under previous policy, when dismissal was allowed only by the crown, dissident advisers frequently used their positions as a forum to rouse discontent during the long months when gubernatorial requests for changes in membership were crossing the Atlantic.

Increased emphasis was also placed on the importance of royal instructions issued to colonial governors. Orders from the King and Privy Council were customarily kept secret from the public. As a result, governors were able to take vastly unpopular stances under the claim that they had been ordered to do so by secret instructions. No one could argue with the assertion.

It would appear that the colonists had no alternative but to submit to

English domination, but even the powerful British were aware that the provinces were far from defenseless in combating the authority of the King and his counsellors. Large segments of the British economy were totally dependent upon America where laborers were estimated to be six times more productive than workers in the mother country. The toil of the provincials sustained thousands of jobs in England, and even the slightest decrease in colonial productivity caused severe economic repercussions across the sea.

The geographic separation between the home isles and the possessions also served as a deterrent to arbitrary rule. Government worked in America only because citizens voluntarily submitted to absentee authority. Ultimately, the sole way in which the British could force compliance with unacceptable policies was by stationing massive numbers of English troops in the New World. Compulsory enforcement, however, was virtually impossible. The depleted English budget would not withstand such a permanent drain. The isles could not be left exposed to attack by European rivals. Even if troops were dispatched, there was no assurance that they would be a match for an inflamed American citizenry. The heavily armed adults of the provinces were far different from the domesticated residents of England. In Britain, guns and shot were reserved only for gentlemen, but in the colonies arms were the everyday tools of all citizens. Provincial men and women were well versed in fighting techniques and not to be trifled with.

But perhaps the strongest weapon available to the colonists was the desire of Holland, France and Spain to curtail the growing power of England. Home officials were well aware that continental enemies would gladly assist the provinces if disaffection with English rule became too great to tolerate.

Because neither the Americans nor the English held dominant power, colonial assemblies and royal governors developed pragmatic methods for modifying the idealistic directives that the Lords of Trade shot across the Atlantic with greater frequency. Despite efforts at centralization, English correspondence continued to be a confused mass of Royal Proclamations, court writs, warrants, instructions, letters and decrees issued by numerous, uncoordinated agencies. Orders that were unworkable or insulting were either ignored in the west, or altered to assure voluntary compliance. Such intentional disobedience might have caused a bloody confrontation between colony and King, but as had so often occurred in the past, British attention was rapidly being diverted from America to London. Charles, whose reign had been marked by dissension and disaster from the beginning, was discovering that the situation did not improve with time.

In the early 1670's, the King attempted to uphold the bargain struck with Louis in the secret treaties of Dover. In what was probably part of a "Grand Design" to return England to the Catholic fold, Charles issued a Declaration of Indulgence that allowed freedom of worship to Catholics and dissenting Protestants. He instigated the Third Dutch War in an effort to help France subdue the Protestants of the lowlands, but the actions only succeeded in arousing English fears that European nations were plotting the motherland's downfall.

By 1673, opponents in Commons had gained sufficient backing to force renunciation of the Declaration and to approve a Test Act that barred from office any citizen who refused to take Church of England sacraments. Enforcement of the measure extended to the highest levels. When Catholic convert James Stuart rejected the test, he was ousted as Lord High Admiral. The heir apparent had held the post since he was four years old.

James had never been an extremely popular figure, but the younger son of Charles I had gained a degree of public respect. During the Dutch wars, he fought bravely and narrowly escaped drowning when his flagship was sunk. The gratitude of the population, however, was surmounted by mistrust; it was suspected that James had become an agent of Rome.

As the power of the anti-court faction continued to increase, Charles was forced to end the conflict with Holland. To the delight of Protestant backers, the King approved a marriage between James' daughter Mary, second in line to the throne, and her cousin William, the Puritan Prince of Orange.

In 1678, resentment between religious factions flared again with the discovery of the so-called "Popish Plot." According to informers, England's highest ranking Catholics were involved in a conspiracy to murder Charles and install James on the throne. The Romanist murderers would then complete their coup by annihilating every English Protestant.

Gory predictions of mass rapes and murders became accepted as fact. Catholics of every degree were haled into court on evidence that was circumstantial at best. Inflamed mobs took to the streets and assaulted known Catholics.

So daring did the zealous crowds become, that even the King's carriage was not safe on London avenues. In one instance, Charles' coach was attacked by rioters who believed that the vehicle was carrying the Duchess of Portsmouth, the monarch's Catholic mistress. Actually the occupant was not the aristocratic Duchess, but Nell Gwynn, a popular actress of common origins who was also a favorite of the King. Nell, a devoted Protestant, had no intention of suffering because of mistaken identity. Leaning from the coach window, she sought to establish her lineage in no undertain terms. "Be silent, good people!" Nell shouted to the multitude. "I am the Protestant whore!" Amid cheers of support the young courtesan victoriously proceeded on her way.

As Catholics by the thousands fled into hiding, the antiroyal faction became even more daring. The clique, which would form the nucleus of the Whig Party, was led by Lord Shaftesbury, Proprietor of Carolina and a former confident of the King. Under Shaftesbury's patronage, a movement was begun to exclude James from the line of succession.

As early as 1668, attempts had been made to remove Stuart as a legitimate claimant. Assorted solutions had been put forth including a plan to force Charles to divorce the barren Queen Catherine so that a union might be arranged with a more fertile bride. Shaftesbury's scheme was not quite as commonplace: James Stuart would be replaced as heir apparent by Charles' illegitimate son James Scott, the Duke of Monmouth.

Despite intense pressure, Charles remained firm to the existing succession by withstanding all efforts to have Monmouth legitimatized and therefore eligible for the throne. Even non-Exclusionists feared that the life of the King was in jeopardy as long as the Duke of York remained a viable claimant. Echoes of the Popish Plot reappeared when the King's brother was accused in Commons of conspiring to kill Charles as part of the "Mealtub Plot." The design was so known because documents implicating the Duke were found in a pantry container.

Amidst the papist and Exclusionist controversies, Scottish Covenanters rebelled again against England. At Bothwell Bridge, a royal force under Monmouth quashed the insurgents. Captured troops were dispatched to America in punishment and the victory made Monmouth an even more attractive candidate for Kingly robes. The rivalry between Charles' brother and his illegitimate son intensified.

Hysteria against Catholics eventually became dangerous even to members of the royal family. York was sent from the country for safekeeping. Accusations were rampant that the Catholic Queen was part of a plan to poison Charles so that James might rule. Only when his consort seemed in extreme peril, did the King begin vigorously suppressing the persecution that had rent the nation.

Charles, forced by financial insolvency to call an unfavorable Commons, was able to disband the body when a new secret loan was forthcoming from Louis. The £400,000 payment assured that Stuart would be independent of legislative pressure and as a result, Charles believed that the time had come to move against the Whig opposition.

Lord Shaftesbury was arrested for high treason. Although evidence against the peer was minimal, there was no assurance that the verdict would be acquittal. Shaftesbury asked to be sent to Carolina, a request that bred speculation that the province was a hotbed of conspiracy against the monarchy. Instead of American exile, Shaftesbury was allowed to escape to Holland. In 1683 he died of stomach gout, dooming the Exclusionist movement and severely hampering the Whig cause.

James was called home and the popularity of the Stuart brothers began rebounding. A major reason was the discovery of the "Rye House Plot," a conspiracy in which high Protestant leaders were implicated. The scheme called for the murder of both Stuarts as they rode past a famous tavern on the road from London to Newmarket. The pair was saved only by a last minute change in schedule.

The aftermath of the discovery brought a variety of changes. Monmouth, who was evidently involved in the plan, fled into hiding in Holland. To assure that at least one Stuart would survive a major assassination attempt, James refused to travel in the company of his brother. Finally, the fledgling Whig Party was severely reduced. Critics of royal policies feared that renewed political dissension would be construed as support for the Rye House design. Persecutions of Catholics abated as Protestants muted their complaints.

Hoping to seize the offensive, Charles marshalled his authority for a direct attack on borough charters. Like many American colonies,

English towns were chartered under documents that gave local governments independent powers and guaranteed specific rights to the individual. Using his new found prestige, the King forced the recall of more than sixty charters, including that of the city of London. Some towns were completely deprived of founding documents, while others were issued virtually useless replacements. The Whigs, whose power base lay in the populated urban boroughs, were helpless to prevent the move.

For four years Louis' subsidies allowed Charles to rule without Parliament. The "French Party" gained ascendancy at court and the way seemed clear for increasing introduction of royal prerogative. In February of 1685, however, the reign of Charles II drew to a close. The King fell dangerously ill. James' supporters closed English ports so that news of the situation would not reach Monmouth. Many monarchists feared that the King's illegitimate son, known to some as the "Booby Duke," would launch an illegal invasion to take the throne as soon as the position became vacant.

On February 6, Charles requested that he be administered the last rites of the Catholic Church. Coincidentally, the priest secretly brought to the royal bedchamber was the same clergyman who had helped Charles to escape from the Roundheads during the civil wars.

James, whom moderates believed would instigate another internal conflict if deprived of the throne, quickly assumed power after Charles' death. The great majority of Britishers were not pleased with the new ruler and the disaffection increased when Stuart attended public mass just two days after taking control. For a time, however, James was reasonably safe. Parliament's Tories, whose allegiance to the legal line of succession was rooted in fears that anarchy would result from deviation, exerted authority to assure that the crown would pass on as required by law.

In June, the first test of James' hold came when Monmouth landed a small party at Dorset. Recalled by remnants of the Exclusionists, the ambitious Duke set out toward London, anticipating that thousands would flock to support his bid for the throne. Despite Monmouth's popularity with the common people, he was unable to attract support from the gentry or nobility. On July 6, his inferior army was routed at Sedgemoor by royal forces under John Churchill, a courtier whose sister had served as James' mistress and had borne several illegitimate children by the new King.

Despite pleas from Monmouth to his uncle, the rebel was beheaded on July 15. Government leaders, believing that the Protestant cause might find fertile soil in the provinces, directed that no word of the Duke's rebellion should be carried on boats leaving for Virginia.

Difficulties were also being created by Archibald Campbell, the Earl of Argyll and the most powerful noble in Scotland. Argyll, a former Stuart supporter, had been estranged by false charges of treason that the brothers had framed in an attempt to curtail the noble's power in the north. Dressed as his step-daughter's footman, Argyll had managed to escape from imprisonment in the Tower and take refuge in Holland.

In mid-June, the Scotsman invaded England in an effort to rally disaffected Covenanters against the Catholic ruler. His rebellion was as unsuccessful as Monmouth's had been. Argyll was captured and executed. His head was placed on public display.

James showed none of the compassion that had marked Charles' treatment of the Cromwellian revolters. A "Bloody Assize" was convened to try supporters of Monmouth and Argyll. More than 300 rebels were hanged and as a warning to others who might challenge the throne, the corpses were strewn along major highways of the island nation. A thousand more fortunate soldiers were transported to America as servants.

The inability of Monmouth and Argyll to attract widespread support among the dissatisfied citizenry demonstrated the natural reluctance of the British to overrule the legal succession. The tumultuous times of the English civil wars and the excesses of the Cromwellians had not been forgotten. James sat on a shaky throne in 1685, but the seat was his. More important, for the first time in more than a century, the crown was openly Catholic.

# Chapter VIII

# New England's Union Upset

THE ASSUMPTION OF a Catholic monarch was not heralded in Massachusetts, but the reaction was much more subdued than would have been forthcoming from the Puritans of Commonwealth days. Far-reaching changes had taken place in the Bay since Cromwell emerged victorious. Ironically, the increasing liberalism had been brought about by the accomplishments of the conservative clergy.

The founding theocrats of Massachusetts were successful in eliminating divisive elements and moulding a stable society dedicated to hard work. The saints' determination brought widespread prosperity based on a vast commercial empire that reached out to ports in England, the sister colonies and continental Europe. Captains and traders skilled in smuggling made New England an important force in seventeenth century commerce. The advancement doomed the closed, Puritan society.

Exposure to differing cultures undermined the singleness of purpose that had safeguarded the early believers. Boston became an urban center whose population was exposed, if not completely receptive, to new and foreign ideas. The clergy attempted to perpetuate sanctity of thought, but the tide of change was too powerful to stem. No longer were village streets filled only wtih the narrow philosophies of a few, reverent ministers.

Nowhere were the changes so obvious as in the arena of politics. Trade depended heavily upon English buyers, sellers and shippers. Freedom of the seas was maintained by British frigates. It was impossible for the Bay to continue as a self-sustaining commonwealth haughtily defying British policy without incurring harm. To maintain their commercial dominance, Bostonians were forced to sacrifice complete independence. The Bay's integration into the realm was a gradual, but irreversible one, involving advances and setbacks covering a thirty year period.

Obviously, the Massachusetts Puritans had not expected the Restoration to alter their Commonwealth status. Long after other provinces had recognized Charles II as King, the Bay colony remained silent. On June 10, 1661, more than a year after the monarch's return, the Massachusetts General Court finally commented on the relationship of the province to the crown. In a *Declaration of Rights by Charter,* the Court made it clear that the 1635 *quo warranto* had not affected the original charter in any way. The saints' basic rights remained inviolate from either King or Parliament. The officials declared:

1. We conceive the patent (under God), to be the first and main foundation of our civil policy here, by a governor and company, according as in therein expressed.

2. The governor and company are, by the patent, a body politic in fact and name.

3. This body politic is vested with power to make freemen.

4. These freemen have power to choose annually a governor, deputy-governor, assistants, and their select representatives or deputies.

5. This government hath also power to set up all sorts of officers, as well superior as inferior, and point out their power and places.

6. The governor, deputy-governor, assistants, and select representatives or deputies have full power and authority, both legislative and executive, for the government of all the people here, whether inhabitants or strangers, both concerning ecclesiastical and civil without appeal, excepting law or laws repugnant to the laws of England.

Three months after the *Declaration,* Massachusetts officials proclaimed Charles as King.

In the confusion following the Restoration, the assertion of independent rights was not struck down by London, but by 1664 officials were ready to act. A royal commission was dispatched to investigate the manner in which New England's colonies were being governed. Ostensibly, the probers were to assure that provincial administrators were faithfully executing charter documents and that no citizens were being denied legal rights. However, the Commissioners had been secretly instructed to seek ways in which the charters might be recalled or modified so that more direct supervision could be applied by the crown. Under consideration was a plan to consolidate all the northeast colonies under the rule of a single, royally appointed governor.

The English Commissioners were presumably able to secure sufficient evidence to prove that large scale abuses of power existed in New England. Unfortunately, as the agents returned home, the Dutch attacked at sea. Before the vessel was captured, an alarmed official threw overboard the carefully documented findings. Without proof of misconduct, preoccupied by the Great Fire and consumed with the plague, officials cancelled plans for the projected change in administration. Once more the 1629 charter had been saved. Puritans attributed the reprieve to divine intervention. Normal government was resumed.

By 1671, conditions were again ripe for a British move against Massachusetts, but even the Commissioners of Trade and Plantations recognized that the province was in a decidedly powerful position. Commissioner John Evelyn perceived that great delicacy was required in even corresponding with New England. Commenting in his diary on a May 26, 1671, Commission meeting, Evelyn wrote of the Massachusetts situation:

> . . . rich and strong as they now were, there were great debates in what style to write to them; for the condition of that colony was such, that they were able to contest with all other plantations about them, and there was fear of their breaking from all dependence on this nation . . . some of our Council were for sending them a menacing letter, which those who better understood the peevish and touchy humor of that colony, were utterly against.

The most effective manner of subduing the arrogant province involved serious debate in Britain. Hard liners suggested that a powerful British fortress staffed by regulars and royal frigates should be built in Boston harbor, but the militant proposals were rejected in favor of less aggressive approaches.

Edward Randolph was sent to America in 1676 by the Lords of Trade to observe government operations and determine how enforcement of the navigation acts was progressing. Randolph was openly impeded by locals, but managed to send back to England copious accounts of abuses supposedly occuring in the Bay. The agent's list included numerous allegations of government infringments upon the rights of the King, Parliament and the people: Anglicans were denied freedom of worship; Quakers were hanged in violation of royal decrees; regicides were harbored; war was imminent because of Massachusetts' grasping designs on neighboring provinces and the navigation acts were virtually ignored. To remedy the situation, Randolph urged than an armed force be sent from England to regulate shipping and insure that abuses did not continue unchecked.

The investigator's reports buttressed English notions that masses of dissatisfied colonials truly desired crown intervention. Colonial representatives were summoned to London to answer the serious charges, but instead of reassuring the officials, the representatives' arrogance and evasions only further infuriated the Lords.

Reaction by administrators in the colony was little better. Only reluctantly did the Puritans admit that England might involve itself in Massachusetts' affairs. On the vital issue of the navigation acts, some in the colony publicly announced that because no representatives from New England sat in Parliament, then measures passed by the body were not binding in America. When British authorities ordered the 1629 charter examined for possible modifications, the Puritans ignored the request.

Such affronts only served to reinforce the Lords' impatience and in 1678 recommendations were sent forth that a *quo warranto* be issued. It was also decided that the navigation acts would no longer be enforced by the Bay's popularly elected governor. Instead, the English declared that Edward Randolph would serve as Collector, Surveyor and Searcher of his Majesty's Customs. Randolph would represent not the province, but the King.

The General Court which had been so adept at delaying tactics produced a sudden flurry of activity. The body agreed to repeal locally-enacted laws that were contrary to English practice, but announced that no measure would be changed if the religious principles on which the province had been founded would be threatened as a result. Despite promises of cooperation, the Massachusetts' leaders refused to accept Randolph's royal appointment. Supposedly, their opposition was based on the contention that all officials serving in the province were to be elected or appointed by the people of the colony. Only when it became obvious that the English authorities had no intention of retreating, was the Collector allowed to begin work.

Plans for the *quo warranto* were suspended after the General Court's conciliatory statement and the outbreak of the Popish Plot. A furor over the mishandling of the navigation acts continued to build, however, as English merchant complaints turned to predictions of mass bankruptcy.

Other disruptions came from the Puritan clergy, an institution that was rapidly losing strength but still dominated life and government in the colony. Randolph considered the political machinations of the ministers to be appalling, a conclusion shared by Walter Barefoote in neighboring New Hampshire. To the Lords of Trade, Barefoote warned:

> No Pope ever acted with greater arrogancy than those preachers who influence the people to their fantastic humors, and debauch them from their duty and obedience to his Majesty and his laws, and are ever stirring them up to disloyalty. . . .

The Lords ordered that an agent be sent to London to discuss changes in the Massachusetts charter, but no acknowledgement was forthcoming from America. Additional calls were sent and still no agents appeared. In the summer of 1680, the King sought to end the insubordination by vowing that if colonial representatives did not arrive in England within ninety days, the issue would be turned over to the courts. The royal directive did not stir the provincials to action. Not until May 20, 1682, did agents Joseph Dudley and John Richards set sail. Unknown to the British, the departure was still another ploy, for neither man was empowered to authorize changes in the patent.

The belligerent attitude of Bay leaders was not endorsed by all elements in the colony. By 1683, a strong opposing faction had emerged that favored compromise with England. The conciliatory wing perceived that Massachusetts was no longer powerful enough to contest British authority. The moderates feared that continued resistance would bring imposition of total crown rule and the loss of all charter rights.

Followers of the soft line were primarily urban Puritans, Anglicans and artisans. A significant number of traders also supported the movement for it was believed that under English domination the navigation acts would be enforced with ruthless severity.

Arrayed against the moderates, was the entrenched "Faction," of conservative Puritans whose center of power lay in the General Court. The Faction's political outlook was inseparable from its religious dogma and to some degree, compromise with England was seen as a betrayal of the covenant with God. The most radical members of the party did not wish merely to preserve the status quo, but desired a return to the early days of settlement when citizens gave unquestioned obedience to the theocrats. The idea that God would protect the colony against Anglicanism and the Catholic-leaning King was a bulwark of the old-liners.

Predictably it was not the moderates, but Edward Randolph that protested the loudest against the Faction. The collector bombarded the Board of Trade with complaints suggesting that the conservatives intentionally hampered the King's interest. On June 3, 1683, the Lords moved for a *quo warranto* on charges of unlawful usurpation of government authority. Legal proceedings were delayed briefly when the sheriff of Middlesex refused to serve the writ because Massachusetts was not included within his jurisdiction. The problem was solved when a writ of *scire facias,* a process not involving service, was issued by the Court of Chancery.

Massachusetts officials were notified of the action but the officeholders, perhaps expecting the difficulty would be settled by God, refused to plead. After a preliminary ruling in favor of the crown, the corporation's charter was officially declared null on October 23, 1684.

Tension rose in New England as word spread that the entire region was to be united under a single governor. The prediction seemed more than rumor when writs were also issued against Connecticut and Rhode Island. Even the most pious Puritans grew disturbed, but in February of 1685, the hoped-for miracle occurred. Charles II died before a new colonial regime could be established, and James, preoccupied by succession problems ordered that the existing administrations should be continued.

The Puritans had been saved still another time. The Faction was vindicated. In May elections, conservatives swept all major posts except that of governor where popular Simon Bradstreet was reelected.

The joy in Massachusetts soon turned to consternation, for James II proved even more concerned with the American colonies than had been his brother. As one who had personally experienced the difficulties involved in provincial government, the new monarch was convinced that only efficiency and uniformity could save the empire. James wasted no time in reclassifying New York as a crown province.

England's Catholic King then proceeded to frame a colonial policy far more ambitious than earlier efforts. Charles had concentrated upon changing proprietorships and charter provinces to crown status, but James intended to merge the fragmented units into comprehensive super colonies. He may have envisioned that eventually all British provinces from Maine to the Indies would be united under a single governor.

New England was selected as the proving ground for the idea of consolidation. Here, James intended to make many colonies into one. The name of the resulting unit would be the Dominion of New England.

Bostonians reacted to the merger with anger. Particularly outrageous was the appointment of Joseph Dudley as President of the interim government that would rule until final arrangements for the Dominion could be devised in England. Suspicions were high that Dudley, dispatched as an agent to fight the *quo warranto*, had betrayed his allegiance to Massachusetts Bay in exchange for high office.

Dudley's commission arrived in Boston on May 14, 1686 and in a typical reaction, the General Court, rather than accepting the inevitability of the new government, pronounced the entire concept as an illegal abridgement of citizen rights. Refusing to have any part in the transaction, the Court adjourned.

The temporary government was not a complex operation. Joined with Massachusetts Bay in the arrangement were Plymouth, New Hampshire, Maine and the King's Province or Narragansett County in Rhode Island. All executive, judicial and administrative powers were vested in the President and a sixteen-member Council appointed by the crown. Popular assemblies and many elective offices that had previously existed in the various independent provinces, were abolished. Edward Randolph was appointed to the powerful job of Secretary and Registrar.

On May 25, 1686, Dudley's government was officially proclaimed and although several councillors refused to accept royal appointment, a workable administration was set in motion. In his inaugural address, Dudley optimistically predicted that the unification would bring a "happy increase and advance" to the province. The cheerful progress did not materialize. Instead, complaints began pouring into the capital at Boston.

Less than a week after the President's installation, citizens submitted a formal petition denouncing the government as arbitrary and contrary to the rights of Englishmen. The hard-liners who had denied for so long that British law was valid in America, now assumed a diametrically opposed position.

More grumbling was heard in matters involving religion. Abstaining Puritans resented that taxpayers were billed £21 for wine used to celebrate the advent of Dudley's administration. A riotous commemoration of the Queen's birthday was deplored as a profanation of the sabbath. Fears were voiced that the hated cross of St. George would be reintroduced into local flags. Resentments were stirred when a Church of England clergyman arrived to organize a local parish. Opposition grew even stronger when Randolph suggested that Puritan congregations should be forced to contribute twenty shillings per week to support Anglican worship.

Although only five of the sixty militia officers were Anglican, Puritans resented even modest attempts to redistribute commissions in a more equitable form. The newly prescribed method of oath-taking brought other complaints. The saints of Massachusetts, who customarily pointed their hand toward heaven while swearing, strongly objected to English practice in which the Bible was held and then kissed. Such a display was seen as idolatrous and papist.

Edward Randolph, who had initially cooperated with Dudley, also grew dissatisfied. Labeling the President as a man of "base, servile and antimonarchial principles," the Secretary alleged that Dudley had profited at the expense of royal revenues. Dudley, who had appointed his sixteen-year-old son to the lucrative office of Collector of Ports in Boston, might have been equally critical of Randolph. During the formation of government, the Britisher had busied himself by selling offices for as much as £10 per year.

Few constructive solutions were produced by the appointed Council, a body that provided little firm leadership and fell into bickering over the most insignificant matters. In describing the chaos, Randolph observed: ''Now, instead of meeting to do public business, 'twas only to quarrel, and that in such heats that it threatened to occasion the disolving of the government.''

Uncertainty as to the specific form that the permanent Dominion would take probably contributed to much of the ill feeling. Additional fear no doubt was incurred because of rumors that Colonel Percy Kirke was under consideration as the area's governor. Kirke was an infamous monarchist credited with summarily executing large numbers of Monmouth's soldiers who had surrendered at Sedgemoor. The prospect that a cruel and corrupt foreigner might replace their popularly elected governor could not have been settling to those in Massachusetts.

The suspense ended during the summer of 1686 when the final Dominion structure was approved. If the citizens of Massachusetts Bay had considered Dudley's near powerless regime to be undesirable, their complaints would increase a hundred fold with the arrival of Sir Edmund Andros, the new Captain-General and Governor-in-Chief of all New England.

Long before Sir Edmund arrived in Boston, residents had become thoroughly disgusted with President Dudley and his administration. Perhaps believing that any replacement would be an improvement, New Englanders showed no immediate opposition when the King's appointee arrived on December 19. Resistence may also have been discouraged by the royal frigate *Rose* and the company of one hundred grenadiers who escorted the Governor to Boston.

Andros, though well connected at court, was an experienced military figure who had helped to put down Monmouth's Rebellion and had served as Governor of New York. His powers under the Dominion, however, far exceeded those delegated to any previous colonial official. The New England post, as envisioned by the King and the Lords of Trade, was a powerful office based on innovative departures from both British and American political tradition.

Andros was given the authority to make laws and levy taxes. Although each measure was subject to approval by the Dominion Council and reviewable in England, no provision was made for citizen involvement. Theoretically, opinions of the populace would emerge in the forty-two member Council, but the body was not intended to be a representative assembly. Members would hold office by royal appointment rather than by popular election. Supposed care would be taken to assure that the councillors were chosen from different geographic sections of the union, but the primitiveness of transportation made it unlikely that members from more remote areas would attend frequently. To compensate for the expected high absentee rate, it was decided that seven members would constitute a quorum and that limited business could be considered by as few as five attendees. The specter that taxes could be levied or laws approved by the vote of this small band of men was not comforting to provincials accustomed to strong elective legislatures.

Andros had also been delegated almost total powers of administration. He was authorized to head the militia, establish courts, conduct war, regulate Indian affairs, collect quitrents and assure that the navigation and other acts of England were fully enforced.

Of significant importance were the Governor's instructions that neighboring jurisdictions should be brought into the Dominion as soon as possible. Connecticut, the remainder of Rhode Island, New York and the Jerseys were all scheduled to be integrated into the system. In some cases, submission required a skilled hand of diplomacy, and Sir Edmund proved equal to the assignment. Connecticut authorities, who had three times refused to surrender their charter to *quo warranto,* were talked into capitulation by the Governor. Other jurisdictions also fell and within sixteen months, a total of nine former colonies had officially become part of the Dominion. It was possible that plans for the eventual inclusion of Pennsylvania and Maryland were also being considered in England.

Technically, each of the former colonies was subject to the same regulation as each other member, but in practical operation the Dominion's influence was minimal in provinces distant from Boston. Life in New York was little changed and the Jerseys were so far removed from the capital that no representatives were even appointed to the Council.

The situation was reversed in Massachusetts Bay where the constant presence of Dominion officials assured that every directive would be rigidly enforced. Citizens would have no respite from government intervention,.a fact that became abundantly clear when Andros launched an English approved revision of land policy. Throughout New England, land titles were a jumbled mass of conflicting claims that burdened the courts with unceasing litigation. Thousands of landowners held no clear titles, but rested property claims on squatters' rights, Indian purchases, corporation grants, sales from private individuals or General Court deeds.

Andros introduced what appeared to be a rational design for solving the problem. All landholders were directed to apply to the Governor for new titles. The various claims would be analyzed and the rightful owners would receive valid and unquestionable titles from the King.

While the reconfirmation may have been based on solid administrative techniques, residents saw the program in a far more sinister light. Not only would the Governor reap windfall profits from fees charged for title issuance, but a complete land list could be compiled and the most choice parcels could be set aside for confiscation. Some basis for the cynicism existed. Andros' favorites had begun receiving tracts of prime land and the treasured town commons were coming under increasing scrutiny by privileged loyalists.

For decades, New England's villages had depended upon the commons for grazing sheep or cattle, gathering firewood, training militiamen and holding public ceremonies. Each green was considered the property of the village and was available to all in joint usership. With the advent of the new government, prior use or town ownership no longer seemed a defense against the designs of speculators. The Cambridge common, held by citizens for fifty years, was surveyed and partially granted. Irate townspeople were imprisoned for pulling up the surveyors' stakes. Edward Randolph made himself even more detested by requesting title to commons in three separate villages.

When Dominion subjects refused to submit their titles for reconfirmation, Andros began issuing writs of intrusion aimed at confiscating the derelicts' property. Less drastic, but equally dismaying, was the Governor's decision to impose quitrents on territory that had long been cultivated.

Quitrents, an accepted practice in England and the southern colonies, were foreign in Massachusetts where land was usually held in fee. Recognizing that the annual payments constituted a valuable new source of revenue, British officials had authorized Andros to levy quitrents of 2s 6d per year per one hundred acres on all territory "yet undisposed of.'' Under the restriction, property already taken up would be forever exempt, but anyone acquiring new land would be perpetually subject to the fees.

Believing that the threat of quitrents could be used to force reluctant landholders to apply for reconfirmation, Andros extended the original intention of the authorization. The Governor announced that rents would be collected not only on undistributed land, but also on that where "royal confirmation might be wanting." Parcels where titles had not been reconfirmed were considered as fitting into this category.

Tensions created by unfavorable land policies were accentuated by what Puritans viewed as a calculated program to erode religious independence. The controversy over oath taking did not abate, and indignation over the impious behavior of the royal grenadiers continued. The church rate, a public assessment historically collected by government agents for the support of Puritan activities, was forbidden. But no religious infringement aroused more emotional response than Sir Edmund's actions in securing a meeting place for Boston parishioners of the Church of England.

Soon after his arrival, the Governor suggested that Puritan facilities should be made available for weekly Anglican rites. The request was refused. Determined to provide a suitable atmosphere for the meetings of the official belief, Andros directed that the keys to the South Meeting House should be turned over to him. Despite incontestible proof that the building and the land on which it stood were the private property of the Puritan congregation, the meeting house was appropriated for Anglican activities. Within weeks, the former owners were forced to schedule their own services at the convenience of the Anglicans. As a further insult, part of the Puritan burying ground was also taken for the English church. Puritans were also upset by the reported Anglican baptism of a "noted whore" and the performance of secret marriage ceremonies.

Andros and his followers were widely suspected of carrying out an organized plan of repression against Puritan clergymen. Though their authority was no longer supreme, the theocrats still held considerable prestige and their learned sermons served as important molders of public opinion. Because the ministers were firmly opposed to the Dominion, their influence was constantly detrimental to the workings of government. To congregations throughout the Bay, it seemed indisputable that Dominion loyalists were determined to suppress the source of dissention.

Charles Morton, minister at Charlestown, was tried for "seditious expressions," supposedly uttered during a sermon. Increase Mather was arrested for slandering Randolph. The Reverend Wiswall of Duxbury was ordered to appear before the Governor in Boston under near inhumane conditions. According to Cotton Mather:

> . . . he was then lame in both feet with the gout, fitter for a bed than a journey, therefore [he] wrote to the Governor, praying that he might be excused until he should be able to travel and engaged that then he would attend any court. But the next week, the cruel officer by an express order from Sir Edmund Andros, forced him to ride in that condition, being shod with clouts instead of shoes. And when he came before the Council he was there made to stand till the anguish of his feet and shoulders had almost overcome him. . . .

Added to the popular discontent over land policies and religious persecution were anxieties created by the Dominion's handling of tax assessment and collection.

In March of 1687, Andros with the consent of the Council, imposed a tax to be collected in each village by locally elected agents. A negative response was immediately returned by the people. Announcing that taxation without consent of the governed was illegal under the ancient laws of England, communities throughout Massachusetts Bay refused to even consider electing the collectors. In Essex County, all but three villages stood firm in disobedience. Nowhere did citizens exhibit more enraged behavior than in Ipswich.

Led by minister John Wise, inhabitants of Ipswich agreed in town meeting that the tax was an infringement on the most basic human rights. Andros was not impressed with the protestations of the Puritans who had denied liberties to non-believers for decades. Throughout the village, townspeople were arrested as "insurrectionists." Many begged pardon for the refusal to pay, but Wise and five others persisted. A special court was convened. According to critics, those called to hear the case were "strangers and foreigners, gathered up" to serve the interests of Andros rather than those of justice.

The judges and jurors, sympathetic to the Dominion, refused to accept Wise's contention that the arbitrary tax was prohibited by the Magna Carta. The minister was informed that English rights did not reach around the globe. The clergyman, denied habeas corpus, was also warned that his only incontestible liberty under British rule, was that of not being sold into slavery. The judgment was swift. Wise was found guilty, fined £50, forced to post a £1,000 bond and forbidden from continuing in the ministry. His accessories were fined and barred from holding public office.

Persecution of the clergyman generated public sympathy, but the trial succeeded in breaking the tax resistance movement. To insure that a repetition of the Ipswich incident would not reoccur, Andros forbade further town meetings. The ban was a blow to anti-Dominionites, for the local gatherings served as a means for informing the people and the venting of grievances. Community meetings had become essential to the citizenry after the popular assembly had been abolished. The practical and historic necessity of town meetings, however, was ignored by Andros, who announced that residents might convene for government business only once a year and then for the sole purpose of electing officers. Discussion of any other matter was prohibited.

The furor over the 1687 tax bill and the abolishment of the town meetings, ended any possibility that the Dominion government would be voluntarily accepted. Incidents that might have been disliked, but tolerated under a more popular administration, became *causes celèbres* under Andros.

When the Governor ordered that fee schedules be established for court litigation, the people interpreted the move as an attempt to endorse profiteering by jurists. Efforts to modernize the legal system brought only complaints. Enforcement of the navigation acts alienated moderate merchants who had originally accepted the British rule. The establishment of designated ports of entry angered those living in towns not selected. Efforts to curtail smuggling and piracy brought discontent from traders and the elimination of Boston's mint drew the wrath of loose money interests.

Any pretense that the Council served as a representative body had been dispelled. Delegates from distant colonies, who had rarely attended, virtually ceased participation when Dominion officials refused to reimburse the men for travel expenses. Moderates, increasingly unwilling to be connected with Andros' policies, resigned. The effect was to leave authority almost totally in the hands of the Governor and a small group of loyalists.

In the fall of 1688, Andros was rudely reminded that internal dissention was not the only threat to the existence of the Dominion. All along the frontier, unfriendly Indians in cooperation with the French in Canada, challenged English pioneers.

Establishment of a comprehensive and effective defense on the northern border had been a primary reason for the formation of the New England union. Canada, united under a single governor, had successfully encroached on the territory of the unaligned provinces for several years. The Puritans, trusting in God for protection, ignored defense needs. The thousands of lives lost during King Philip's War had been the bloody harvest of the short sighted policy.

Interpreting even the war as God's will, provincial governments continued to ignore the frontier menace. Attempts by Andros to organize an adequate defense were not welcomed as sensible precautions, but resented as costly and unnecessary burdens.

Friendly or "praying" Indians had been confined to reservations, but little success had been forthcoming in controlling less amiable tribes. Encouraged by the French, Canadian Indians began warring against the Iroquois, traditional allies of the British. At stake was the profitable fur trade that appeared to be slipping from French to English control.

Andros attempted to woo the Iroquois confederation into supporting the Dominion by bringing tribal leaders to Boston. The effort did not impress urban residents who muttered that the red men were not coming as allies, but as spies to scout the city's weaknesses.

Attacks spread from New York into the Connecticut Valley and Maine. The Dominion Council authorized a major expedition, but experienced New Englanders were reluctant to lead the poorly organized troop. Andros was forced to take personal charge of the seven hundred man army.

From the beginning, the operation was ill-fated. Supplies were inadequate. Long marches were undertaken in extreme weather. Morale was low and the Indians skillfully avoided the expedition by disappearing into the heavy forests. According to Cotton Mather, the job of cornering the natives was as difficult as "hedging in the cuckoo." Little support was contributed on the home front. While Andros and his men struggled in the wilderness, Boston merchants reportedly took advantage of the Governor's absence by selling arms to the French and Indians.

As winter approached, the expedition settled into rude forts on the frontier, prompting speculation in the capital that the military failure had been intentional. Rumors of a conspiracy, headed by Andros, raced through the port city. According to one line, the Governor had insisted on the invasion in order to bankrupt the Dominion. Another theory was that no Indian threat had actually existed, but that Sir Edmund had created the menace in order to divert the militia and leave Massachusetts vulnerable to French attack. Reportedly, Louis' fleet stood ready to take Boston at any moment. Assisting the Europeans were blood-thirsty savages who had been secretly armed by Sir Edmund. The intention of the combined enemy was to capture all of New England for the Romanists.

That Andros, who had long been condemned by Puritans for avid Anglicanism, could be considered in league with Catholic France revealed the extent to which the American possessions had been influenced by the religious turmoil gripping the mother country. In 1688, England was a nation torn by the old rivalries of Catholic verses Protestant, King verses Commons. At the center of the struggle was a monarch whose impositions had proved more disastrous than those that had prompted the regicide of Charles I.

The initial confidence placed in James began to erode even before the Bloody Assizes. The King, unable or unwilling to recognize that the crown was his only because of Tory support in Parliament, embarked on a course to eliminate all restrictions that had been placed on Catholics. Thirty years earlier, the monarch had barely escaped Roundhead armies by disguising himself as a peasant woman. The experience and years in exile had left their mark. Stuart retained little sympathy for Protestants, be they high Anglicans or dissenters.

Ignoring the Test Act, James began dismissing Protestants from power and issuing commissions to Catholic supporters. In the summer and fall of 1686 alone, five papists were placed on the Privy Council. Catholics became chief of the Navy, Lord Treasurer and Keeper of the Privy Seal. Trustees at Oxford were ordered to approve Anthony Farmer as President of Magdalen College. Young Farmer, who had been expelled from Cambridge for seducing undergraduates, providing a naked lady for student entertainment and participating in drunken quarrels, had only one apparent qualification for the honored job; he was a Catholic.

The appointments of Catholics to high positions in the Army was particularly alarming to the Protestants. The large force that had been organized to fight Monmouth's and Argyll's rebels had not been disbanded.

Despite Parliamentary laws forbidding such action, James issued a Declaration of Indulgence that removed sanctions from non-Church of England believers. When the King's power to override laws passed by Commons was upheld by a friendly court in the case of *Godden v. Hales,* opposition in the House stiffened. In answer to mounting protests, James prorogued the assembly.

In both England and the colonies, it was generally assumed that James was in league with Louis XIV. The mistrust was heightened by the English King's seeming acceptance of France's violent reprisals against Protestants after revocation of the Edict of Nantes. An estimated half a million Protestants were forced to flee the Bourbon state to save their lives. Many chose the American colonies as a new home, but the King remained silent on the persecutions.

During April of 1688, James ordered that a second Declaration of Indulgence, a document that eliminated all criminal penalities against Catholics, should be read in Anglican churches throughout the nation. Declaring the decree a violation of Parliamentary supremacy, Church of England ministers refused. As a result, seven high ranking churchmen, including the Archbishop of Canterbury, were arrested.

Despite increasing resentment toward Stuart, most Englishmen refused to force a confrontation that could mean the beginning of a new civil war. The hesitance was reinforced by the assurance that James would be followed to the throne by a strong Protestant. Because no male heir had been born, the King's eldest daughter, Mary, would ascend. The future Queen's husband, William of Orange, had long and bravely lead the Protestant lowlands against France. After Mary would come her sister Anne, a zealous supporter of the established church.

The certainty of a Protestant successor was shaken by the announcement that the Queen, Mary of Modena, was pregnant. Mary had borne several children but none had survived. In this instance, however, Catholic confidants unhesitatingly announced that the expected infant would be a hearty boy who would live long and lead his country. The pronouncements were chilling to Anglicans, for male heirs of any age took precedence over all females.

In early June, one month before the expected arrival of the royal baby, the crown quarters at Whitehall were the scene of hurried activity. Mary was moved to seclusion in St. James Palace. Few Protestants were included in the entourage.

Strong rules of procedure had grown up around the event of a royal birth. In order to assure that no deception was practiced, unimpeachable representatives of the church, family and government were customarily present during the delivery. These served as witnesses for the people of England, insuring that the newborn was indeed of royal parentage and that foul play had not been perpetrated.

On July 10, Mary of Modena gave birth. By choice or chance, witnesses tended to be Catholics or foreign intimates of the Queen. Not present was the Archbishop of Canterbury, who was conviently installed in the Tower awaiting trial. Anne Stuart, second in line of secession was also absent.

Within hours the news rang out across England. A healthy child had been born. The new heir, who would be raised a Catholic, was named James Francis Edward.

Disbelief in the legitimacy of the birth wracked Britian. Some claimed that an unknown male child had been smuggled into the bedchamber in a warming pan and substituted for a female or stillborn infant actually delivered to the Queen. Others maintained that Mary had either never been pregnant, or had miscarried early in her term. Dissident Anglicans began intriguing to remove James. It was decided that William and Mary would be asked to invade the country and assume leadership of England.

All London was astir with uncertainty when Increase Mather arrived in the summer of 1688 to present grievances against Andros and the Dominion. The minister's hope was to secure both the elimination of the unpopular government and a new charter that would provide for popular rule in Massachusetts Bay.

Mather's journey had almost been terminated before it began, for Randolph, learning of the intended trip, attempted to imprison the clergyman. Fortunately, Mather was able to hide undetected and ship out disguised in a long cloak and wig.

Surprisingly, Mather's requests met with limited acceptance among court circles. The concessions he was able to obtain, however, were not the result of skillful diplomacy, but a reflection of a new policy on which James had embarked.

The monarch belatedly recognized the strength of the opposition and in an attempt to recoup Protestant support, reversed direction. He agreed to call Parliament, abolish his ecclesiastical court and restore the London charter revoked by Charles. But even as the English monarch courted liberal favor, William was at the Hague preparing to cross the channel. On October 16, James made what would be his last pronouncement to the American colonies. All provincial governors were commanded to prepare for war with Holland. It was announced that a foreign invasion of the plantations was likely and imminent.

The Prince of Orange issued his own declaration and called upon all officials who had been removed by enemies of the true church to retake their posts. William also warned that the fight to save England from the papists was about to begin.

In Maine, where the Dominion troops were secluded in winter camp, Andros received James' order, but had no word of William's declaration. The Governor acceded to the King's demand and instructed all New Englanders to be "vigilant and careful" in watching for enemy fleets. If such a force was sighted, the people were directed to use their "utmost endeavor to hinder any landing or invasion. . . ."

Throughout the length of America, settlers waited anxiously for news of developments in the mother country. In Boston, tension was high and rumors rampant. It was said that William Penn, who had been assisting Mather, had been executed as a Jesuit. Washerwoman Goody Glover was hanged for witchcraft by the nervous population. In January, a letter arrived from Mather claiming that action on the charter was imminent, but the clergyman did not include any new information on the political situation in England.

Because of the distance that separated the New World from the old, none in the colonies could have known that the drama in Britain had already been played. On November 5, William landed at Torbay and thousands flocked to the Protestant standard. Even Princess Anne and John Churchill deserted the crown to welcome the foreign claimant. James was left virtually alone.

The revolution of 1688 was bloodless and indeed glorious to the nation's Protestants. In late December, a defeated James fled to France. After an abortive attempt to raise forces in Ireland and an unsuccessful plea for arms and men from the Vatican, Stuart appeared to accept the inevitability of defeat.

As spring approached, residents in the Dominion remained unaware of any occurrences after James' October proclamation. Only Edmund Andros had become privy to more current information and he had chosen to keep the intelligence secret. In New York, Deputy Governor of the Dominion Francis Nicholson had learned of William's landing and informed the Governor in Maine. Andros promptly returned to Boston and used every means to assure that word of the Torbay invasion did not reach the population.

On April 4, Sir Edmund's delicate maneuvering was upset when copies of William's declaration from the Hague arrived in Boston on board a ship inward bound from Nevis. Although the passenger carrying the proclamation was arrested for transporting treasonous papers, the contents soon leaked to the citizenry.

Meanwhile, word was received overland that the Maine force had mutinied and abandoned the primitive forts. Enraged militiamen alleged that Andros had tried to poison the force's rum. Some claimed that doctors in the company had been instructed by the Governor to kill the sick. Andros himself, was accused of spending each night in the company of Indian women.

Uneasiness in the port was intensified by an alarm that a large group of red men were gathering at Spy Pond near Cambridge. Citizens raced to arms, but when the defenders arrived at the waterway, they discovered that the herds of attackers were actually six Indians fishing peacefully. Back in town, word spread that bombs had been planted underneath Boston by the enemy. The charges were supposedly ready to be detonated.

Andros realized that the capital was on the verge of panic. On April 16, he noted that there was a "general buzzing among the people, great with expectation of their old charter, or they know not what." The following evening, the first contingents of the rebellious troops arrived in Charlestown from Maine.

April 18, was Lecture Day, a time of great excitement when Puritans from surrounding communities traditionally flocked into the port city to hear clergymen preach the gospel. The hubbub which filled Boston on that morning in 1689 was far greater than usual.

About 8 a.m., word flew through the southern end of town that vast numbers of citizens were arming in the northern sector. Simultaneously, word in the north was that southerners were showing peculiar activity. Mobs formed throughout the city and within minutes, Captain

John George of the *Rose* was apprehended. The port's beacon was lit in a general alert and drums beat in a militia call. Andros took shelter in the fort. Randolph and several other Dominion officials could not reach the installation and were taken prisoner.

As increasing numbers crowded into the city, moderate leaders converged on the Town House for a secret meeting. At noon, the group publicly presented a lengthy petition detailing the problems that had occurred under the Dominion and recommending courses of action that should be taken.

The proclamation was entitled *The Declaration of the Gentlemen, Merchants, and Inhabitants of Boston and the Country Adjacent.* In an opening salvo, the signers denounced the "bloody dévotoes of Rome," who had plotted against the English people. Part of the papist plan, the gentlemen claimed, had been the revocation of the Massachusetts charter, a protection that had kept the saints safe from the "wild beasts of the field."

The *Declaration* continued by claiming that the Dominion had subjected the peaceful New Englanders to a plague of self-serving locust. Andros had placed unqualified strangers and "haters of the people" in high positions so that the colony could be ravaged. The proclamation announced:

> . . . a small volume [could not] contain the other illegalities done by these horse-leeches in the two or three years that they have been sucking of us . . . Doubtless a land so ruled as once New-England was, has not without many fears and sighs beheld the wicked walking on every side and the vilest men exalted.

According to the *Declaration,* the people of Massachusetts had been "peeled, meeted out and trodden down," but suffered the indignities peacefully because of a basic love for England. They rebelled only when learning that the Prince of Orange had been sent by God to save the realm from the "horrible brinks of popery and slavery."

By 2 p.m., Boston's streets were thronged with thousands of colonists and an estimated fifteen hundred others waited in Charlestown to be ferried across. Andros still held the fort, but a long boat from the *Rose* attempting his rescue was taken by the rebels. Heavy guns were turned on the British frigate where loyal officers were preparing for battle. In the face of imminent bloodshed, Andros agreed to meet with the moderates at the Town House.

Initially, the Governor refused to surrender the installations remaining under Dominion control, but Sir Edmund capitulated after a night in jail. Captain George begged that the *Rose* be spared from striking the flag, a request granted by insurgents who compromised by removing the ship's sails. Andros, Randolph, Dudley and nearly thirty other officials were placed in confinement; many were locked into heavy chains. Throughout the Dominion, those who had held prominent posts in the union were apprehended. The rebellion that had occurred so suddenly, had completely succeeded.

The confinement of the English appointees was perhaps as much for their own protection as for the people's safety. After the initial excitement had passed, a "rabble" ready for action began pouring into the city. One observer suggested that the pioneers flocked in like "wild bears and the leader mad with passion, or rather drunk with brandy." According to prison rumor, even a Puritan minister had become so carried away that he suggested the throats of the captives should be slit.

Calm was restored on April 20, when twenty-two gentlemen organized a temporary governing body named the Council for Safety of the People and the Conservation of the Peace. Octogenarian Simon Bradstreet was selected to head the administration. Undoubtedly, Bradstreet's restoration was pressed so that the rebellion could be justified under William's proclamation that illegally removed officials should resume their posts.

By basing the overthrow of the Dominion on William's instructions to the English people, the New Englanders were maintaining that the provinces had been disrupted by the same conditions that had occurred in Britain when charters and officers had been unjustly removed by the Stuarts. In view of the prevailing attitude at Whitehall, the contention was tenuous at best.

Officials in England had already accepted the concept that the Glorious Revolution was launched almost solely to correct abuses in the isles. William had ordered Catholics removed from office in England, but on February 19 he issued a proclamation declaring that all royal appointees in the colonies should continue to exercise their duties. Under this edict, Andros and the Dominion loyalists, all strong Anglicans, had indisputably been reconfirmed. Obviously, the 1688 revolt was to be officially construed as an administrative change primarily affecting the homeland.

The likelihood that the April 18 insurrection was indeed a spontaneous outpouring of citizens seeking to obey William's recommendations from the Hague was subject to some dispute. Edward Randolph disagreed with the contention that the overthrow had been spontaneous by declaring the entire affair was a well calculated and "notorious" plot by the Puritan clergy. Perhaps more significant than Randolph's evaluation, was the fact that on April 18, Bostonians had no idea if William's invasion had indeed succeeded. England could have been engaged in a bloody civil war. James, with the help of Catholic France, might have been able to defeat the Prince and restore arbitrary rule. Even as they rose up, a repeat of the Bloody Assizes may have been confronting Englishmen who had opposed the Stuart King. Equal punishment for Americans who deposed royally-appointed officials was a distinct possibility.

Fears of retribution were not sufficient to deter passage of reforms. In mid May, representatives from forty-four Massachusetts towns met in Boston and agreed to return to the government that had been in operation before the charter revocation. The Dominion was to be viewed as an illegal interlude imposed unjustly by an arbitrary monarch.

Other jurisdictions took similar positions. Previous governments were restored in Connecticut, Plymouth and Rhode Island. New Hampshire, the former royal colony, had no previous government to which citizens might return. Leaders asked to be annexed to Massachusetts Bay.

The situation in New York was more complicated. Francis Nicholson, who had been serving as presiding official in the colony and as Deputy Governor of the Dominion, was authorized to take control of the union if Andros were out of the colonies or dead. No legal provision, however, had been made for instances in which the Governor was physically unable to perform his duties for any other reason. As a result, Nicholson left the Hudson colony to secure new instructions from England. Behind he left a confused province in which old line conservatives were pitted against a more liberal middle class.

News of William's victory in driving James from the isles arrived in Boston by ship in late May. The apprehension that reprisals would be lodged by a victorious Stuart was eased, but the Prince's attitude toward the Dominion uprising was still undetermined. Leaders of the new government grew even more anxious when the order confirming existing appointees arrived. From Cambridge on July 30, Thomas Danforth wrote Increase Mather: ''I am deeply sensible that we have a wolf by the ears.''

In the aftermath of the rebellion, great emphasis was placed on Andros' supposed plot to deliver the Dominion to the French. Witnesses stepped forth with evidence that the Governor had recruited native mercenaries to help in the treason. One resident swore that a Weskeskek Indian named Wessecanow had been offered £12 by Sir Edmund to organize a tribal attack on Manhattan. The Governor reportedly had promised to support the raid with five hundred soliders.

Indians known as Waterman and David vowed that the Maqua tribe had also been approached. In exchange for helping to annihilate the British, Sir Edmund had allegedly promised to pay one bushel of white wampum, one of black and three cartloads of trading goods. Colonial Lenox Beverley swore that four Indian women visiting Andros at camp in Maine, departed drunkenly with large baskets filled with powder and shot. It was also charged that ammunition for the northern troops was intentionally malformed, so that soldiers would be forced to beat the bullets into correct shape while the enemy seized the military advantage.

Andros and his colleagues remained under guard in Boston. Their accommodations were far from pleasant. Randolph revealed the seamier side of prison life in a letter to a friend when he wrote:

> T'will be a favor to me and the rest of the gentlemen with me if the poor wounded man, who has lain 16 days rotting in his own excrement, might be taken and removed to some other warm place, that we be not infected with the vehement stench. . . .

In August, the ex-Governor made a bid for freedom and succeeded in breaking jail. Andros, dressed as a woman, fled the Bay but was arrested in Rhode Island supposedly because he had forgotten to exchange his boots for more feminine footwear.

Throughout the remainder of 1689 and 1690, Increase Mather labored in London to present the insurgents' verson of the rebellion. Petitions, broadsides and pamphlets poured forth in his effort to secure a new charter from William and Mary. The struggle was a difficult one, for as early as February of 1689, British authorities had recommended that the Dominion be retained.

Basic to Mather's arguments was the proposition that the rights of the realm did not halt at the English coast. The illegalities of the Dominion—abolishment of town meetings, imposition of taxes without consent of the governed, challenges to valid land titles, arbitrary court actions and the elimination of the assembly—constituted due cause for rebellion in England and therefore justified the revolt in America.

If this argument was not valid and the rights of the mother country did not extend to the possessions, then neither did the law. Writs of *quo warranto* and *scire facias* could not have been legally used to revoke the old charter. If such was the case, then the rights of the 1629 document remained in effect.

By mid-1690, it seemed that Mather was making progress, but the debilitating war between England and France dampened the momentum. The idea of a unified New England became increasingly attractive to English militarists and politicans. The fragmented defense that had failed so miserably in pre-Dominion days held little allure for those charged with halting Louis' expansionist desires.

Additional impediments came from Andros, Dudley and Randolph, who had returned to England to answer a total of 364 charges. Although the King had ordered the men's transfer on June 30, 1689, the departure was delayed for seven months. English leaders spent little time dealing with the prisoners; because official complaints from Massachusetts arrived unsigned, allegations of misconduct by the trio were dismissed. After being freed, the deposed officials began speaking out against the insurgents who had overthrown the Dominion.

The quality of the reestablished Massachusetts' government did little to arouse enthusiasm in London for charter restoration. Administration in the colony had deteriorated. Old rivalries between the Faction and the moderates returned. Taxes were not collected. Property was taken without due process. The legality of legislative measures was questioned by the citizenry.

On October 7, 1691, nearly two and one half years after the Boston rebellion, a new charter was at last granted to Massachusetts. The Bay area was joined with Maine and Plymouth in a single crown colony. Although a royally appointed governor would head the province, significant local autonomy would be allowed and a representative assembly would be authorized. Town meetings and other prerogatives of a free colony were restored. Liberty of conscience was made universal and suffrage was extended to all freemen.

Old line leaders were dismayed by the document and irate that Mather had consented to such liberal provisions. The minister who had worked against the aristocratic Lords of Trade, hostile merchants and an arbitrary King received little thanks. Instead, the clergyman stood condemned by the Faction for not securing complete restoration of the old charter.

Despite the beliefs of the conservatives, the crown had been generous with the rebels of New England. For insurgents in New York, the treatment would not be so gentle.

# CHAPTER IX

# Leisler Humbles New York

CONFUSION FOLLOWING the overthrow of the Dominion was far greater in New York than in the provinces around Massachusetts Bay. Government on the Hudson was rooted in strong, appointed leadership and lacked the tradition of self-determination that was present in England's charter colonies. Since the earliest Dutch settlements, important decisions had been made not by representative assemblies, but by foreign dictate. As a result, New Yorkers merely watched while residents of Puritan areas confidently organized new governments to replace the Dominion.

Francis Nicholson attempted to form an interim administration to provide stability and defense. From a democratic perspective the Deputy Governor's efforts were singularly inadequate.

James had appointed eight advisers from New York to serve on the union's Council, but by spring of 1689, only Nicholas Bayard, Stephen Van Cortlandt and Frederick Philipse remained. Nicholson appointed the trio as advisers in the temporary government, a selection that could not have reassured New York's population that the interests of the common citizen would be considered important. A group less representative of the colony's diverse population could hardly have been chosen.

Each of the Councillors was extremely wealthy, Dutch-born and associated with the oligarchy of landowners and merchants who had long opposed popular demands. In addition, Bayard, Van Cortlandt and Philipse were related as brothers-in-law and were politically among the most conservative men in the colony.

Nicholson did attempt to secure instructions from Andros who technically remained head of government despite his confinement in Boston's jail. The effort was complicated by interference from New England rebels, and when orders from the deposed Governor eventually reached Manhattan, the messages were concerned with the problems of the Boston prisoners instead of Nicholson's attempts to establish a working government in New York.

The Deputy Governor sought to avoid a repetition of the Boston uprising by summoning a "General Convention" composed of local officials such as justices of the peace, magistrates and commissioned military officers. Public confidence in the body, however, was destroyed by the announcement that all deliberations would be kept secret.

The Convention was primarily concerned with protecting New York from physical threats presented by internal rebellion and attack from outside enemies. The use of citizen labor in repairing fortifications was approved by the body which also authorized collection of funds for a war chest. It was obvious that the Convention, like Nicholson, believed that preservation of the existing government overrode equally pressing economic and social concerns.

On April 26, copies of the Boston *Declaration* were made public in Manhattan and opposition to Nicholson's hastily constructed administration began to crystallize. On perusing the document, New Yorkers discovered that the Bay area insurgents had suffered from many of the same problems that were common on the Hudson.

Perhaps the most obvious bond between the provinces was a shared dislike and mistrust of Sir Edmund Andros. During his governorship in New York, Andros had frequently been suspected of fraudulent practices, dispensing unequal justice and catering to a select group of loyalists. In 1680 when authorization for tax collection had expired, the Governor had ordered his deputies to continue collections without legal justifications. The assessments infuriated New Yorkers as strongly as Sir Edmund's similar move under the Dominion had disturbed Boston's Puritans.

Labeling the taxation as an infringement of Magna Carta, a usurpation of parliamentary jurisdiction and repugnant to the "known ancient and fundamental laws" of England, residents arrested collector William Dyer. Dyer was indicted for high treason, but the prisoner challenged the authority of the grand jury and the New York Court of Assizes to rule on the activities of a royal officer. He insisted on being taken to Britain for trial, and once safely across the Atlantic was able to secure his release.

Controversy between the people and the government over the role of a representative assembly was a second experience shared by inhabitants of New York and dissidents in Boston. The Hudson colony's 1664 patent had delegated to the Duke of York near total discretion in organizing provincial administration. The Proprietor had refused to include the concept of a popular assembly in his plan. The ommission was widely resented, but nowhere as strongly as on Long Island. Here, communities settled by Massachusetts and Connecticut immigrants became hotbeds of contention. In 1673 Long Islanders showed no resistance to the temporary takeover of the colony by the Dutch. England's recapture of the territory one year later was met with threats that unless more liberal provisions for self-government were forthcoming, the Island would secede from the Duke's province. Andros stifled the opposition by declaring that further insubordination would be construed as treason and rebellion. The Puritan settlements reluctantly returned to the English fold.

In October of 1683, the government made a limited concession by allowing a Convention of eighteen elected delegates to meet. Permission had been granted only after residents in Manhattan and on the Island refused to pay taxes, claiming that the levies had been illegally imposed. Results of the assembly only confirmed conservative suspicions that popular legislatures were inherently threatening to established authority.

Participants in the meeting devised a "Charter of Liberties and Privileges" that called for establishment of a permanent assembly, citizen control over taxation, provisions for reasonable bail, verification of basic civil rights and provisions for religious conscience. The document was widely applauded in New York, but local enthusiasm was rudely ended in May of 1686 when the Privy Council declared the Charter "inconvenient" and a possible infringement on British prerogatives. To assure that no misunderstanding existed, the Lords emphatically declared the Convention's work "repealed, determined and made void."

After the veto, revolts sprang up in Jamaica and Richmond counties, but the disturbances did not spread to other sections of the province. The situation was quite different when the Dominion collapsed in the spring of 1689.

Suffolk County citizens demanded that the Manhattan government be organized along more democratic lines. Residents of Queens and Westchester replaced appointed officials with locally elected representatives. In Manhattan, New Yorkers refused to pay taxes on the grounds that no legitimate government existed to authorize collection. At Jamaica, eighty militiamen gathered for a politically-motivated march on the seat of government. According to Nicholson and his advisers, "ill affected and restless spirits" were rallying others into rebellion throughout the colony.

As in Boston, physical fear was the catalyst that joined together diverse elements of dissatisfaction. Like rebels in the Bay area, New Yorkers were beset by dread of Catholic domination. Yet unlike the hatred that had long scarred Puritan communities, intolerance of Catholics was a new development in Manhattan. Since the days of Dutch control, members of the Roman sect had been accepted as merely participants in one of the many religions allowed under the province's policy of toleration.

The emergence of anti-Catholic prejudice did not result from actual evidences of conspiracy, but was an outgrowth of the Protestant hysteria that permeated England. Fears were increased by the influx of French Huguenots who settled in the colony after revocation of the Edict of Nantes. Increasingly, New Yorkers became apprehensive that Romanist domination might suddenly erupt from internal plotting or conquest by French Canadians. In the uncertainty that followed disintegration of the Dominion, incidents that previously had seemed ordinary, suddenly became ominous signs that a Catholic conspiracy was afoot.

Catholic, ex-Governor Thomas Dongan was an early victim of the religious bias. Dongan, who had voluntarily pawned his personal silver to secure funds for the province's defense, was increasingly portrayed as a villain whose intention had been to betray the area to the

French. Although Dongan had remained in New York as a private citizen, he was suddenly vilified for imposing arbitrary rule, plotting the enslavement of the people and perhaps serving as an agent for the exiled King James.

Accusations also turned against Nicholson. The Deputy Governor was known as a practicing Anglican, but underground gossip reported that he was actually a devoted Catholic who practiced the detested rites in secret. Public suspicions were strengthened by a series of unfortunate decisions that the official made during the final days of the Dominion. Instead of publicizing news of William's invasion, the Deputy Governor notified only Andros of the Torbay landing. He had secretly and unwisely ordered £773 12s earmarked for New York's defense to be removed from the public treasury and hidden away. Other errors in judgment followed: Nicholson publicly compared William to Monmouth and even after it had become obvious that Stuart had been defeated, he refused to proclaim the Protestants William and Mary as rightful monarchs.

At least two other high-ranking Catholics were also targeted as potential enemies. Mathew Plowman, collector of customs, had incurred the enmity of powerful New York interests through his enforcement of the navigation acts and his removal of provincial defense funds on Nicholson's order. Jarvis Baxter, commander of the military garrison at Albany, also came under mounting attack from Protestants. The northern outpost was of supreme importance as the first line of defense against invasion from the French and Indians. That the fort rested in Catholic hands was a matter of grave concern. It was feared that Baxter might not use every available means to repel enemy attacks or that he might voluntarily surrender the garrison without a struggle.

Growing panic over the vulnerability of the colony made the existence of a conspiracy seem more obvious each day. To increasing numbers, Catholics were undoubtedly planning to overthrow English rule by taking control of the political, economic and military instruments of government. By May, a large element in New York was as consumed with hatred of Romanists as were the Puritans in Boston.

Suspicion became a fever breeding on the germs of rumor: the Governor's three advisers were Catholic; war with France was imminent; James in exile was planning to use Louis' forces to retake the crown; Indians from the north were preparing to go on the warpath as part of a grand design of conquest.

New Yorkers reacted swiftly to the supposed plots. Baxter was removed from authority at Albany and Plowman was forced to relinquish his civilian duties. Dongan fled to New Jersey. Sentries were posted at critical points to watch for the arrival of the French fleet.

The expulsion of Catholic military and civilian leaders temporarily alleviated anxiety over an internal threat, but those in Manhattan were still fearful that their fortifications were inadequate to withstand foreign encroachment. Most of the regular soldiers had been dispatched with Andros on the Maine expedition or had been sent north to guard the frontier. Only twenty regulars were left at Fort James, the city's major garrison. Most of the men were old or infirm.

Manhattan's six militia captains were ordered to assist in manning the fort, but little confidence was placed in the ability of the home guard to turn back a full scale attack. By May 15, the situation had become critical, but the problem was not a foreign enemy. Nicholson and his Councillors informed the Lords of Trade that the "seeds of sedition" that had been sown in New England were blossoming into rebellion in New York. The Council urged the Englishmen to dispatch new instructions post haste.

Nicholson sought conscientiously if ineptly to preserve the peace, but his frustrations instead provided the impetus for complete breakdown of the fragile government. In late May, the Deputy Governor became involved in a heated argument with a militia lieutenant. During the confrontation, Nicholson brandished a pistol and promised to burn the city rather than see a continuation of the chaos that was verging on anarchy.

News of the threat shook the community. It was widely reported that Nicholson and a band of Catholic cohorts intended to destroy Manhattan in a bloody Protestant massacre. Citizens in the city had no intention of waiting to discover if the story was real or imagined.

On May 31, large crowds of armed men began milling in the streets. Van Cortlandt and Philipse reportedly attempted to dispel mobs assembling around the house of militia Major Jacob Leisler. Instead of disbanding, the demonstrators set out to the beat of drums toward Fort James.

The Convention was called into emergency session, but deliberations were interrupted by a squadron of armed residents who broke into the chamber and demanded that Nicholson surrender keys to the installation. Within hours, the fort was in the hands of the insurgents.

By evening, dissidents had composed and issued a proclamation that explained the motives involved in capturing the city's defenses. More than four hundred militiamen and their officers were credited with approving the document that was entitled *A Declaration of the Inhabitants Soldiers Belonging under the Several Companies of the Train Band of New York.*

Like the Boston manifesto, the New York *Declaration* proclaimed that locals had peacefully suffered under "wicked, arbitrary power" that had been imposed by Catholic-leaning governors. Established authority had been challenged only after Nicholson had brazenly threatened to burn Manhattan. The signatories continued: ". . . we have thought fitt . . . to be liable to answer for the life of every Protestant that might have perished, and every house burnt or destroyed, if we had remained longer in security. . . ."

Declaring themselves "entirely and openly opposed to papists and their religion" the militiamen vowed that the fort would be held in safekeeping for William's new government. It would be surrendered, however, to any Protestant representative appointed by the King and Queen.

Despite the importance placed upon possession of the garrison, the post was of little defensive significance. Major Leisler claimed that only fifteen of the installation's thirty-three cannon were workable and only a single barrel of powder was "fit to sling a bullet halfway [to] the river."

Nicholson, believing that the militia was entirely beyond control, asked the Convention for suggestions on ways in which lawful order might be restored. The assembly, recognizing that the Deputy Governor would be able to rally only minor support, replied that the disturbances could not be halted by force. Instead of mounting what would be futile opposition, the group recommended that no action be taken. It was presumed that the excitement of the moment would pass and that the mobs would melt away from lack of direction.

The Convention's advice was not wise. Without overt opposition from Nicholson, the anti-government faction grew stronger. The spontaneous rioting of May 31, matured into a stable, political movement that attracted even moderate citizens. Within a week, the leadership problem was solved when Jacob Leisler assumed control.

Leisler had been born in Frankfurt am Main in 1640, but little is known of his life before 1660 when he arrived in New Amsterdam as a mercenary soldier in the pay of the Dutch West India Company. Spurred by ambitions higher than a soldier of fortune, Leisler left the company employ to become a merchant and broker. His rise to wealth was aided significantly by a marriage to a rich widow whose family included the prominent Bayard clan.

During a European voyage in 1678, Leisler and a small group of other New Yorkers were apparently captured by Turkish pirates. A ransom of 2,050 pieces of eight was raised by public subscription to secure the hostages' release. Leisler returned to New York and even further increased his financial holdings, but the economic advancement was not matched by political appointment to high office. Leisler remained outside of the formal power structure and his relations with the elite remained strained, perhaps as a result of a legal dispute between his wife and the Bayards.

Critics charged that the merchant's participation in the 1689 uprising was motivated by personal financial interests, but it appears that power rather than money was the goal that drove the militia officer to rebellion. Leisler possessed few of the charismatic qualities that endear followers to a leader; he was brash, uneducated, quarrelsome, loud and domineering, but in times of instability, such characteristics are often mistaken for strength of character.

Even if Leisler's unrefinements had been recognized, it is unlikely that the traits would have been considered defects by the movement's earliest participants who were primarily workers and artisans of Manhattan. Loyalists to the established government saw the insurgents as a drunken rabble with no ideology or legitimate grievances, but more than alcohol motivated the working class provincials that held the fort.

Strong undercurrents of resentment had long divided the rich from the poor. High government posts were unfailingly reserved for members of the wealthy classes. The most favorable trading monopolies went to merchants from prominent families. Huge tracts of land were engrossed by patroons while commoners found even small parcels difficult to acquire.

It was perhaps a desire to preserve this favorable condition that froze the Deputy Governor and his Council into indecisiveness when dealing with the situation. Without complete intelligence on the success of William's invasion, the officials were reluctant to either join the rebels in acting against James, or to use force against the popular movement.

Leisler and his men showed no such inertia. All were eager to acknowledge the Prince of Orange, a Dutchman like the majority of New Yorkers. When news that England had proclaimed William and Mary arrived in Manhattan, the insurgents immediately recognized the couple as the official heads of the British realm.

Assurance that the Protestants had triumphed in England did not cause the dissidents to lower their defenses. Guards remained at their posts and alarms periodically rang out that French invaders had been spied in nearby waters. Each alert proved false, but the city's population was kept in a constant state of readiness by the beating of drums and summons to arms. The preoccupation with danger resulted in near paranoid behavior. On one occasion, five hundred men rallied when news was spread that four strangers were approaching Manhattan. The intruders were apprehended and found not to be papist agents, but students on vacation from Harvard College. A similar scare resulted when reports spread that Governor Andros had been seen in the area.

The population's growing dependency upon Leisler and the militia emboldened the insurgents. A particularly ugly incident occurred when four merchants, including Bayard, were appointed to replace Mathew Plowman as collector of customs. Although the arrangement was temporary, the dissidents were far from pleased. The less than cordial reception given the appointees was described in an anti-Leislerian pamphlet entitled *A Letter from a Gentleman*. The anonymous author wrote:

> . . . as soon as those gentlemen entered upon the office, Captain Leisler with a party of men in arms and drink fell upon them at the Custom House, and with naked swords beat them thence, endeavering to massecre some of them, which were rescued by Providence, upon said Leisler beat an alarm, crying about the city "Treason!", and made a strict search to seize Col. Bayard who had made his escape and wherein departed for Albany where he stayed all summer in hopes that orders might come from England to settle those disorders—.''

Satisfactory instructions were not forthcoming from England, and on June 11, Nicholson set sail for London. In his absence, a de facto government began to emerge under the insurgents.

Lieutenants of the rebellion were placed in official posts and a "popular assembly" was called. To counteract any ill reports which Nicholson might spread, two Leislerian followers were dispatched to Britain as colonial agents. The pair was instructed to explain why the takeover had been necessary and to secure a charter assuring that the old regime could not be reinstated.

Authority in Manhattan was temporarily vested in a Committee of Safety that would serve until elections could provide more permanent administrators. Leisler was named Commander-in-Chief of the province, the civilian as well as military head of government.

Leisler unhesitatingly used his official powers to silence voices raised against the rebellion. According to the *Letter,* the Commander-in-Chief:

> . . . sent several parties of his armed men out of the fort, dragged into nasty goals within said fort, several of the principal magistrates, officers and gentlemen and others that would not own his power to be lawfull, which he kept in close prison during will and pleasure, without any processes or allowing them to bail, and he further published several times, by beat of drums; that all those who would not come into the fort and sign their hands, and so thereby to own his power to be lawfull, should be deemed and esteemed as enemies to his Majesties and the country, and be by him treated accordingly, by which means many of the inhabitants, tho' they abhorred his actions, only to escape a nasty goal and to secure their estates, were by fear and compulsion drove to comply, submit and sign to whatever he commanded-.''

Repression of dissent was more difficult in areas distant from Leisler's urban power base. A complete refusal to submit came from Albany where the frontier settlers had established their own government. The villagers resisted all directives from Manhattan and announced that only lawfully appointed representatives of the crown would be recognized.

The Albany stance proved so threatening to Manhattan's economy and defense, that in November, Leisler dispatched a troop of soldiers to subdue the resisters. Leading the force was the Commander's son-in-law Jacob Milburne. Milburne was no stranger to extra-legal operations. The Englishman had reportedly been deported from the isles for "clipping coins," and had spent five years in forced servitude for the crime. The punishment had little effect for in 1678, he was arrested in New York for behaving "scandalously and reproachfully. . . .

thereby encouraging others to be mutinous.'' Such a raucous past did not deter Milburne from a meteoric rise under the Manhattan rebels. In a note of nepotism, the ex-servant was named as Secretary of the colony, a position second in importance only to Leisler.

When diplomacy failed to sway Albany officials, Milburne marched his men on the town garrison. The show of strength was ineffective, for it was evident that the fortress' defenders would not surrender peacefully. Also likely, was that Mohawks friendly to the villagers would join in opposing the invaders. Milburne discretely ordered his contingent to withdraw. For the time being, Albany would remain under local control.

On December 8, 1689, Leisler was able to obtain somewhat questionable ammunition to use against those who cried that the rebels had illegally seized government and were ruling without valid authorization. At issue was a packet of correspondence from the King that arrived in the port city addressed to Nicholson or whomever in his absence was exercising powers of government. The material had been prepared long before either Nicholson or news of the fort's capture reached London. In the Deputy Governor's absence, the papers should have been automatically presented to the Council, but Leisler confiscated the documents for himself. Included among the correspondence was a decree authorizing the holder to ''perform all things,'' customarily done by a royally-named Lieutenant Governor. The grant of power was a temporary one, effective only until a permanent official could be named.

Leisler refused to relinquish physical possession of the decree. Instead, he announced that his own authority had been confirmed by the crown and that he would henceforth assume the title and responsibilities of Lieutenant Governor.

An unrestrained campaign was launched against opponents who remained unwilling to swear obedience to the insurgent. Homes of high-ranking critics were plundered. Bayard was arrested for ''high misdemeanors against his Majesties' Government.'' The imprisoned Councillor at last recognized that continued resistance was futile and agreed to acknowledge Leisler. The concession came too late. Leisler refused to release the former official. Stephen Van Cortlandt was more fortunate and managed to evade apprehension by fleeing the colony.

Consistent with the dignity of his newly exalted position, Leisler attempted to correspond on an equal basis with other provincial governors. Maryland's John Coode was particularly receptive. Coode, who had assumed leadership under circumstances as questionable as Leisler was delighted that a fellow Protestant had joined the fight against the Catholic menace. The Chesapeake official wrote that both New York and Maryland were fortunate to have escaped a "great design that was on foot to betray and ruine their Majestys' and the Protestant interest."

Albany's citizens were less impressed with the crown authorization and continued to resist rule from Manhattan. Instead of succumbing to the Lieutenant Governor's demands, the frontiersmen submitted petitions to London, requesting aid and accusing the rebel of attempting to incite local citizens against a legally constituted government.

On the evening of February 8, 1690, an unexpected tragedy intervened to eliminate opposition from the frontier post. In the darkness, a combined force of Indians and French raced unopposed through nearby Schenectady. The entire town was burned and only a handful of English escaped death or capture. Panic broke out in Albany. In exchange for the assurance of southern troops, Albany officials agreed to recognize the rebel administration. From Long Island Sound to the northern frontier, Jacob Leisler now controlled the province.

In the capital, loyalist William Nicholls was appalled. Writing to his friend George Farewell in Boston, Nicholls confided:

> The villain gives himself the title of Lieutenant Governor. Out of hell certainly never was such a pack of ignorant, scandalous, false, impudent, impertinent rascals herded together. They are the shame and infamy of all that may be called government. . . . In a passion I could say with the poet: "Can he from his so lofty throne, behold such villains prosper and his thunder hold?"

In the spring of 1690, it did indeed appear that Leisler had established his government in a near invincible position. But even as the citizens of the frontier reluctantly submitted, divisions were noticeable among the administration's supporters. The frictions would increase as the problem of protecting the colony became more intense. Just as fear of outside domination had enabled Leisler to rise in power, so would that same emotion become a major element in his downfall.

Canada's surprise attack on Schenectady was seen as merely one stroke in a major French offensive against English possessions. The prediction that other incursions were likely was correct, for a wide-sweeping plan to vanquish British America had been approved by the Paris court.

To combat the Catholic peril, Leisler invited delegates from other colonies to a joint conference held in Manhattan on April 16. The highlight of the meeting was the unveiling of the Lieutenant Governor's scheme for a coordinated invasion of the north. Representatives from Connecticut, Massachusetts and Plymouth agreed to join in raising men, funds and supplies for the venture.

Leisler's plan for Canadian conquest involved attacks on New France's two major strongholds. Land forces under Milburne and Connecticut's Fitz-John Winthrop would march northward from Albany, down the Champlain Valley and into Montreal. An estimated eighteen hundred friendly Iroquois were expected to join the troop. At the same time, more than two thousand New Englanders under Sir William Phips would leave Boston by ship, sail down the St. Lawrence and strike at Quebec.

Though the design seemed reasonable on paper, the implementation brought unexpected results. The overland venture was marked by disaster from its August beginning. Small pox, inadequate leadership, quarreling among the troops and a loss of morale dogged the soldiers. Instead of rendezvousing with masses of Indian allies, less than one hundred Iroquois appeared. Because no provision for boats had been made, Lake Champlain proved an impassable obstacle. In anger and disarray, the men turned back, defeated without confronting the enemy.

The sea borne wing fared little better. In the unfamiliar northern waters, the Massachusetts vessels ran aground or broke up on rocky coasts. Word of the force's progress preceded them, and by the time the New England ships arrived off Quebec, the French had been able to retrench into invulnerable positions. Like the Montreal contingent, the Bay area expedition was forced to withdraw without victory.

Leisler reacted to the failure with customary fury. Instead of accepting personal responsibility for the ill-planned invasion, the Lieutenant Governor ordered Winthrop and several of his aides imprisoned. According to Leisler, it was the Connecticut leader's cowardliness rather than poor strategy that had doomed the takeover.

Critics at home were also becoming more vocal. Among the most dissatisfied were Manhattan merchants who had initially supported the new regime. Hopes that Leisler, as a former tradesman, would act favorably to the commercial community had been dashed by several oppressive measures. A three pence per pound tax was set on all property, and even more damaging, was the government's standing order that merchants must make supplies available for the use of the army. If tradesmen refused, Leisler's agents were instructed to break into shops, warehouses and private homes to take what was required. Huge amounts of goods disappeared without accounting into official hands. Annoyed partisans suggested that the material was not being used to supply soldiers at all, but was being shipped to foreign ports and sold at high profits. Less likely were rumors that Leisler was preparing to confiscate an entire vessel and put to sea as a pirate.

Unwilling to bear the oppressive atmosphere any longer, thirty-six leaders of the Manhattan community formally petitioned William and Mary for protection against rule "by the sword, at the sole will of an insolent alien." That Leisler was not English born was a point increasingly pressed by opponents who saw in the rebellion a possible "Dutch plot" to return the colony to Holland.

Three weeks later, opposition was even more pronounced when the Lieutenant Governor was attacked in the street by approximately fifty men armed with clubs, swords and canes. Official depositions describing the incident reveal that the assault was a serious one. Hendrick Van Bre Voost swore that as several assailants grappled with the official, one John Crooke "strooke a full blow with his cooper's adz" at Leisler's head. The Lieutenant Governor was able to escape the blow only by quick footwork. With sword drawn, the executive managed to make good his exit. The public guard was able to disperse the dissidents, but the remnants, uttering "threatening and seditious words," vowed to rise again.

The steel hand of government descended. An uncooperative assembly was suspended. The public mails were searched. Opponents were jailed without warrant. Residents of Albany were forbidden to leave their community without special permits from Leisler. Even Protestant ministers were not exempt. According to the *Letter:*

> . . . Mr. Selyns, minister of New York, was most grossly abused by Leisler himself in the church at the time of Divine Service and threat-

ened to be silenced, etc.—Mr. Dellius, minister at Albany, to escape a nasty goal was forced to leave his flock and fly for shelter into New England. Mr. Varick, minister of the Dutch towns on Nassaw Island, was by armed men dragged out of his house to the fort then imprisoned without bail. . . .

Long Islanders were not long in joining the growing opposition. In October, one hundred and fifty persons gathered in Queens County to march on Manhattan. Declaring the crowd to be traitors, Leisler ordered Milburne to disperse the mob and arrest all leaders. Directives were given that "sloops, boats, canoes and any other vessels," in the area were to be searched in case an amphibious assault on the capital was being readied.

Milburne successfully suppressed the revolt, but his tactics were not calculated to pacify a resentful populace. On November 7, a petition to the King and Queen announced that the troops were looting the homes of innocent people, stripping women of their clothing and indiscriminately shooting citizens. Reportedly, more than one hundred settlers had been driven off their land.

Petitions such as the Long Island protest were unnecessary to stir action in Britain. The issue of who would rule had already been decided by the English and the answer did not involve the popular faction. In September of 1689, the King named Sir Henry Sloughter, a military official, as Governor of New York. Bayard, Van Cortlandt and Nicholls, all old critics of Leisler, were appointed to serve on the royal Council together with members of the conservative Philipse and Schuyler families.

Sloughter delayed leaving England for more than a year, and was shipwrecked in Bermuda, but on January 31, 1691, an advance guard under Major Richard Ingoldesby arrived off Manhattan with two companies of British soldiers. The real battle for control of the province was about to begin.

Two widely differing versions of the events occurring after Ingoldesby's appearance emerged in the heated political environment that engulfed New York. Anti-Leislerians reported that the Major announced he wished only to quarter and refresh his men in the city hall, and requested that Leisler hold the fort until Sloughter could arrive. Leisler supposedly reacted to the officer's statement by flying into a hysterical rage, labeling the British contingent as "papist dogs," and vowing that the redcoats would be slain. Refusing to acknowledge Ingoldesby's commission, the Lieutenant Governor began stocking the fort with provisions and ordered that English soldiers should be shot if they appeared on the streets.

Supporters of the rebel government saw the confrontation in a different light. Their scenario suggests that Ingoldesby arrogantly demanded the immediate surrender of the fort, but refused to show any authorization for the ultimatum. In refusing to turn over the King's fortification, Leisler had merely displayed admirable caution. The real villain of the affair was the British Major who repaid Leisler's kindness by stirring local citizens into rebellion.

Until Ingoldesby's arrival, the popular faction in New York was probably on safe ground. Although many of the administration's acts were of dubious legality, most infringements were less than felonies and probably would have gone unpunished. Further, a long list of mitigating circumstances could be made to rationalize the 1689 assumption of authority.

It could have been argued that during the post-Dominion confusion, no legitimate government existed against which rebellion could have been waged. Leisler's followers had acted promptly to proclaim William and Mary, a commitment that had not been given by the old royal Council appointed by James. Similarly, although unlawful seizures of property had taken place, the confiscations were supposedly to equip an army so that English men and women could be protected against French invasion. The abortive attack on Canada had failed, but the attempt had temporarily consolidated the New England colonies into a strong position and had perhaps, aided England in the war with France. Finally, Leisler's government had consistently repressed all Catholic conspiracies and had come out strongly at every juncture against the Stuarts.

If Leisler had peacefully surrendered the fortification to Ingoldesby, the official might have been temporarily imprisoned, but it is almost certain that all involved would have received royal pardon. William, whose own seizure of the throne had been scarcely legitimate had been generous in showing leniency in cases that would have brought severe retribution under previous monarchs.

The Lieutenant Governor, however, rejected any claim that Ingoldesby held authority in the city. On January 31, Leisler issued a public declaration calling out the militia and announcing that the Major was organizing dissidents on Long Island contrary to the crown's interest. In the names of William and Mary, New Yorkers were ordered to "suppress and repell by force" the English troops.

Ingoldesby returned a quick answer. He accused Leisler's men of unjustly firing upon the redcoats and vowed that his only intention was to halt the outrages committed daily on helpless citizens by the government's troops.

The battle of the proclamations continued. On February 4, Leisler announced that Ingoldesby had been led astray by "flagitious councellors" bent on revenge. He directed that suitable arrangements be made for quartering the English soldiers in the city, but warned all Manhattanites not to "abbet, comfort, countenance, aid, assist or any ways to join" with the Major in attempting to set aside the established government. The order was disregarded by approximately five hundred loyalists who attached themselves to the English force.

For six weeks, Manhattan was caught in a stalemate. British forces bivouacked in the city hall while about three hundred Leislerians held the fort. The interval was not peaceful. Four redcoats who inadvertantly trespassed on the garrison's grounds were arrested. On March 16, Leisler's men, claiming that they had been fired upon, began shooting wildly toward the city. According to contemporary accounts, the rebels stepped up their barrage by bombarding the sector where the redcoats were housed. In the indiscriminate firing, the fort's defenders killed or wounded several civilian bystanders. By March 19 when Sloughter at last put into port, nine British soldiers had become casualties.

The legally appointed governor wasted no time in assuming control. His commission was immediately made public and all guns in the city were fired in recognition. Sloughter then sent word to the fort that Leisler should surrender the installation. The Lieutenant Governor answered that such an act would be impossible.

Leisler's refusal was supposedly based on the contention that he was not sure that the individual claiming to be Sloughter was actually the new Governor. The rebel suggested that the man might actually be an impersonator deceitfully attempting to capture Manhattan for the enemy.

Joost Stoll, a former colonial agent in London, was dispatched to identify the claimant, but even after confirmation had been made, the fort was not given up. By some accounts, Leisler again refused to capitulate on the evening of March 19. This time his rationale was that it was not sound military practice to turn over fortifications during darkness. However, the following morning proved just as inconvenient. Ignoring the Governor's demand that the garrison be immediately evacuated, Leisler dispatched Milburne and a fellow rebel to negotiate terms of surrender.

Sloughter would tolerate no more. The two envoys were clamped into jail, but Leisler still refused to yield. It appears that only when the fort's defenders threatened to mutiny did the insurgent official finally capitulate.

When the militia marched out of the fortress, Leisler discovered just how deeply the people's resentments had become. Spectators shouted curses and spat at the former leader. The behavior of conservatives allied with Sloughter was even worse. Supposedly government leaders attacked Leisler like "raging furies," put irons on his legs and threw him into a "dark hole, underground, full of stench and filth."

Emerging out of just such a dark hole was Nicholas Bayard, finally freed from jail after fourteen months imprisonment. As the rebel official adjusted himself to confinement, Bayard was sworn in as a member in good standing of the new royal Council.

Ten days later, Leisler, Milburne and eight accomplices were indicted by a grand jury on charges of high treason and felony murder. The homicide count stemmed from the death of a civilian killed by gunfire from the fort during the Leisler-Ingoldesby confrontation.

Prospects for an impartial trial appeared remote, for the court was composed entirely of Sloughter's entourage and anti-Leislerians. Joseph Dudley, the ex-Dominion loyalist, was named President of the court. He could hardly be expected to look kindly upon men accused of overthrowing legitimate government.

Leisler and Milburne refused to plead to the indictment, maintaining that they were royal appointees answerable only to William and Mary. Twice the trial was delayed so that the men might reconsider, but twice more the defendants contested the court's jurisdiction.

Verdicts were returned on April 17. Two of the prisoners were found not guilty and were released. Leisler, Milburne and six associates were declared guilty. As punishment, the traitors were sentenced to be hanged, decapitated, drawn and quartered.

Sloughter stayed the executions in accordance with English custom that rebels against the crown, unless killed in the heat of battle, received final word of their fate from the monarch against whom the revolt had been waged. Dudley agreed with the cautious approach, but the remaining members of the Council were in no humor to stand by as the rebels went unpunished. One anonymous official wrote:

> . . . many here of considerable fortune and knowne integrity to the crown . . . are uneasy thinking it will never afterwards be safe for them to live in this province nor can their lives or fortunes ever be secure if such men do survive to head an ignorant mob here upon occasion, and if some example be not made of such criminals to future generations. . . .

The rebels' accomplices received a temporary reprieve, but on May 16, Sloughter capitulated to those calling for immediate execution of the provocateurs. Leisler and Milburne were hanged, and buried in common ground near the gallows. A bill of attainder was passed ordering confiscation of the rebels' estates. Claims for compensation rained forth from those who had suffered at the hands of the revolters.

Anger over the execution was muted by a series of reforms introduced by Sloughter in an attempt to provide increased self-government for the people of New York. The new Governor, however, was not able to enjoy the relaxed atmosphere that the liberalizations brought about. In July, less than two months after the executions of Leisler and Milburne, Sloughter died of natural causes and Ingoldesby became temporary head of the colony.

The two rebels had not been completely forgotten. Sons of the executed dissidents left for England to argue before the Privy Council and Parliament. The popularist-minded Britishers were receptive to the heirs of men who had supported William in the fight against James and Catholic France. The attainders of rebel property were reversed. Final pardon was granted to the six convicted felons who had been condemned but not executed. It was formally declared that Leisler had acted legally and properly in administering the government of New York in the absence of a duly appointed crown official.

In 1698 the transformation of Leisler and Milburne from rebels to heroes was completed. The men's corpses were exhumed and reinterred in holy ground. Twelve hundred people attended the grand ceremony and a solemn day of fasting was declared to commemorate the event.

# CHAPTER X

# Maryland's Catholics Imperiled

THE FEAR of Catholic domination that sparked rebellion in Boston and New York also beset Maryland, but revolt on the Chesapeake did not emerge as a sudden reaction to the Popish Plot, James' conversion or William's invasion. Resentment and suspicion of Church of Rome adherents had existed for years in the Proprietor's colony.

Unlike the northern provinces where Catholics composed an insignificant fraction of the population, Maryland was home to a large minority of "Romanists" who controlled not only government, but economics as well. Interjection of the religious issue into the basic colonial problem of civil liberties versus authoritarian control made the division in Maryland the most complex in America.

During the decade following the Restoration, disagreements between the people and the Proprietor were temporarily set aside by more pressing needs such as defense. The elimination of Puritan rule and the reconfirmation of Lord Baltimore's patent, only eased the symptoms of discord. Beneath the surface, the basic conflict remained unsolved.

In April of 1669, ill feeling erupted briefly as a result of a rousing address delivered to the Protestant-dominated assembly by Reverend

Charles Nicholett. The Puritan clergyman condemned the body for cowardliness in demanding liberties equal to those enjoyed by other British subjects. Nicholett was fined forty shillings for speaking seditiously, but the oration succeeded in spurring the legislature. Members approved a list of grievances that supposedly plagued the colony as a result of Baltimore's maladministration.

The conservative, Catholic-led Council, which also sat as the upper house, decried the measure as potentially treasonous. Under the advisers' interpretation, criticism of the Proprietor implied condemnation of the crown, and as such was not to be tolerated. Instead of agreeing to consider the complaints, the upper house ordered the list erased from the assembly's official journal. Governor Charles Calvert was equally dismayed and threatened to dissolve the legislature. In the face of united opposition from more powerful instruments of government, the Assembly disgustedly agreed that the journal could be "contradicted, expunged, obliterated, burnt, anything . . ."

Radical measures to discourage opposition in the lower house were not considered astute in view of the crown's expanded use of *quo warranto* to halt supposed citizen oppression. Because dissent appeared to be more annoying than threatening, Maryland officials chose a more inconspicuous means of eliminating radical ideas.

In 1670, the vote was limited to freemen who owned at least fifty acres of land or personal property worth at least forty pounds sterling. This restriction disenfranchised most tenant farmers, small-scale artisans, laborers and newly freed indentured servants. As a further means of control, the number of assemblymen from each county was reduced from four to two.

Although the regressive suffrage measure had in effect deprived large numbers of Marylanders of a voice in government, no corresponding change was made in the tax system. The poll remained. Voteless citizens found themselves paying the same levies as more privileged neighbors who enjoyed the ballot.

The amount as well as the method of taxation came under growing attack as the long peace between red and white began fracturing and government levies were hiked to finance defense budgets. The 1670 assembly was forced to authorize a two shilling per hogshead tobacco tax that was awarded to Baltimore on the provision that at least one-half of the proceeds would be spent in the colony for pressing needs such as defense. Payments were faithfully collected, but no accounting of the expenditures was made public. There was no evidence that the Proprietor was indeed returning the specified amounts to the colony.

Cecil Calvert's death in 1675 seemed to provide hope for those saturated by rule from England. Cecil had not been completely attuned to the democratic spirit of the colonial situation. He had once suggested, for example, that special medals be worn by every individual so that the aristocracy could be separated from the common people. The second Lord Baltimore was replaced by Charles Calvert, resident Governor of Maryland since 1661 and the first Proprietor to actually live in the colony.

Dissidents were unappeased by the possibility that improvement might take place sometime in the future. Soon after Lord Charles left for London in June of 1676, rebellion broke out.

The revolt began when sixty men assembled near the Patuxent River to frame a petition of complaints involving exorbitant taxation, limited suffrage, poll taxes and the oath of supremacy. The Council had not softened its visceral opposition to the use of petitions. The conferees were ordered to disperse on pain of being declared rebels. It was suggested that only the assembly could act on such citizen problems.

Confronted with a hierarchy that refused to yield, the protesters armed themselves and formed a military company under the leadership of William Davyes and John Pate. A small group marched off to beating drums with threats that the militia would be fired upon if summoned to quell the revolt. The insurrection, however, attracted no widespread support. When the operation was officially declared a rebellion, members lost courage and returned home under the promise of a pardon. A price of 2,000 lb. tob. was placed on the heads of Daveys and Pate, and the ringleaders did not remain at large for long. Both were apprehended and hanged on the cliffs of Chesapeake Bay.

The hard-line stance adopted by the Maryland officialdom was partially influenced by anxiety that mass insurrection would erupt if any leeway was given. The winds of freedom were gusting throughout the colonies, and nowhere were the forces for change so strong as in neighboring Virginia. Undoubtedly Baltimore's Councillors saw that compromise with Bacon's rebels had only increased popular fury against authority. Even Sir William Berkeley, the King's own representative, was not safe from the mob. Surely, they believed, an unpopular Proprietor whose charter had been constantly questioned could maintain control only by strict enforcement of the law.

Conditions in Virginia no doubt also affected Marylanders who wished to enlarge local rights at the expense of established authority. Berkeley's unrelenting prosecution of the rebels, the mass hangings and the reluctance of royal commissioners to protect the insurgents probably intimidated potential dissidents in Maryland into remaining temporarily silent.

In 1678 the lull was briefly enlivened when physician Edward Husbands was charged with endangering the lives of assembly members by putting poison into their duck pie. In punishment, the doctor was given twenty lashes and exiled.

Josias Fendall, forbidden to hold office as a result of his 1660 rebellion, was less secretive than the physician in opposing the administration. An opportunity for the ex-Governor to vent his malcontent came in 1677 when voters of Charles County disregarded the prohibition and elected Fendall to the General Assembly. When Fendall was barred from taking the seat, he laid plans to organize other radicals in a drive to push Baltimore from the colony. The Council reacted swiftly to crush the revolt. The movement disintegrated and Fendall escaped.

Anti-proprietary forces seemed stymied. After nearly a half century, Lord Baltimore's descendants still ruled with virtual unchecked power. Peaceful attempts to gain reforms had failed as surely as had more violent protests by Claiborne, Ingles, Fendall, the Providence Puritans, Davyes and Pate.

The inability of dissidents to force improvements was attributed to many causes, but the most important was the repugnance for rebellion that was held by the colony's moderate majority. Like their English counterparts, Marylanders held abiding respect for constituted authority. The fast-moving changes that occurred in England during the late 1670's, however, began to reverse the hesitation at contesting lawful government.

Hysteria and religious hatred fanned by the Popish Plot crossed the Atlantic as easily as the British fleet. By 1681, the conflict of Catholic against Protestant had become firmly entrenched in Maryland. Moderates who earlier refused to rise up on political grounds, were being rapidly drawn into the struggle against Baltimore as a result of the religious issue.

At the center of the apprehensions, was the control over Indian affairs that was vested in a small group of Catholic officials. As horrible tales of the Popish Plot filtered into the colony, speculation became centered on the possibility that Baltimore's agents had formed an unholy alliance with the red men. The purpose of the conspiracy was the destruction of all Protestants.

Acerbating the suspicions was the growing prosperity of Jesuit missionaries, popularly known as the "Pope's messengers," who dwelt among the frontier tribes. Because their ministry took place far from Protestant oversight, it was suspected that the holy men were not totally concerned with spiritual matters. According to rumor, the Jesuits had become so wealthy that the sect could afford to equip and maintain a private army. The most likely footsoldiers, of course, were the clergymen's Indian charges.

Intimate relations between Indians and white officials had been an integral part of the strategy of each Lord Baltimore. Cecil Calvert had attempted to protect "friendlies" by setting aside an 8,000 to 10,000 acre tract on the Wicomico River. It was planned that this reservation would be forever safe from white encroachment and under the protection of the state. Despite Baltimore's good intentions, the design was not a success and the official policy of coexistence came under mounting attack.

Periodically, breakdowns did occur between the two diverse societies that shared the land. Non-resident Indians and splinter groups from peaceful tribes presented occasional threats. In such instances, provincial officials approved punitive expeditions, but each military commission carefully limited the hostile action that could be taken by the Marylanders. Blanket approval of war against all Indians was unknown.

The rapid disintegration of Indian-white relations had begun soon after the Restoration, when Maryland experienced a rapid increase in population. Laws governing behavior of tribes became increasingly more severe. By 1666, it was illegal for a red man to come into an English area unannounced, carrying arms or with a painted face. Anyone who ignored these regulations could be shot on sight and no punishment would be imposed on the killer.

Mistrust was fostered by the gross misconceptions of Indian behavior held by most colonials. Indentured servant George Alsop, for example, helped to spread grisly superstitions by announcing unreservedly that the red peoples worshipped the devil, sacrificed infants every four years and practiced exotic tortures. Accounts of Indian cannibalism were not unknown in the colony where most small farmers viewed the tribes as truly representing the forces of evil.

Josias Fendall saw the rising terror of Indian attack as a conduit for ousting the proprietary government. In the spring of 1681, the ex-Governor joined with John Coode in raising a force of insurgents in southern Maryland. Fendall openly scored the Proprietor as a "traitor" and berated the citizens of the province as fools for paying taxes to support an arbitrary government that was in league with hostile Indians. Apparently, the pair concocted a desperate scheme to end Catholic rule by kidnapping Baltimore. The rebellion met with considerable success on both sides of the Potomac. According to the Proprietor, Fendall and Coode managed to enlist "most of the rascals" in northern Virginia. However, before the insurgents could be organized, both ringleaders were imprisoned.

Cavalry Lieutenant George Godfrey of Charles County saw no reason that the revolt should be abandoned merely because the masterminds had been seized. Godfrey devised a plan to rescue Fendall and Coode, but news of the intention reached authorities who promptly arrested the militiaman. In August, Godfrey was condemned to death, but the sentence was commuted to life in jail. Fendall and Coode fared better on charges of sedition and conspiracy.

Although Coode was acquitted, he was censured for displaying an insubordinate "tongue." Fendall was found guilty of the crime, a serious felony that was legally punishable by amputation of the ears, boring of the tongue, whipping, branding and imprisonment. Compassionate officials rejected the more gruesome penalties: instead, Fendall was fined 40,000 lb. tob. and exiled.

Success in halting the revolt did not assure Baltimore that Maryland would remain tranquil. Unresolved difficulties seemed to be propelling the colony toward an ultimate confrontation.

Falling tobacco prices and decreases in the availability of land proved as disastrous to Maryland farmers as the problems had been to Virginia planters. In an effort to end land speculation, it was announced that all territory on which taxes were three years in arrears would revert to the Proprietor. The practical result of the measure was not to reduce holdings of the wealthy, but to create a hardship on poor farmers who suffered cash flow problems. Some claimed that the escheated fields were taken without due process and then distributed to Baltimore's cadre. In addition, land acquisition by newcomers was changed from the traditional system of headright to a purchase procedure.

The judicial system was also a source of conflict. Among the most numerous complaints were those involving excessive bail, cruel punishment, unequal justice, illegal imprisonment and the inclusion of unqualified persons on juries. The trying of matters of law before the Council, rather than the courts was also criticized by dissidents. Some alleged that the processes of law had become so distorted, that innocent Marylanders had been arrested in large numbers during 1685 so that officials might have an impressive number of convicts to pardon in celebration of the birth of James' son.

Charges against administrative officers were similar to those raised against the judiciary. Most civil servants in the colony received no salary, but depended upon fees for their livelihood. To many residents, the payments these men charged for services were outrageously high and bordered on extortion. The Secretary of the province earned as much as 200,000 lb. tob. annually while naval officers routinely earned £200 sterling. Complaints also centered upon the exclusion of Protestants from office holding. Only rarely were Anglicans included on the Council, and those who were named, were usually connected to the Proprietor through marriage or business.

Complaints from dissatisfied citizens were not the only difficulties confronting Baltimore during the last years of Charles II's reign. Influential William Penn was pressing land claims to a large portion of the eastern shore and even collecting taxes in areas that had been cultivated for years by Marylanders. Wishing to halt the encroachment as quickly as possible, and perhaps fearing that the eastern shore inhabitants might prefer Penn's leadership to his own, Charles Calvert returned to England during May of 1684.

The trip may also have been intended as a fence-mending exercise to pacify London officials. Although the King was sympathetic to the Catholic cause, the Proprietor must have realized that the increasing stream of charges arriving in London from Maryland would not have gone permanently unnoticed. News of the *quo warranto* proceedings against the New England colonies must have severely unnerved the lord.

Baltimore's reception in London was not that customarily given to returning heroes. Particularly damaging to Lord Charles' reputation had been reports that the King's revenues in Maryland were being intentionally impaired so that Proprietary interests could be advanced. At the center of the controversy was Collector of Customs Christopher Rousby, a royal appointee who alleged that fraud was involved in the collection of the Plantation duty. Rousby did not confine his accusations to official correspondence. In a public interview with Baltimore, the Collector had suggested that the Proprietor was a traitor who should be shipped back to England in chains. Baltimore retorted by labeling Rousby as the "most lewd, debauched, swearing and most profane fellow" in the government. Despite Lord Charles' protestations, Rousby's charges were increasingly accepted as valid by English officials.

Much was tolerated by the British from their overseas subjects. Rebels might be pardoned. Murderers receive commuted sentences. Sedition and libel against the monarch might be overlooked, but manipulation of royal revenues was considered a virtually unpardonable crime.

The Maryland situation, already considered insufferable, became even worse in October of 1684 when Rousby was stabbed to death during an argument aboard a British revenue ketch. The assailant was George Talbot, Baltimore's nephew. Talbot was taken to Virginia for trial, but with the help of his wife and a corps of supporters, the accused murderer was able to escape back to Maryland.

The death of Charles II saved the Proprietor from defending his charter in the courts, but the hiatus was only temporary. On April 30, 1687, James ordered that a *quo warranto* be served against the lord.

Trouble was also boiling on the Chesapeake. Calvert had left Maryland under the control of eight Councillors, but in 1688 the Proprietor dispatched William Joseph from England to head the province as Deputy Governor. The choice was unfortunate, for Joseph was an absolutist whose views on popular government were reminiscent of the early Stuarts.

In November, the Deputy Governor delivered an insulting address to the assembly in which the divine rights of kings and the duty of citizens to obey the Proprietor without question were emphasized. The somewhat prudish official also took care to condemn the assemblymen for allowing public and private sins to go unpunished. Scored as especially dangerous to the colony were adultery, breaking of the sabbath and drunkenness, a crime labeled as the most serious of all sins. Joseph may have been attempting to counter charges by Anglicans that Catholic Maryland was a pig sty of decadence. Reverend Joseph Yeo for example, had notified the Archbishop of Canterbury that the area was a "Sodom of uncleaness, and a pest house of iniquity."

Even more astonishing was Joseph's insistence that each assembly member again swear the oath of fidelity to the Proprietor rather than to the King. After "hot and high" debates, the legislature refused. Joseph, branding the action as treasonous, prorogued the assembly and threatened to permanently banish any representative that continued the holdout. The Council supported Joseph on the grounds that if citizens were allowed to deny the supremacy of Baltimore's leadership as proclaimed in the oath, then rebellion might be the next insolence. Only when the legislators agreed to take the pledge was the group reconvened.

In such an atmosphere of discord, little was accomplished. A long list of grievances approved by the body was rejected by the Council. Stymied, by the unbreakable line of no compromise, the legislature adjourned until April of 1689.

On January 19, the upper house notified the Proprietor that "all things are peaceful and quiet." The appointees had greatly misjudged the public temper. Although the climate in Council may have been agreeable, things were far from tranquil among the citizenry.

In early 1689, hints of William's invasion provoked the advisers to recall government arms that had been distributed to the public for protective use. The official explanation was that the guns were being collected for routine maintenance and would be returned after repairs had been made. Actually, the Council planned to redistribute the weapons only to those who could be depended upon to defend the interest of Baltimore and James.

The subterfuge did not convince the public, for dissatisfaction with the handling of provincial defense was already a heated issue. Though laws required that public magazines be established in each county, most stores were actually kept in a central arsenal under the control of the Catholic-led militia. In addition, impressment of supplies for military purposes had been carried out for many years, but little of the materiel was evident and cynics believed the goods had been appropriated for private sale.

Recall of the provincial arms only confirmed the Protestant conviction that a conspiracy existed and that a large scale atrocity was imminent. According to rumors, nine thousand Indians were massing at the Governor's estate and three thousand Senecas were at the head of the Patuxent. Nine thousand French and Indians were said to be poised on the Bay and natives on the eastern shore were reported to be ready to do battle as Catholic mercenaries.

An investigatory commission was established to confirm the tales of fright, but no trace of the great masses of invaders could be found. On March 27, the Commissioners made their findings public by explaining:

> . . . people in several places of the said counties, had gathered themselves in great parties to defend themselves, as they were persuaded, against a groundless and imaginary plot and design contrived . . . by Roman Catholics inviting the Indians to join with them in that detestable and wicked conspiracy . . . we have made an exact scrutiny and examination into all circumstances of this pretended design, and have found it to be nothing but a sleeveless fear and imagination fomented by the artifice of some ill-minded persons who are studious and ready to take all occasions of raising disturbances for their own private and malicious interest.

The report, coupled with word that William had succeeded in deposing the Catholic King, stifled fears of a conspiracy, but ill feelings against the proprietary regime remained, for the assembly had been prorogued until the fall and Marylanders were angered by the arrogant handling of their representatives. Many citizens believed that Baltimore had subverted the legislature's prerogative of approval over taxation by imposing special fees and duties. The announcement that the Council would serve as the upper house had also created resentments from residents who saw the move as an illegal investiture of legislative power in a non-elective body. Constant vetoes by the Proprietor of popularly passed bills added to the mounting tension, and tempers rose even higher when two petitions, drawn up for presentation to the crown, were confiscated by government officials and forwarded to Baltimore instead of the monarchs.

Calvert's hand-picked advisers were not as assertive in proclaiming William and Mary as they were in regulating the legislature. Even after it had become clear that James had been driven from the isles, the Council remained silent, evidently hesitant to act until instructions arrived from the Proprietor. The men waited in vain. Baltimore had dispatched orders that a proclamation should be issued, but the messenger carrying the directive died en route and the message did not leave England.

In an attempt to force recognition, a Protestant organization was formed in April. The group's unwieldy title was "An Association in Arms for the Defense of the Protestant Religion, and for Asserting the right of King William and Queen Mary to the Province of Maryland and all the English Dominions." The leader of the Association was John Coode, the rabble-rouser who eight years earlier had aided Josias Fendall in an abortive rebellion.

By mid-July, disharmony between the Proprietor's agents and the Association reached crisis levels. The tension was no doubt increased by the spirit of revolt that seemed to surround the Chesapeake colony; the Dominion provinces had already overthrown the union; Leisler seemed certain of maintaining control in New York; dissidents in neighboring Stafford County, Virginia, had revolted in response to a supposed Indian-Catholic plot.

Several hundred men, angered that the public guns had not yet been returned, began rallying under Coode for a march on St. Mary's. An investigator dispatched by the Council to reconnoiter the situation was arrested. In response, the militia was called out and Coode's men were declared in rebellion. A pardon was announced, however, for all those who desisted.

The insurgents answered the offer of pardon with an eloquent *Declaration of the Reasons and Motives for the Present Appearing in Arms of His Majesty's Protestant Subjects in the Province of Maryland*. Signed by Coode and seven lieutenants, the document aimed at attracting citizens to the cause and displaying an image of respectability rather than barbarity.

The Maryland *Declaration* was remarkably similar to those issued by rebels in Boston and New York. Like the northern insurgents, the Association members claimed to have suffered patiently from abuses and risen only when William emerged to show that the "inudation of slavery and popery" should no longer be tolerated. According to the *Declaration,* Catholics throughout the colony were feverently praying for James' success, and a victory over England by Louis' forces. The paper continued:

> We are every day threatened with the loss of our lives, libertys and estates of which we have great reason to think ourselves in eminent danger by the practices and machinations that are on foot to betray us to the French, Northern and other Indians of which some have been dealt withall, and others invited to assist in our destruction. . . .

An extensive list of complaints was included in the manifesto, but few new allegations against the Proprietor were enumerated. Primary attention focused on Baltimore's usurpation of kingly power, imprisonment of citizens without trial, illegal impressment of men and property, excessive fees, operation of Catholic cabals, obstructions of justice, lack of due process and harsh sedition laws. It was also suggested that Maryland's papists had condoned murder and illegally confiscated Anglican property for Popish use. Even the raising of Protestant orphans by Catholic families was scored.

The *Declaration* promised that a free assembly would be called immediately so that William and Mary might be proclaimed. Although the permanent removal of Baltimore's proprietary was cited as a major goal, neutrals were assured that no outrages would be committed on their property as long as they did not attempt to help the establishment.

Coode's proclamation was indeed a powerful device. Loyalists were able to garner only four hundred men willing to fight in support of the established government. On July 27, the St. Mary's fort was surrendered by militiamen who refused to engage the insurgents.

Despite the capture of the capital, Baltimore's most prominent appointees remained at large. Most had taken refuge at Calvert's plantation, Mattapany. It was considered imperative that the loyalists be peacefully forced to resign all claims of government. A violent purge by the rebels would alienate many moderates from the cause.

The Mattapany defenders rejected all calls for surrender and prepared for either armed confrontation or a long siege. On August 1, however, an accommodation was reached. In return for the removal of all Catholics from governmental posts, Coode pledged safe conduct home for the loyalists and protection of all property against looting.

Within hours the issue had been decided. Baltimore's representatives relinquished control and Coode stood in charge of a new, Protestant-led Maryland.

The inability of the Proprietor's deputies to rally more than a handful of the province's twenty-five thousand citizens, illustrates the degree to which residents had become alienated from the government. Popular support for the goals of the new administration, however, did not translate into personal loyalty to John Coode. The emergent leader was a disreputable character whose past conduct inspired little admiration.

English-born Coode had immigrated to America about 1672 and soon after had chosen a common course to quick economic rise. He contracted a favorable marriage with a wealthy, middle-aged widow. In 1676, the newcomer was sufficiently well-known to be elected to the assembly as a delegate from St. Mary's. Evidently, the legislator had kept secret his status as an ordained Anglican minister, for clergymen of all persuasions were disqualified from sitting in the lower house. In 1681, however, he was expelled for participation in the Fendall revolt.

Eight years later Coode, now a rabid opponent of Baltimore, had no intention of allowing the faction that had subjected him to abuses, to regain power. Two days after the fall of Mattapany, the Association recognized William and Mary, an action that was but the first move in a program calculated to sway the monarchs into revoking the Proprietor's rights.

The Association pressed on with formation of a new government. Calls were issued for elections in which representatives to a provincial Convention would be selected. Catholics were barred from voting for the delegates, scheduled to convene at St. Mary's in August.

Not all Maryland Protestants were enthusiastic over the new rulers' plans. In several areas, officials refused to call for the balloting and Associators were compelled to force the elections. The delegates ultimately chosen were far different from those who had traditionally led the colony; most were younger, inexperienced in politics and relatively new to Maryland.

Lack of a popular mandate did not prohibit the delegates from voting decisive changes in government. The colony's legal code was totally revised. The Church of England was made the official religion. Regular and periodic assemblies were made mandatory and a Committee of Safety was appointed to report upon the supposed Catholic-Indian conspiracy. Not surprisingly, the investigators uncovered what they claimed was valid proof that Baltimore's deputies had plotted to betray the area to the French and Indians.

The righteous proclamations of the Association were somewhat tarnished by the delegates' failure to reduce the fees that had been considered so excessive under the Proprietor. Presumably, when the Protestants became the receivers, the amounts no longer appeared either unreasonable or unnecessary.

A decision to dismantle the central government so that administrative and judicial powers could be vested in local authorities was the Convention's most startling alteration. However, emphasis on grass roots government was a natural outgrowth of the movement's philosophy and composition. For the first time, hundreds of qualified Protestants were able to exercise political power in their communities and it was unlikely that once securing such authority, the long-barred Protestants would voluntarily relinquish the rights to provincial-level administration.

On September 4, the Convention adjourned. Only a skeleton committee remained organized on a colony-wide basis.

Despite the seeming unassailable control enjoyed by the Protestants, Coode was wary of allowing prominent Catholics to remain at large. Baltimore's men had shown an amazing proclivity to rise from defeat and reestablish proprietary control. Lack of border guards had allowed many former officials to escape to Virginia or Pennsylvania. It was of utmost importance that loyalists be prevented from reaching England and spreading biased tales of the July rebellion.

Coode requested that Leisler be on constant guard in New York so that dangerous Catholics heading north could be arrested. Opponents who had not fled were subject to harrassment and placed under house arrest. Anne Arundel's Richard Hill, claimed that forty armed Associators looted his house and turned their horses into his cornfield. His ship, worth approximately £700 was reportedly taken and a warrant was issued for his apprehension dead or alive.

Hill fled to Virginia, but Barbara Smith, whose husband had been imprisoned for failing to join the Associators had wider objectives. Goodwife Smith managed to evade the Protestant net and sail for England to place anti-Association arguments before home officials. In Maryland, the repression of opponents continued. The guns of Catholics were confiscated while private correspondence was opened and censored.

Despite the lack of overt challenges to their power, the Associators were discovering that governing a colony was not as simple as it appeared. The scheme of decentralization was faltering, for local officials were often uncertain as to their duties or jurisdictions. In addition, many citizens refused to acknowledge the authority of the claimants.

Popular cynicism with the self-proclaimed insurgents was not lessened by the somewhat questionable reputation and marginal talents of many Associators. Henry Mitchell, who was made a justice of the peace, boasted a long record of court appearances on charges involving rabble rousing, assault and pig stealing. Gilbert Clarke, named sheriff of Charles County, had been convicted of perjury and was removed from office after being found guilty of extortion. Charles James, one of the initial recruiters in the Association, was forced out as sheriff of Cecil County because of charges involving perjury, suborning perjury and false imprisonment.

Because even moderates were growing dissatisfied with the new organization, Coode found it increasingly more difficult to stifle complaints. A violent and most unexpected incident, however, provided the new administration with an opportunity to regain support by reviving anti-Catholic prejudice.

The episode involved Nicholas Sewall, Baltimore's son-in-law and a former Deputy Governor who had fled into exile in Virginia. Sewall returned temporarily to Maryland and during the visit his vessel was attacked by a group of men under one John Payne, an Associator and Militia Captain who also served as Collector of Customs. During the confrontation, Payne was killed, allegedly by a Sewall follower named John Woodcock. Baltimore's kinsman, who claimed to have been at home in bed during the action, escaped back to Virginia with a band of followers.

Leaders of the Association seized upon the killing as an example that the Catholic menace still flourished. According to their reports, Payne, acting as royal tax collector, had been treasonously murdered in broad daylight by an agent of the Pope. Sewall's explanation was quite different. The former official claimed that Payne and his vigilante henchmen had attacked without warning in the middle of the night. Their purpose involved no official duties, but was an illegal act of revenge on a lawful nominee of the true government.

Virginia authorities evidently believed Sewall's explanation, for extradition requests were denied. However, four loyalists involved in the fracas were apprehended and put on trial in Maryland. In the politically-charged atmosphere, three of the defendants were convicted and Woodcock was subsequently executed.

Payne's murder dealt a severe blow to Baltimore's efforts to have the Association government declared invalid. With the help of loyalists such as Richard Hill and Barbara Smith, the Proprietor had been frantically working to show that England's interests were being damaged by the rebels who had usurped power on the Chesapeake. The news that still another collector of customs had been slain by a kinsman of Baltimore did little to convince the Lords of Trade that the King's business would be better promoted under proprietary government.

The Association was also seeking to impress the British and at the same time improve its position at home. By the time a second Convention convened in April of 1690, it had become obvious that a provincial-wide body was desperately needed to supplement local government. Representatives approved formation of a Grand Council of Twenty, composed of two delegates from each county and headed by John Coode. Ironically, this steering committee proved to be as unrepresentative of the province's population as had been Baltimore's Council.

In late May, the stamp of legitimacy for which the insurgents had hope arrived in a message from the King. The plantation Lords, fearing that Catholic France might overrun the colony and use the Chesapeake as a base for attacking British settlements, had decided that the Association should continue to head the province until final disposition of the Proprietor's claims could be made. In the meantime, Baltimore's deputies were not to be molested while collecting quitrents and customs legally due under charter rights of the soil.

With the rights of government at least temporarily secured, the insurgents dispatched several agents including John Coode to London. Their task was to convince the Lords of Trade that the existing government should be permanently recognized and that Maryland should be converted into a crown colony. Nehemiah Blakiston, Coode's brother-in-law became temporary head of area. Although married to a wealthy Catholic, Blakiston held authentic Protestant credentials, for his father John Blakiston had been among the judges who condemned Charles I to the executioner's axe.

Things were progressing well in Britain for the Protestant cause, but the outlook for the Association was not as bright. The inability of the rebels to organize and maintain a stable government no doubt made the Lords hesitant to entrust the future of the colony to the insurgents. According to reports from America, the navigation and Plantation Duty acts were not being enforced. Funds that were collected were being diverted into private pockets. The haphazard and perhaps fraudulent administration of the Associators stood in poor contrast to the firm leadership that had existed under Baltimore.

A true dilemma confronted the Lords. It was obvious that insufficient grounds existed for the granting of a *quo warranto,* but it was equally apparent that the people of Maryland would not tolerate a return to the old system of Catholic-dominated government. Baltimore had offered to make significant concessions: he would appoint Protestants to high office, pardon the Association rebels and investigate all citizen grievances. The belated allowances, however, were believed to be insufficient to justify a complete restoration of the Proprietor's authority.

In June of 1691, an arrangement was approved that satisfied both the crown and Baltimore. The Proprietor would retain rights of the soil, but government would revert to the crown. Maryland would be administered as a royal colony under an appointed Governor and Council.

The agreement, which included provisions for freedom of conscience, was well-designed to de-fuse radicalism on both sides of the religious issue. In early 1692 when Sir Lionel Copley arrived as the province's first royal Governor, peace had been restored. Copley continued the drive toward conciliation, but the Britisher had strong doubts that permanent peace could be achieved without major changes. On September 15 he notified the King: "This province will never be happy till my Lord Baltimore's interest be bought out by His Majesty, for while his interest continues, his party will be considerable and on all occasions will be able to disturb the public peace and quiet. . . ."

Another new face appeared in Maryland with the arrival of Edward Randolph, the ex-Dominion officer who had been appointed Surveyor-General of the new crown colony. Randolph was as little impressed with the Maryland Council as he had been by the Massachusetts Bay advisers. The Cheasapeake officials, he suggested, were a "contemptible crew" who behaved like "silly animals."

The Councillors scorned by Randolph included many former Associators, but conspicuously absent was John Coode. The former leader had been passed over for any major appointment and was named merely as a collector of customs. He had no intention of overlooking the slight and allowing the crown government to proceed unchallenged. For the next fifteen years, Coode agitated against three successive royal governors. His dissension ranged from mere rabble rousing to virtual rebellion and he was ultimately forced to flee the colony in order to escape arrest warrants.

Despite Coode's attacks, Maryland remained firmly under crown control until 1715 when Charles Calvert, the fifth Lord Baltimore managed to secure restoration of charter rights. His method, however, was not by conquest or the courts, but by eliminating the religious problem through conversion to the Protestant faith.

The return of the proprietary did not plunge Maryland into the chaos that had characterized the first half century of settlement. The Glorious Revolution in Maryland and subsequent rule by royal appointees made reestablishment of authoritarian government by a private individual no longer feasible.

# CHAPTER XI

# Carolina Lords Overthrown

ILLIAM AND MARY, as well as their successor Queen Anne, presided over an England vastly different from the semi-feudal country of crisis that had existed under the early Stuarts. The Glorious Revolution had indisputably ended the contention that through divine right, any monarch might supersede the wishes of the people as interpreted by Parliament.

Attitudes toward government, characterized for nearly a century by violent upheavals and rancorous discord, had changed dramatically. The eighteenth century emerged as an age of politics in which the arts of persuasion and subtlety replaced the heavy hand of military power.

Despite the rejection of absolute monarchy in England, royal prerogative still formed the basis of government in the colonies. Unrepresented in Parliament, the 250,000 white, English citizens of the North American provinces still failed to enjoy the full civil protections against arbitrary rule that were the birthright of those dwelling on the home isles. However, political realities, the growing wealth of the colonial economy and the failure of the Dominion made it clear that complete administrative control could not be secured by fiat.

In the hope that greater supervision could be established, the British machinery for dealing with the plantations was reorganized in 1696.

Power was centered in a Board of Trade that was charged with exercising comprehensive oversight of the entire colonial situation. Under the organization's auspices, long-range planning was to be substituted for crisis management.

Americans would grow to detest the prestigious Board as the hated enforcer of British power and the instigator of thousands of detailed orders relating to virtually every aspect of colonial life. However, members of the group did act aggressively in attempting to eliminate several of the basic problems that had contributed to the spate of provincial rebellions during the seventeenth century.

To prevent arbitrary and unequal justice, the Board reviewed all colonial laws to see if "mischief" was being done to crown interests. As a result of these examinations, selfish Proprietors and corporations found it increasingly difficult to impose orders that conflicted with British policies or rights. The Board also served as a hearing body for individuals charging that "oppressions and maladministrations" were being committed by provincial officials upon the citizenry.

English authorities made serious attempts to improve the quality of colonial administration by filling governorships with technically qualified appointees. The long-standing custom of nominating executives because of personal connections had not proved successful in creating either good will or good government. Overly lax governors had been unable to enforce collection of British revenues and had frequently strengthened the power of local assemblies by default. In the opposite extreme, unnecessarily forceful executives had tended to impose such rigid controls on the populace that citizens had been estranged from fidelity to the monarchy.

To appease the English element that had come to view appointment to American posts as an inherent right and at the same time to assure provincials that quality of leadership would be provided, a system of sinecure was adopted. Under this concept, prominent but unqualified Britishers continued to be named as provincial governors. The appointees, however, remained in England and were vested with no powers or responsibilities. Each received an annual stipend, but actual control of the plantation was delegated to a more capable Lieutenant Governor who actually resided in the colony. In those instances where sinecure was applied, the system proved imminently more successful than traditional appointment based on political reward.

Limited attention was also given to development of a corps of professional colonial administrators. Francis Nicholson, perhaps the most prominent of these career executives, served as Governor or Lieutenant Governor in New York, Virginia, Maryland, the Dominion, South Carolina and Nova Scotia.

Genuine efforts were also made to eliminate corruption in office. In 1700, Parliament approved the first act specifically authorizing trial and punishment for governors who committed crimes in the course of their duties. The measure served mainly as a deterrent, for Walter Douglas, Governor of the Leeward Islands, appears to be the only individual tried under the measure. Douglas, accused of various irregularities including embezzlement of the communion silver entrusted to him for provincial use, was found guilty under the statute and sentenced to five years' imprisonment.

As British administrative techniques were being improved, colonial society was undergoing alterations that simultaneously contributed to political stability and reduced the danger of violent rebellions.

Religion gradually became less than an overriding concern, depriving rabble-rousers of the power to inflame the population against dissident minorities or supposed conspiracies. The Church of England became so firmly entrenched that freedom of conscience was either legally guaranteed or informally condoned in every province.

The emergence of an economically-oriented culture brought significant shifts in the placement of power. Large concentrations of wealth were accumulated by merchants and planters who developed strong, vested interests in maintaining internal peace. These gentlemen, who served on royal councils or as leaders of the assemblies, became effective buffers between the radical demands of the people and the more conservative inclinations of crown appointees. In their leisure time, the new aristocrats studied political theory and became eloquent spokesmen capable of presenting colonial viewpoints to English authorities as adeptly as any titled lord.

British acknowledgment that representative assemblies indeed were integral parts of government also helped to ease tensions in the population, but perhaps no factor proved as significant as the development of an intra-colonial outlook among provincials who had earlier seen events only in terms of isolated self-interest. As the years passed, improved communications and transportation linked the provinces into

a more cohesive unit. Americans were still a rural, independent peo- ˒
ple, but as villages became towns, and towns became cities, more
sophisticated ideas came to the fore.

Yet arrayed against the forces of change in government, economics,
society and politics were the anachronistic and increasingly prosperous
proprietary colonies. Though each passing year made it more evident
that the ownership of vast tracts by private individuals was an obsolete
system, charters remained unassailable. The Board of Trade attempted
to correct this situation by framing four bills which would convert the
proprietary plantations to crown status, but each of the measures was
defeated in Parliament.

No territory demonstrated the undesirability of proprietary control
more clearly than the Carolinas where absentee owners had proved
consistently unable to maintain the peace. Unlike the crown, the Proprietors had made few efforts to upgrade the quality of government or
the techniques of administration.

Charleston merchant Thomas Cary had been named Deputy Governor of the northern section of Carolina, a position he was most ill
equipped to fill. From the first, Cary encountered opposition. Much of
the dissension stemmed from the Quaker sect whose members were
aggressively moving into positions of authority in the colony.

To eliminate the rivalry of the Friends, Cary ordered strict enforcement of a controversial Vestry Act that specified that only communi-
cants of the Church of England who agreed to swear an oath to the
Queen, might sit in the Assembly. By rigidly enforcing the stipulation,
Cary assured that not only Quakers, but other religious dissenters were
prohibited from exercising a voice in government.

A protest to the Proprietors by non-Anglicans was upheld. The
London lords ordered that Cary be removed from office and the oath
suppressed. The Carolina Council consented and elected their own
President, William Glover, as the new chief executive.

Cary refused to accept the decision of the Proprietors and the election of Glover. In an extreme example of shifting political allegiances,
the deposed official joined with the religious dissenters to retake the
government by force.

Fortunately for Carolina, cooler heads prevailed and the opposing
parties agreed to submit the decision of who should rule to an assembly that would be specifically chosen in new elections, to be held on

October 3, 1708. It was soon obvious, however, that partisanship had not been buried. Widespread irregularities occurred at the voting precincts and confusion resulted over precisely who had been elected. In most areas, two sets of delegates claimed victory, but neither faction could muster sufficient strength to dominate the other.

Cary tired of the credentials fight and reverted to his original plan of settling the matter by show of force. Virginia Governor Alexander Spotswood, monitoring the disturbances from Williamsburg, was appalled by the entire procedure. According to Spotswood, Cary had treacherously:

> . . . gathered together a rabble of the looser sort of people and by force of arms, turned out the President and most of the Council, and by his own authority assumed the administration of government.

The Proprietors did not take kindly to the usurpation of power. Large segments of the population refused to acknowledge Cary and continued to support Glover who had fled in fear to Virginia. Rejecting the claims of both factions, the lords dispatched Edward Hyde, a cousin of Queen Anne, as the new Governor.

Hyde arrived in Albemarle during August of 1710, and although his official commission had not arrived, he was sworn into office. The new Governor set about to correct existing abuses by establishing courts and calling for the election of still another assembly.

Initially, Cary and his followers cooperated with Hyde, but the inclusion of Glover as a Council member, the elimination of Quakers from positions of power and unfavorable moves by the legislature soon dampened the faction's enthusiasm. The assembly not only voided all of Cary's legislation, but the representatives reestablished Church of England membership as a qualification of officeholding. It was rumored that anti-proprietary officials would be called to account for abuses of power that had occurred during Cary's governorship.

Both Hyde and the assembly had vastly underestimated the power of the dissident party. Claiming that both the Governor and the legislature were acting without legitimate authority, Cary reorganized his followers. He warned that no opposition would be tolerated, and according to critics, sent agents to the frontier to arouse the Tuscarora against the proprietarians. More unlikely were rumors that he was planning to seize the colony's treasury and abscond to a pirates' den in Madagascar.

Cary was arrested in March of 1711 for high crimes, but he managed to break jail and return home to begin fortifying his plantation against possible attack by Hyde's followers. The Governor's attitude toward the colonists, however, was not calculated to attract a wide following. Instead of praising the settlers, he declared the locals were "naturally loose and wicked, obstinate and rebellious, craftly and deceitful."

The situation was even further complicated by the arrival of Richard Roach, a proprietary deputy who allied himself with the rebels and asserted that Hyde's claim to power was baseless. By June 30, so many had flocked to Cary's standards, that the insurgent leader concluded that the time was right for eliminating both the Governor and the Council. Cary announced that he was assuming the reins of government, and with seventy supporters set off on a brigantine to launch a surprise raid on the officials who were meeting at a plantation on the Chowan River.

Hyde, probably forewarned, had managed to organize a near equal force of loyalists. The rebels' sneak attack was turned into a rout. Cary's men fled in disarray, pursued by the Governor who captured both the brig and a large supply of ammunition. The victors of the battle, however, had not yet won the war.

Resentment of the proprietary refused to abate. Despite Hyde's offer of pardon for all rebels who agreed to submit to his rule, large numbers of malcontents returned to Cary. Supposedly, great quantities of rum and brandy were used to lure the common folk into supporting the insurgent, while physical threats were made against more reluctant planters. Hyde, realizing that his force was inadequate to contain the revolt, appealed to Spotswood for the help of the Virginia militia.

Spotswood, a royal appointee in the absolutist mold, deplored uprisings by the masses, but the official was a most realistic politician. The old colony Governor believed that Virginians would be reluctant to march against fellow farmers who were protesting aristocratic rule. If citizens ignored a militia call to arms, then Spotswood's own authority would be severely damaged.

Thus instead of dispatching locals to put down the rebellion, Spotswood offered to mediate the controversy. The offer was ultimately rejected by Cary, who had become so certain of his invulnerability, that he was publicly comparing the Carolina movement to an insurrection that had taken place in Antigua during 1710. The island revolt had been a bloody affair in which an uncontrollable mob had literally torn Governor Daniel Parke limb from limb. The riot was well-known to Spotswood, for Parke's daughter Lucy was the wife of prominent Virginian William Byrd.

Spotswood reacted by devising a logical plan whereby legitimate authority could be reestablished in Carolina, but not imperilled in Virginia. Instead of militiamen, he would send a British man-of-war and a company of royal marines to aid the beleaguered Hyde.

The show of English force was decisive. No longer was the target of the Carolina rebels a civilian appointee of private Lords Proprietors. The rebellion, if it were pressed, would be against the military arm of the crown. Cary's force was no more willing to commit high treason than Bacon's men had been. The insurgents drifted away while Cary fled into a supposedly friendly area of Virginia. Even the small farmers of the old colony were reluctant to harbor the fugitive. The rebel leader was apprehended and dispatched to England for trial, but as in the case of Culpeper's revolt, the Proprietors were not anxious to acknowledge that control had been lost in the overseas dominion. Cary was allowed to return home unpunished.

Residents in northern Carolina would not long enjoy the peace that resulted from Cary's defeat. In September of 1711, a confederation of Indians led by the Tuscarora invaded the territory and attacked as far east as New Berne. Destruction was widespread. Tales of massacre emerged from every area. The warriors were beaten back only with the assistance of frontiersmen and friendly Indians from the South. The sacrifice of those in the neighboring colony was a considerable one, for the province headquartered at Charleston was also verging on revolt.

Relations between South Carolinians and the Proprietors had shown no improvement since the days of Seth Sothell. Rather, the alienation had intensified as a result of continually unfavorable actions such as the English lords' refusal to approve a habeas corpus act passed by the legislature, failure to order retaliatory raids against pirates ravaging the eastern coast and reluctance to provide a workable monetary system so that rampant inflation might be controlled.

Most divisive, however, was the Proprietors' continued mishandling of defense problems. No colony was as vulnerable as South

Carolina, an area confronted by the Spanish in Florida, the Indians on the frontier, the French in the Mississippi Valley and an assortment of renegades on the sea.

The volatile issue of survival separated not only the people from the Proprietors, but caused intrasectional strife as well. A violent outbreak of the ill-feeling came in 1703 when widespread panic gripped the area as a result of an anticipated invasion by the Spanish. Realizing that the lords would not finance a preventive strike at St. Augustine, the Assembly drew up legislation providing local funding for a major expedition. The measure was popular among the fearful citizenry, but a majority of religious dissenters, led by pacifist Quakers, refused to be present for a final vote on the measure. Because a quorum could not be obtained, the bill was doomed.

Frightened residents exploded against the dissenters. Legislators were threatened with death and assaulted by street mobs. For four days a riot raged out of control in Charleston and according to the victims, the Governor made no effort to suppress the disturbances or provide safety for the targets.

During the ensuing years, power flowed from the office of the appointed governor, into the hands of the Chief Justice, a post held by Nicholas Trott. The jurist, considered by many to be the most venal officeholder in the colony, had cannily allied himself with the English lords against a progression of governors who were generally sympathetic to the public's interest. Citizens, disquieted by the unresponsive rule, began submitting petitions to the crown, suggesting that the colony be taken under royal control.

Contention increased after the absentee owners refused to assume any costs of the 1711 Tuscarora War. The colonists' defense had saved the province, but the effort had contributed to crippling inflation. Perhaps believing that the threat from the red men had been permanently quashed, the Proprietors refused all requests that large amounts of hard currency should be interjected into the local economy.

The Indians were far from vanquished. In April of 1715, thousands of Yamassees, Creeks, Choctaws and Catawbas attacked exposed settlements. Frontier families raced to Charleston for protection. One-half of the land under cultivation fell into weeds and the resulting famine was so severe that one observer noted that the colonists were "ready to eat up one another for want of provisions." In desperation, even black slaves were armed.

Total annihilation was avoided only when the powerful Cherokees and Chickasaws elected to remain neutral in the struggle, but a heavy loss of life as well as economic hardship resulted from the conquest. Inflation reached new levels and still no corrective action was forthcoming from London. The Proprietors continued to neglect needed reforms and instead embarked on a course seemingly designed to enrage the population even further.

Revenue measures designed by the assembly to check inflation were vetoed. The granting of new land was specifically prohibited without direct approval of the lords. Territory captured as a result of the Yamassee War was closed to citizens so that the tract might be divided among the Proprietors. Funds for protecting these giant manoral plots, however, were not forthcoming. It was apparently assumed that local pioneers would continue to defend the area at their own expense. The provincial Council was reorganized to eliminate all opponents to the established government.

In July of 1719, the lords received an urgent message from Governor Robert Johnson who begged for immediate help in deterring an invasion of six hundred Indians being armed by the Spanish. The absentee owners did not move to assist the colonists and instead ordered the dissolution of the angry assembly.

By November, the rumored Spanish invasion appeared so imminent that members of the legislature met in unauthorized session to deal with the crisis. The gathering resulted in a drastic decision: Johnson would be asked by the body to take control of the province in the name of the King.

The Governor was indeed disillusioned with the neglectful attitude of his English employers. He would not, however, consent to what might be construed as rebellion. Instead of accepting the legislature's offer, he ordered the rump Assembly to disperse.

Instead, the delegates formed a "Convention" and on December 21 named James Moore as Governor. Following accepted practice for those who depose an existing administration, the assemblymen issued a proclamation listing the abuses of power that the Proprietors had exhibited. The charges were familiar: the English owners were accused of acting arbitrarily and illegally in repealing lawful acts of the legislature. They had deprived citizens of free rights and administered the province contrary to the statutes of England. They had left the colony "naked" to foreign attack and placed the area in a "sinking condition." For these reasons, the Convention announced:

> [We] hereby declare the said James Moore, his Majesty's Governor of this settlement, invested with all the powers and authorities belonging and appertaining to any of his Majesty's governors in America, till his Majesty's pleasure herein shall be further known.

Johnson's efforts to raise a counter force were impeded by a large concentration of armed citizens who had come to the capital for Muster Day exercises. Moore and a twelve-man Council, also appointed by the Convention, received the militiamen's support. The new government was soon firmly entrenched.

Fears that the disposal of proprietary authority would be punished as rebellion were quickly eased. Neither King nor Parliament showed an inclination to act against those who had delivered the colony into crown hands. In the summer of 1720, South Carolina came under official royal rule. Francis Nicholson was appointed as the King's lawful Governor.

The Proprietors, though losing rights of government, retained rights of soil for a decade. In 1729, all owners but John Carteret agreed to withdraw claims in exchange for approximately £2,500. At last the 1663 charter was given up.

Although a period of relative satisfaction with government emerged in the province after the 1719 rebellion, all the American colonists were not contented. A large and potentially powerful new group was beginning to take up the tools of revolt, and these dissidents appeared capable of channeling their opposition into most bloody directions.

Like earlier insurgents, the new faction sought personal freedom and a release from oppressive government. However, no Magna Carta or Petition of Rights could be used as a philosophical justification for their challenge. No erudite friends stood by in London to influence the courts and no powerful colleagues sat in the assembly. These rebels, men and women who instilled cold terror in the hearts of other Americans, were the unfranchised, landless, powerless and enslaved blacks.

# CHAPTER XII

# *The Black Rebellions*

THE ORIGINS of slave rebellion in North America are far older than English colonization. In 1526, black laborers at a Spanish enclave on Carolina's Pedee River revolted against their white owners in what was probably the first slave challenge to European domination on the continent. The Pedee dissidents were subdued, but several managed to escape westward to seek refuge with the Indians. Although the conspiracy was quashed, basic tensions in the village were not eased: Spain was forced to abandon the colony after only six months of operation.

English settlers fared little better in controlling their "human chattel"—men and women considered servants for life and thus ineligible for common law rights. From 1619, when the first black slaves reached Virginia, until the Emancipation Proclamation in 1863, transported Africans and their descendants were widely feared by the slavocracy as an "intestine enemy" capable of launching bloody rebellions without warning.

While revolts by white colonists were usually rooted in a variety of causes, insurrections among the Negro population were invariably directed at one of three simple goals: freedom from bondage, improvement in living conditions or retribution against oppressive masters.

229

Most of the undertakings had little chance of success, for vigilant owners and provincial governments maintained a united front that made large scale violence virtually impossible. The opportunities for interplantation plotting were limited by watchers and searchers kept on continuous patrol to apprehend slaves breaking curfew or travelling without permits. Arms and ammunition were carefully kept from black hands so that the slave arsenal of clubs and farm implements would be little match for the guns available to whites. Even if a temporary military victory could be achieved by rebelling slaves, there was only a remote possibility that insurgents could escape recapture. Without permanent supply lines, blacks would eventually succumb to hunger or the elements. Unlike runaway indentured servants who might melt unnoticed into the white population, residents of African origin could be instantly identified as outsiders by their skin color.

Until the early years of the eighteenth century, when the first large numbers of blacks were imported into America, individual escape was a far more effective way of achieving freedom than mass insurrection. However isolated outbreaks of group uprisings did occur during the settlement era. One of the first was a 1657 revolt near Hartford in which blacks and Indians combined in an abortive attempt to displace English rule. Race relations in New England remained strained throughout the colonial period, but at no time did the threat of slave rebellion against the Puritans approach the constant danger posed to whites in the tobacco and rice cultures of the south.

Environmental and economic factors rather than a basic preference for slavery transformed the farmers of Maryland, Virginia and the Carolinas into eager purchasers of human merchandise. The short growing seasons which made slavery financially unattractive in the north were absent in the agricultural tidewater where huge masses of unskilled labor were in constant demand. Alternatives to slavery were attempted, but each proved inadequate. Indians were found to be undependable workers whose bondage presented grave dangers to frontier settlers. White Europeans could not be attracted in sufficient numbers to tend the fields, and those who did agree to indenture themselves, generally would not tolerate the relatively inhumane conditions imposed by planters upon their workers.

The advantage of importing blacks from Africa and the sugar islands appeared overwhelming. Because virtually no laws protected the interests of blacks, masters could work their charges at will, while providing only minimum food, clothing and shelter. Rigid discipline could be maintained, for almost total control of slaves was vested in individual owners rather than in the courts. Most important, planters profiting by the system of slavery for life, did not face loss of their acquisition investment through expiration of a set term of service.

British commercial interests were quick to recognize that the slave needs of provincial farmers offered attractive avenues for profit. Acting through the crown-chartered Royal African Company, prominent Englishmen began outfitting hundreds of slave ships for the trans-Atlantic journey. Despite the high numbers of blacks who died en route, returns of one hundred percent over investment were not unusual for individual voyages.

But planters in America soon discovered that the supposedly ideal solution to their labor problem was not without disadvantages. Nowhere was this lesson more obvious than in Virginia.

Officials in the old colony readily acknowledged that the province's large, ill treated minority—individuals who held no expectation of freedom—constituted a potentially deadly force. Conditions that had prompted Birkenhead's Plot in 1663 went unaltered and by 1680, the Burgess attempted to deal with mounting black dissention by approving "An Act for Preventing Negroe Insurrections." According to the legislators, the law was desperately needed to counter dangerous conspiracies being hatched by slaves meeting "under pretence of feasts and burials."

Funerals did provide one of the few opportunities for blacks from neighboring plantations to gather without direct white surveillance. To the slaveocracy, the natural topic of conversation at such observances was not the dead, but rebellion.

Some jurisdictions attempted to eliminate the opportunity for conspiring by setting limits on the number of slaves that might attend final rites. In 1687, the Virginia Council took more extreme precautions after discovering that blacks in the Northern Neck area had used funerals as a cover to organize revolt. The officials reacted to the unsuccessful rebellion by banning all public burials for slaves.

Colonial fears of internal revolt were magnified by the Glorious Revolution and the subsequent war with France. Of major concern, was the possibility that blacks might join with Bourbon and Catholic

forces to overturn Protestant rule in America. Such apprehensions
were particularly widespread in Maryland where Baltimore's deputies
were repeatedly accused of conspiring with servants and Indians to
massacre Anglicans and Puritans.

In 1691, New Jersey agitator Isaac Morrill was arrested in New-
bury, Massachusetts, on similar religiously oriented charges. Allegedly,
Morrill had plotted to lead Indian and black workers in a bloody attack
against local whites. At an Ipswich hearing, the defendant confessed
that his plan was part of a more ambitious scheme to bring down England's Protestant outposts. Under Morrill's design, the rebels would
seize a boat, escape en masse to Canada and conduct lightning raids
against New England pioneers along the northern frontier.

Despite the seeming threat posed by dissident blacks, few conspirators in the early years of colonization were punished by death or
serious injury. Blacks represented a significant financial investment to
their owners and the loss of even a single worker might prove disastrous to a small farmer. Even after provincial governments agreed to
compensate the masters of slaves executed for rebellion, provincial
courts were hesitant to impose punishments that might be physically
damaging. Slaves were branded or mutilated, but rarely were culprits
sentenced to lose a hand or foot, for dismemberment severely reduced
the value of a worker. Similarly, slaves were seldom imprisoned for
extended periods. It was believed that long-term incarceration unjustly
deprived a planter of sorely needed labor.

The most acceptable modes of punishment for black rebels were
flogging or transportation out of the colony. In James City, Virginia,
for example, a slave convicted of repeated attempts to raise a revolt,
received a relatively lenient punishment. Instead of being hanged, the
felon was severely whipped, permanently confined to his master's
plantation and sentenced to wear a heavy iron collar about his neck.
According to the court's decision, death would be imposed only if he
escaped or removed the manacle.

The tendency of courts to deal lightly with convicted rebels
changed dramatically after the turn of the century when the importation of slaves reached critical levels and whites in many areas found
themselves outnumbered by their laborers. In 1680, blacks composed
slightly more than four percent of the colonial population. Thirty years
later the figure had increased to nearly fourteen percent. The new ar-

rivals constituted a potent and violent reservoir of insurrectionists.

During the spring of 1710, a conspiracy of major proportions was organized in Surrey and Isle of Wight counties Virginia. The plot was a simple one: on Easter Sunday morning, while local whites were occupied in church, hundreds of blacks and Indians would rise up in arms. The rebels would march in formation towards freedom, killing all who blocked the way.

Before the plan could be put into effect, word of the outbreak was brought to authorities by a slave informant named Will Ruffin. Warrants were swiftly issued for the arrest of known conspirators, but ringleader Peter Thompson managed to evade capture despite a reward of £10 alive or £5 dead which was placed on his head. Thompson's chief cohorts, Scipio Edwards and an Indian slave named Salvadore Jackman were not so fortunate. Both were apprehended and taken to stand trial at Williamsburg on charges of high treason. After their conviction, the men were sentenced to be hanged, drawn and quartered; lesser participants were ordered flogged and returned home. To demonstrate that loyalty to the white establishment would not go unnoticed, Will Ruffin was purchased by the colony for £40 and given his freedom.

News of plots such as the Virginia rebellion spread rapidly to other colonies. The most lurid and obscure details of conspiracies were given wide publicity in towns hundreds of miles from the scene of the disturbance. Often reports of the intended horrors were exaggerated to outrageous degrees, perhaps in an effort to keep slave owners alert and justify ill usage of local blacks.

Urban areas in the north were not immune from the tensions that gripped southern plantation society. Apprehensions were particularly acute in Manhattan, for the largest population of slaves north of Maryland was clustered around the port city. Here, bonded-for-life workers had become a major force in the commercial economy.

Slaves were present in Dutch-ruled New Netherlands as early as 1626, and though small numbers of Africans were sold to farmers along the Hudson, most blacks remained near the provincial capital. Hollanders viewed slavery in a significantly different manner than did English colonists. Under Dutch law, favored blacks might achieve "half-freedom," a status of near independence which allowed workers to contract with private interests for short term employment. In exchange for the privilege, slaves were required to maintain themselves, pay an annual fee to the government and labor if needed on public works projects.

New Amsterdam's commercial environment produced a class of slaves vastly different than those bred in agricultural areas. Instead of serving as field hands, most of the Dutch-owned slaves were semi-skilled workmen, domestic servants or highly trained artisans who provided indispensable services. While positive relations between owner and owned were inherently impossible, racial tensions appeared to be far less strained in New Netherlands than in neighboring British colonies.

The English conquest of the province ended the informal, unregulated system of slavery that had developed under the Hollanders. The Duke of York, a power in the Royal African Company, encouraged importation of forced labor and high profits from trade in human commerce induced even the most prominent Manhattanites to participate in slave trafficking. As a result, overt hostilities emerged in the city.

New York's white work force complained of unfair competition from skilled slaves. For the first time, resentment toward free blacks became obvious. Authorities joined other jurisdictions in imposing limitations on the activities of slaves. All travel after dark was prohibited. The sale of liquor to those in bondage was outlawed. The right of blacks to contract for independent labor was curtailed.

Formal statutes failed to produce a docile and obedient servant class, for the essential skills possessed by the capital's blacks were vital to the city's operation. In an economy where even a slave splitting wood received three times the wages of a white soldier, few citizens demanded strict enforcement of measures that might alienate a vital segment of the work force, and perhaps disrupt the entire economy.

Despite laws forbidding the gathering of more than four slaves at a time, large crowds began congregating in "tippling houses." Soon these unruly assemblies spilled into the streets causing disorder at all hours of the night. In 1696, New York's royal Governor was assaulted by the members of one such mob, and although a slave convicted of the attack was whipped eleven lashes at every intersection in the city, the tavern celebrations did not abate.

A decade later, Governor Edward Hyde was so shocked at the

"great insolency" of New York's blacks, that he directed local law-men to use any steps necessary in controlling slave crowds which might produce "ill consequence" for the area. Justices of the Peace were delegated the power to summarily kill or otherwise destroy any slave refusing to desist "ill practices or designs" such as rebellion.

Suspicions of the white population were also aggravated by activities of the Manhattan unit of the Society for the Propagation of the Gospel in Foreign Parts, the SPG. In 1704, missionaries of the organization began working to convert local slaves to Christianity. The effort made few inroads among the black population who viewed the religious precepts of kindness and forgiveness as irrelevant to the realities of life in bondage.

Because it was feared that permanent bondage of Christians might be construed as immoral by English powers in the established church, most masters refused to allow their slaves to be baptized. Similarly, acceptance of blacks as equal brothers and sisters in religion could have undermined the contention that slaves were a sub-human species, incapable of making their way alone and thus destined to be ruled by whites. Opponents of the Society also proposed that education and baptism would arouse unhealthy longings for freedom, and thus encourage rebellion against the entire institution of slavery.

During the winter of 1711–1712, external factors contributed even further to the anxiety of those in the port city. According to rumors, the French, once again at war with England, were readying a fleet to attack Manhattan. In the north, the once friendly Iroquois were not only sheltering runaway slaves, but were said to be intriguing with Louis' agents in Canada. The growing air of nervousness did not go unnoticed by the black minority.

In late March, a select group of slaves met in secret to plan a rebellion aimed at transforming the capital into a black-dominated enclave. Ironically, ringleaders in the conspiracy were members of the Coromantee and Pawpaw clans, African tribes whose members were considered to be the most loyal and faithful of all workers.

The plotters were apparently aware that the greatest threat to the rebellion's success was presented by slave informants who might reveal details of the design in hope of achieving freedom. To insure that no word leaked to unfriendly forces, each participant at the surreptitious gathering forced to take a sacred oath of silence, a rite that involved self-mutilation and blood sucking. As a further assurance of victory, a conjuror involved in the scheme blessed the participants and distributed a supply of "magical" powder. This charm, when rubbed on clothing, supposedly made the user invisible to all human detection and thus able to roam at will slaying whites with impunity.

For several weeks, the conspirators collected weapons and finalized details of the rebellion. On the evening of April 6, the men were ready to act.

Shortly after midnight, about two dozen slaves stole into a centrally located orchard owned by cooper John Crook. All were well armed with axes, swords, guns or knives. Success seemed certain, for the battle plan was not complicated: a large fire would be set to attract attention. When whites appeared to fight the blaze, each would be cut down by invisible hands. Hundreds of other slaves would then join in the rebellion, and the city would be taken before a general alarm could be given.

While the main body of insurgents secreted themselves in hiding, Cuffee, a slave of Peter Vantilborough, torched his master's outhouse. Within minutes, whites began straggling onto the scene.

Initially the strategy was totally effective. Adrian Hoghlandt was fatally stabbed by his own slave while Henry Brasier was hacked to death by axe-wielding dissidents. Fourteen other early arrivals soon lay dead or wounded and there appeared to be no opposition forming against the rebels.

The slaves, however, had miscalculated by not depending entirely upon silent weapons. Gunfire from the ambush carried tellingly in the evening stillness. Governor Robert Hunter, correctly surmising that a revolt was in progress, ordered out the city's troops and called upon all citizens to arm.

As bells rang throughout Manhattan, the plotters found themselves confronted by a united opposition of overwhelming numbers. The sorcerer's magical powder failed to provide safety in invisibility. The conspirators broke ranks and fled northwards into the woods bordering the community, but escape was only temporary. When light dawned, white sentries were posted on all major routes leading out of the area and militiamen from neighboring settlements were streaming toward the capital in case a renewal of the rebellion erupted. Enraged citizens began combing the forest for the revolters.

Most of the plotters surrendered or were forcibly taken prisoner, but six slaves chose to commit suicide rather than return to face a capricious judgment of the law. So great had local wrath become, that authorities ordered the arrest of any black who might have conceivably had prior knowledge of the uprising. During the following fortnight, seventy men and women were jailed.

Justice against the detainnees was swift for New Yorkers shared the colonial belief that quick punishment was an essential deterrent in all crimes involving slaves. With the assistance of black informants, twenty-seven blacks were condemned in trials that relied upon the worst features of English procedure. Even Governor Hunter was appalled at the frequent miscarriages of justice, and the official acted decisively to stay the execution of slaves convicted under dubious circumstances. Particularly unseemly to Hunter, was the case of one Mars Regnier, a slave twice acquitted before being convicted on the same evidence at a third trial. According to Hunter, the continued harassment of the black man was solely due to a "private pique" between the prosecutor and the defendant's owner.

Hunter also objected to the condemning of two "Spanish Indians." Several years earlier, a group of dark skinned individuals claiming to be free citizens of the Bourbon King had been taken at sea by English privateers. Because of their complexions, the captives were sold into slavery as prizes of war. The victims proved particularly resistant to bondage and bitterly complained of their detention. It was perhaps the Indians' reputation as troublemakers which prompted an aroused jury to declare two of the party guilty of rebellion in connection with the uprising.

Labeling the Indians innocent as the "child unborn," Hunter refused to carry out the death penalty ordered by the courts. Instead, the office holder forwarded their names, together with those of three condemned blacks, to the Lords of Trade, with the plea that Queen Anne issue a formal pardon. He also stayed the execution of a black woman who "pled her belly", until after the delivery of her unborn child.

The twenty-one convicted rebels not recommended for clemency were duly carted to the gallows and burning stakes. Most were executed unceremoniously, but three leaders of the conspiracy were subjected to particularly painful deaths: Claus Jarrett was broken on a wheel and allowed to die without treatment, Robin Hoghlandt was hanged in chains and left to starve, and Tom Roosevelt was roasted over a slow fire.

Retribution was also forthcoming against the SPG. Though only two of the convicted rebels were remotely connected with the Society, missionary John Sharpe reported that the group's "pious design" had been much obstructed and the Christain religion "much blasphemed" as a result of the revolt. Elias Neau, founder of the SPG mission school, was forced from Manhattan's streets by threats from angry New Yorkers who attributed the conspiracy to his Christian movement.

The angry population also demanded that firmer controls on slaves be adopted to insure that future rebellions would not occur. On December 10, 1712, the colonial assembly complied with public opinion by approving "An Act for Preventing, Suppressing and Punishing the Conspiracy and Insurrection of Negros and Other Slaves." The measure set unprecedented regulations upon the servant class. Trial by jury would not be permitted unless such hearings were financed by masters of the defendants. Slaves were prohibited from engaging in private trade, meetings by more than three blacks were outlawed and manumission was discouraged by a clause requiring owners to post £200 bonds for each freed worker.

Transmitting the measure to the Lords of Trade, Hunter attempted to explain the bill's passage by announcing: "I am apt to believe, your Lordships will still [find it] too severe, but after the late, barbarous attempt of some of their slaves, nothing less could please the people."

The Governor, perhaps believing that peace could never return to the city as long as a large portion of the residents were kept in bondage, suggested that the colony return to dependency upon indentured labor. The idea did not receive support. Despite vivid reminders of the narrowly averted rebellion, blacks continued to be imported into the province.

In December of 1717, assemblymen voted to compensate owners of the executed insurgents. In exchange for the loss of each laborer, masters were allotted fifty ounces of "Sevil, Mexico or Pillar Plate." The legislators explained that no payment had been approved at the time of the revolt because of the "general disorder and confusion" which had prevailed.

If the danger of slave rebellion created alarm in Manhattan, the specter of black revolt wrought total horror in South Carolina where forty percent of the citizenry were held as chattel. Labor demands of the rice culture and the encouragement of four Carolina proprietors who also served as members of the Royal African Company had made trafficking in blacks a mainstay of the Charleston economy.

The provincial assembly endorsed the slave trade, but deplored the constant ''fear and terror'' to which the white colonials were subjected. The prevailing dread was not groundless, for conspiracies were discovered in the province during 1711, 1713, and 1714. In desperation, the assembly levied high customs duties on each imported slave in the belief that ''foreign'' workers were more likely to rebel than native born blacks. In other legal action, planters were ordered to maintain one white servant for every ten slaves. Presumably, the white workers would form a defense pool in case of insurrection and would act as informants.

For a brief period, the regulations seemed to bring quiet, but in May of 1720, a large corps of slaves intent on capturing Charleston killed several whites before being subdued. More than a dozen insurrectionists, hoping to reach freedom with the help of friendly Creeks, managed to escape toward St. Augustine. After the Indians refused to become involved, the ''half-starved'' rebels were captured by a contingent of colonials from Savannah. The runaways were returned to South Carolina where leaders of the revolt were hanged or burned.

The prospect of an alliance between slaves and Indians was as unsettling to Southerners as the dread of a black-Canadian compact was to those in the North. Runaways were found living with the hostile Yamasees and Creeks in South Carolina while the Appalachian Cherokees were known shelterers of slaves. Legislatures, seeking to woo tribes away from harboring renegades, offered rewards for the return of all escapees. The Virginia government, for example, approved a bounty of one gun and two blankets for every slave brought back into bondage by the Five Nations. Despite the incentives and constant patrols which ranged the back country, slaves continued to pass to safety among the mountain tribes.

The idea that entire communities of runaways lived beyond the English frontier was widely accepted in the South. Self-sustaining villages probably did not exist, but escaped blacks did congregate beyond the fall line. In 1729, a band of slaves from plantations along the

James River were tracked into the mountains and discovered readying the land for planting. After a pitched battle with Virginia whites, the slaves were returned home.

Of particular concern to Virginia authorities was the link that supposedly existed between slaves, free blacks and rebellion. Freemen were believed to serve as messengers between groups of slave plotters, and principal organizers of insurrections. To halt the exchange, the Burgess outlawed all meetings between slaves and free blacks, and because the very existence of unbonded Negros was considered unhealthy, the assembly also forbade manumission without the expressed approval of the Governor and Council. Instead of decreasing black unrest, the elimination of potential freedom only removed a major incentive to good behavior and faithful service.

In the fall of 1730, it appeared that a significant change was about to occur in the status of slaves in the old colony. Word raced through the black community that ex-Governor Alexander Spotswood, recently returned from England, had brought back a royal proclamation ordering the immediate freeing of all Christian slaves. When officials denied the report, the slave grapevine contended that local authorities intended to ignore the crown order.

All across Virginia it was obvious that a major insurrection was imminent. Slaves suspected of inciting unrest were apprehended and whipped to extract confessions. The Council, announcing that illegal conspiracies were rampant, ordered total enforcement of anti-meeting laws. Local militias were called out to disperse the large concentrations of blacks who refused to disband.

About six weeks after the original rumor had been circulated, an estimated two hundred slaves in Norfolk and Princess Anne counties concluded that freedom could be achieved only through violent means. The laborers carefully elected a group of rebel officers and began recruiting others who would be willing to risk death in a revolt.

Before the uprising could be launched, authorities managed to stifle the plan. Four principals were executed and the general hope that manumission would be forthcoming was totally dispelled.

Governor William Gooch, writing to the Bishop of London, deplored the attempted rebellion, but sympathized with the "poor wretches" who had been forced into slavery. According to the Governor, inhumane treatment of blacks was not unusual, for many farmers in the colony were content to "use their Negros no better than their cattle."

The belief that emancipation of Christian blacks had been approved in England also lay behind a 1734 insurrection in Burlington County, New Jersey. Here, several hundred slaves hatched a bloody plot involving the mass murder of all white males and the raping of white women. After the initial carnage, the conspirators planned to race toward the frontier on stolen horses, burning and pillaging along the way to create chaos.

When details of the rebellion were inadvertently revealed by a drunken slave, mass arrests were instigated. Supposedly, many of those taken possessed supplies of lethal poison, evidently prepared for use on unsuspecting masters. One of the thirty blacks arrested in connection with the revolt was hanged, while the remaining felons were punished by flogging or ear cropping.

As the eighteenth century progressed, colonial governments became increasingly skillful in blocking avenues of escape for disgruntled slaves. In the north, squads of rangers obstructed the way to freedom in Canada. Ships leaving ports such as Savannah, Charleston and Annapolis were searched for stowaways. Systematic rewards and promises of freedom resulted in the creation of a large network of slave informants. Punishments were swift, severe and public. In South Carolina, the head of a runaway clubbed to death by his master was placed on a pole as a warning to others who might seek freedom.

But even the heavily armed planters of South Carolina could not completely encircle their restless slaves with impenetrable barriers. Escape to the north, east and west was indeed hazardous, but a dim glimmer of freedom lay to the south in Spanish St. Augustine.

England's old rival made no attempt to assist the plantation owners of the tidewater in regulating the unwilling slave force. Instead, the Iberian power made every effort to increase conflict between the races in British possessions.

In 1733, Spain's King Philip V decreed that every English owned slave who managed to reach Florida would be freed, but despite the royal seal, the announcement was only partially enforced by officials in St. Augustine. A decided change in provincial attitude, however, took place as the European sea rivals pushed toward war.

By March of 1738, Philip's proclamation seemed an ideal means for hampering English war efforts through the creation of a fifth column. Florida Governor Don Manuel de Montiano proclaimed that full compliance would be given to the declaration: all runaways would be protected by the Spanish as free, armed to fight against the British and resettled in a special enclave about three miles north of St. Augustine. The black village, known as Fort Moosa, soon became the ultimate destination of discontented slaves throughout the south.

Word of Don Manuel's offer flew through the British plantations, bringing hope to thousands of blacks and despair to their owners. Planters realized that even without the Spanish incentive, safety was precarious at best. Total black population in the two southernmost colonies stood at six times the number of whites available for militia duty. The discrepancy grew wider each year, despite continued increases in the import duties.

Although additional precautions were undertaken by the provincial establishment, slaves continued to reach St. Augustine. In the spring of 1739, twenty-three runaways from St. Helen's, South Carolina, maneuvered their way through Georgia and received a warm welcome from the Spanish. Each successful escape raised concerns in English communities. It was announced that Spanish envoys were infiltrating the provinces in order to promote a general slave uprising that would make way for a full scale invasion.

Formal word that war had been declared between England and Spain reached Charleston during the second week of September, 1739. Hours after the news arrived, a band of approximately twenty blacks met near Stono, an outpost about twenty miles from the capital. The obsessive fears of the South Carolineans were about to be confirmed.

In the pre-dawn darkness of Sunday, September 9, the conspirators successfully attacked a warehouse where guns and ammunition were stored. After arming themselves, the slaves set out for Florida, decapitating two white prisoners and leaving the severed heads on display.

Making no effort to conceal their riotous march, the rebels moved down the Pons Pons Road toward the nearest ferry crossing into Georgia. The insurgents evidently hoped to attract a slave following by appearing totally unafraid and capable of overcoming all resistance.

Their progress was slow, for at every house the contingent stopped to slay local whites and collect additional weapons. Only one colonist, a tavernkeeper named Wallace, was spared, reportedly because of his reputation for kind treatment of slaves.

Although some laborers were coerced into joining the movement, most workers fell willingly into ranks. Shouting the cry of "Liberty," beating drums and displaying colors, the band continued to grow with each passing hour.

About 11:00 a.m., the insurgents met five horsemen heading northward toward Charleston; included in the party was William Bull, Lt. Governor of the colony. Bull narrowly escaped capture by galloping into the countryside where he began racing from farm to farm calling planters to arms.

During the late afternoon, the rebel force, estimated at from sixty to one hundred members, encamped in an open field about ten miles south of Stono. The elated men and women began celebrating their freedom with loud singing and dancing supplemented, by some accounts, with large quantities of stolen rum. In their joy, the revolters failed to post adequate sentries.

About 4:00 p.m., Bull's recruits fell upon the slaves in a frontal attack. During the confusion the rebels were unable to organize a countermove and the planters gunned down more than a dozen runaways. The blacks scattered in panic while the slave owners seized captives for questioning. Anyone failing to prove he had been forced into the movement was shot. Those found to have been compelled into participation were returned home. Reportedly, heads of slaves slain on the field were stuck on poles along the Pons Pons Road at one mile intervals.

As night fell, twenty whites and approximately thirty blacks lay dead as a result of the day's action. At least thirty additional rebels were believed to be still at large.

During the following week, as many as sixty blacks were apprehended and executed in connection with the Stono Rebellion. Georgia Governor James Oglethorpe, wishing to protect his own colony from the outside agitators set guards at border crossings, ordered rangers into the back country, and dispatched Indian trackers to trace undetected escapees.

Few in South Carolina believed that the danger had passed. The assembly called for increased vigilance during the winter holidays and approved £1,500 in rewards for slaves who had shown bravery in protecting their masters during the rebellion. Two Indians were voted £75 for helping to pursue the fugitives.

Increased surveillance did not deter slaves from attempting a conspiracy at Charleston during the Christmas season. The scheme was discovered and repressed, but six months later a rebellion even larger than the Stono affair was revealed by a black informant. Reportedly, an estimated 150 to 200 plantation slaves had agreed to attack the capital and capture sufficient weapons to impose black rule. With the advanced warning, the militia was able to subdue the conspirators. Sixty-seven rebels were tried and fifty were hanged in batches of ten prisoners each day. The informant received £20 and a new set of clothes.

In reaction to the dissension of 1739 and 1740, the assembly enacted measures supposedly designed to improve treatment of local slaves. In a sinister reminder of who ruled the province, however, the legislators also established a bounty system for the scalps of runaways.

The Spanish, believing that English provincials might invade Fort Moosa to retrieve the ex-slaves, disbanded the black village. Florida, however, remained a haven for fugitives until 1763 when the Spanish agreed to leave the continent under provisions of the Treaty of Paris. North America became English from the Penobscot to the Caribbean, but the runaways of Florida were not destined to be returned to their old masters. The Spanish did depart the mainland, but with them went the entire population of Fort Moosa.

South Carolina's posses were still tracking down the last of the Stono rebels when the scene of insurrection shifted to tidewater Maryland. In Prince George County, several hundred slaves had joined in a conspiracy to capture the arsenal at Annapolis and establish a black-run state. The plan was doomed when a heavy thunderstorm disrupted the timetable and authorities were able to capture enough of the rebels to thwart the revolt.

Provincial councilmen, shaken by the attempted takeover, hurriedly called for depositions from blacks who had knowledge of the affair. According to Council records, the statements clearly revealed that a "most wicked and dangerous" rebellion had narrowly been averted. On December 21, authorities directed that at least twelve militiamen were to stand constant guard to prohibit a mass escape by the imprisoned revolters. Local lawmen were ordered to be on the alert for accomplices who had not been arrested, and all slaves were forbidden from entering Annapolis on weekends without special passes. In addition, blacks found "wandering" and unable to account for their movement, were to be automatically jailed.

After trials before a special Court of Oyer and Terminer, one of the plotters was executed, but the sentence may have been both premature and unnecessary. A detailed investigation by members of the House of Delegates later revealed that the insurrection had not constituted a real threat to the colony.

The difficulty in distinguishing between real and imagined conspiracies was a continuing problem in the South, where slave secrecy and black protest seemed basic to the very institution of permanent bondage. But in comparison with the fortress state established by the whites in the Tidewater, the atmosphere in Manhattan appeared almost relaxed, at least on the surface.

New York's 1712 slave law had been replaced by an even harsher anti-rebellion code, yet enforcement of the measure was not severe. As a result, the capital's slave community—about one-sixth of the total population—remained relatively unhampered in their activities. The urban slaves, however, were pressed by unique frustrations which stemmed from the crowded, commercial environment in which they dwelt.

Unlike plantation laborers, New York's blacks were intimately exposed to white values and life styles. Many worked side by side with their owners, sharing the same tasks but receiving far less for their toil. The proximity of a free-wheeling port and the allure of foreign values and customs, no doubt prompted a special longing for freedom that was unknown in the closed world of the rural farm slave.

Word of the Stono rebellion intensified fears of the capital's whites, for the news closely followed notification that war with Spain was again a reality. In 1740, as some predicted imminent invasion by the Bourbon fleet, rumors circulated that the city's blacks were bent on poisoning the local drinking supply. Vendors raced into the streets to hawk supposedly untainted water, but when the expected catastrophes failed to materialize, a calm settled back over the city. The quiet was short-lived.

On March 18, 1741, a devastating fire erupted in Fort George, headquarters of New York's royal government. In the intense heat, the garrison's store of hand grenades exploded and for a time it was feared that the entire city would be set ablaze. The fire was eventually contained, but the fortress and all provincial records were totally destroyed. Without a military roster, no one was certain precisely how many men were available to defend the city.

The fire was initially attributed to a careless plumber who had supposedly failed to extinguish live coals used to repair a gutter on the building. The finding of accidental cause, however, was soon reexamined for the embers of the fort were not yet cool when other fires broke out without apparent reason. All were brought under control without widespread damage, but for three weeks, alarms sounded almost daily.

In some instances there was evidence that robberies had been committed before the conflagrations, and it was considered possible that the fires had been set to cover evidences of burglary. This seemingly reasonable explanation was discarded after April 6 when a slave was seen racing from a newly kindled blaze. On the same day, a black man of Spanish origin was arrested at a separate fire.

Nervous residents suggested that a far more sinister motive than robbery lay behind the series of burnings. Many were certain that, as in 1712, arson was somehow being used to promote a full-scale slave rebellion. If decisive action were not taken to uncover the plot, then all whites in the capital were in danger of being slain in a bloody internal war.

An increased fire watch did not halt the outbreaks or the panic that spread throughout the city. According to Lt. Gov. George Clarke, most householders became more concerned with protecting their families and property from slave vengeance than in helping to extinguish fires on others' estates. General reluctance to join in firefighting only increased the possibility that all of Manhattan could be destroyed by a single blaze.

The fear of death by insurrection continued to override concern over property loss. Blacks discovered near the scene of fires were placed under arrest and in one instance, even slaves who were attempting to control the blazes were taken into custody.

As whites began leaving the city for safety in the countryside, a house to house search was instigated to uncover evidences of arson or intended rebellion. Citizens carrying suspicious packages were examined on the streets. Strangers were questioned. No proof was found to support the contention that an insurrection was imminent, but the lack of support did not diminish the alarm.

On April 11, the Common Council approved a series of rewards for information leading to the capture of those responsible for the reign of terror. In exchange for worthwhile information, the Council agreed to reward informant slaves with £20 and freedom. Whites would receive £100, and like black recipients, would be pardoned for any involvement in the arson or supposed rebellion.

No one stepped forward to admit participating in the conspiracy, but the reward did produce a seemingly reluctant informant named Mary Burton. Mary, a 16-year-old indentured servant, claimed that she expected to be murdered at any moment for cooperating with the authorities, but despite the danger she confirmed that the fires were indeed manifestations of a slave rebellion. According to the servant, the mastermind of the hideous scheme was not a black man, but her own employer, a white innkeeper named John Hughson. Hughson, she reported, intended to use the city's slaves to become King of New York.

Mary's accusations were plausible to the desperate leaders of the city. It seemed reasonable that a white was behind the plot, for it was accepted that blacks were intellectually incapable of the intricate planning necessary for a governmental take over.

Hughson's reputation also served to confirm the charges. The innkeeper was a most unpopular citizen who openly flaunted the city's curfew laws and sold liquor to blacks. His tippling house had become notorious as a den of thieves where nightly drinking bouts were held by slaves and free blacks. It was well known that Hughson and his wife had established themselves as major fences in a large network of black housebreakers known as the Geneva [Gin] Club. Even as the charges of conspiracy were being presented, the tavern owner and his wife were in custody on allegations of receiving stolen goods.

By Mary's account, a small cadre of blacks and at least one disreputable white woman were also involved in the insurrection. Most prominent were a tavern habitué named Prince and his friend Caesar, a slave who had supposedly been selected to become Governor of New York after the uprising had been launched. Abetting the pair was Peggy Kerry, a white prostitute who resided at the inn and who reportedly had mothered an infant by Caesar.

Somewhat dubious corroboration for Mary's charges came from prison inmate Arthur Price who applied for a reward in exchange for valuable information he supposedly obtained after Peggy Kerry's arrest. Price claimed that Peggy had privately confessed that Hughson's tavern was a breeding ground of conspiracy. She had also informed

Price that if Caesar and Prince were harmed, then all of the city's slaves would take bloody revenge on the white population.

Mary Burton was not to be outdone. The servant girl expanded her original testimony by announcing that a large cache of gunpowder had been secreted at the inn by a band of black revolutionaries who intended to set explosive charges throughout the city. At a given signal, the powder would be detonated, and whites rushing to quench the resulting fires would be cut down. When sufficient weapons had been secured, the insurgent rebels would take control of the city and force all of Manhattan's white women to become their mates.

Authorities had no intention of allowing Prince and Caesar to remain in jail and become possible martyrs for dissident slaves intent upon a reenactment of the 1712 insurrection. Instead of waiting for incontestable proof that the pair had been involved in a plot to take the capital, the court condemned the men to death on more easily proved counts of burglary.

On May 11, Prince and Caesar were led to the gallows where a large crowd of jeering spectators awaited the hanging. Both felons were urged to make public confessions admitting involvement in the slave rebellion, but according to Justice Daniel Horsmanden, the prisoners died ''very stubbornly,'' in silence. As a posthumous penalty, Caesar's body was hanged in chains and left to rot unburied. The following day, John Hughson, together with his wife and daughter, were indicted on charges of conspiring to destroy New York.

May 13 had been set aside as a day of fasting and humiliation to thank God for deliverance from the dreaded insurrection, but as colonials flocked into churches, Mary Burton remained busy at work. On her word, three additional blacks were arrested. She indicated that others would soon be implicated. It seemed that the commemoration of thanks was most premature.

During the following days, many in the city began neglecting their work in the excitement of new revelations. As quickly as Mary could recall the name or face of some new plotter, authorities dispatched arrest warrants. Jails neared capacity. Court dockets became swamped. Arthur Price, armed with copious amount of intoxicating punch, was shifted from cell to cell to extract incriminating evidence from unsuspecting detainees.

Prosecution officials no doubt realized that it would be difficult to obtain guilty verdicts solely on the testimony of an indentured servant and a prison inmate. As a result, Lt. Gov. Clarke announced that pardons would be given to any accused conspirator who freely confessed guilt and named others who were involved in the rebellion. Sixty-seven slaves clamored to avail themselves of the chance at freedom.

Because pardon was granted only if the confessors implicated others, scores of new suspects were identified. Virtually every confession, however, confirmed that the original Hughson cadre had been instrumental in planning and financing the black rebellion. After an emotionally charged trial, the innkeeper and his wife were sentenced to death. Peggy Kerry was also condemned but sought a pardon by admitting guilt in the matter. Authorities accepted her testimony and then announced that it was insufficient to deserve a reprieve. The prostitute followed the Hughsons to the gallows after recanting her admission.

Instead of lessening the anti-black hysteria that seemed in control of the near paralyzed city, the deaths of the supposed ringleaders only created additional cries for punishment. An atmosphere reminiscent of the Salem witch hunt a half century earlier descended upon the capital. At the provincial court, suspects were rushed to judgment with amazing speed. Albany Carpenter was arraigned, convicted and burnt in four days. Ben Marshall was executed one week after his arrest.

Judge Horsmanden, who presided at many of the trials, detested the "craft" with which blacks sought to escape guilty verdicts, and the "unintelligible jargon" used by defendants to present their cases. Despite the language problem, juries had little difficulty in handing down verdicts against the unlearned blacks.

Some provincials were disturbed by the quality of evidence on which a lengthening progression of slaves were being sent to the gallows. Of major concern was the fact that most suspects were being convicted upon the testimony of other imprisoned blacks—individuals whose very lives depended upon the acceptance of their testimony against others. Also abhorrent was the practice of admitting testimony from unsworn slaves. Justices defended the breach of procedure by claiming that because blacks were incapable of understanding the concepts of religion or God, it would be a profanation to administer a sacred oath to them.

The controversy over oath taking did not stem the flood of confessions that continued to pour forth from imprisoned suspects. So many admissions confronted the lawmen, that it became impossible to record each confession in proper legal form. Instead of separate depositions, large charts were devised on which many admissions could be recorded together. The forms included columns listing names of various suspects and charges. Anyone wishing to make an accusation, merely checked the pertinent column. An equally efficient means of expediting the prisoners was through the imposition of mass trials.

That confession did not always mean freedom was a fact clearly impressed on convicted conspirators Quack and Cuffee. On May 30, the pair was hauled through a large and restless crowd to the public stakes where neat piles of wood stood ready. The spectators were impatient for the executions to begin, but the provinces' Deputy Secretary observed that both men were anxious to confess. Quack and Cuffee eagerly accepted the official's offer of reprieve in exchange for confession, and within minutes the prisoners had admitted participating in virtually every possible crime.

The statements were recorded for use as evidence in the trials of other blacks, but as the two men stood waiting for the return trip to jail, a sheriff announced that any stay of the burning would be impossible. According to the lawman, the crowd was becoming highly aroused at the delay, and would not tolerate a cancellation of the spectacle. Without further pause, the slaves were put to the torch.

In mid June, Manhattanites were horrified to learn that a treacherous new element had been uncovered. According to Lt. Gov. Clarke, it had become obvious that a far more dangerous power than the Hughson mob was behind the intended destruction of New York. Without doubt, the "hand of popery" was the real instigator of the slave rebellion.

Suspicion had fallen upon the Roman church partially as a result of a gubernatorial letter forwarded to Clarke by James Oglethorpe. The Georgian, still dismayed by the Stono Rebellion, wrote that Spain was attempting to cripple England's war effort by promoting slave insurrections in the provinces. Spies and secret agents had been sent into towns and villages to incite blacks. The Spanish infiltrators were disguised as itinerants such as physicians and dancing masters.

When Oglethorpe's report was disseminated in Manhattan, residents suddenly remembered that the Hughsons and Peggy Kerry had displayed telltale signs of secret Catholicism. The suspicions were confirmed on June 25 when a "Spanish spy" was uncovered living peacefully in the midst of the city. The alleged intruder was John Ury, a Latin teacher who found himself accused of being both the mastermind behind the entire rebellion and a priest in disguise.

Ury was promptly arrested and although the testimony of unsworn blacks was not admissible against him, Mary Burton's charges were allowed. Joining in the allegations was Sarah Hughson, daughter of the executed innkeepers. Sarah, convicted of conspiracy, had originally denied all guilt, but on the day appointed for her execution, she requested a reprieve in exchange for cooperating in the government's cases against others.

According to various witnesses, Ury had not only taken part in wild, drinking bouts at the alehouse, but had heard confessions and offered dispensations in advance for murders committed during the uprising. Sarah Hughson announced that Ury had assisted in the conspiracy by making the sign of the cross over assembled blacks and warning that anyone prematurely revealing word of the rebellion would burn in hell.

Other anti-Catholics stepped forward to accuse the teacher of behavior consistent with priestly purpose; he had supposedly built altars, baptised an infant with salt and bought wafer-like candies, undoubtedly for use in celebrating mass.

Ury's protestations of innocence were ignored and on August 29 he became the fourth white to be executed in connection with the slave insurrection.

Little attention was wasted on the suspected priest's hanging, for the introduction of the Catholic element prompted a frantic hunt to uncover other papists. The questionable justice that had sprung forth now seemed beyond the control of even the most rabid jurist. Rumors suggested that the plot had been four or five years in the making and that Spain's fleet had been readied to take the city as soon as local blacks had succeeded in the rampage of murder and pillage. Some reports claimed that slaves on Long Island were also involved in the revolt and that companies of black officers had already been formed to govern the colony.

An almost blasé attitude had developed toward the official burnings and hangings, but excitement was generated anew by reports that Hughson's unburied corpse had mysteriously assumed the characteristics of a black man. The body, left in chains, had supposedly turned dark in color and had grown a mass of curly hair. At the same time that this miracle was occurring, the body of the slave Caesar, was said to have become white.

According to Horsmanden, huge crowds of ''amused'' Manhattanites raced to the gallows to observe the startling changes, but the innkeeper's transformation was not to be seen. Without warning, the body suddenly burst and ''discharged pail fulls of blood and corruption.''

The ghoulish behavior of the citizenry and the seemingly endless line of defendants at the bar prompted growing numbers of opponents to protest the trials. By September, commercial interests were loudly predicting that few workers would be left alive to provide the services needed to run the city. More often, slave owners appeared at hearings in an attempt to prevent their laborers from making confessions.

No doubts were voiced by hard-core conservatives such as Horsmanden and Clarke, men who believed that the prosecutions should continue until every vestige of conspiracy had been rooted out. Mary Burton, also anxious to prolong the purge, proposed the names of still more connivers. Her testimony, instead of aiding the prosecution's effort, became a major factor in ending the trials. Increasingly her accusations centered not upon blacks, but upon white residents. When she dared to accuse several of the city's most prominent citizens of aiding the revolt, Mary's credibility was destroyed and the courts were closed by high level pressure.

By fall, life was returning to normal, but scores of New Yorkers who had seen spring arrive were no longer present. Twenty-two men and women had been hanged and thirteen burned at the stake. Seventy blacks had been deported to the West Indies, the Madeiras, Newfoundland and the Spanish Main. Many of the estimated one hundred and seventy-five persons tried in connection with the rebellion were still in jail.

Also gone were John Hughson's father and four brothers, all of whom had been imprisoned without trial for nearly five months. Only when the entire Hughson clan agreed to depart the province were the men released. Mary Burton had also vanished, but only after being rewarded with £81 and freedom from her indenture.

Termination of the court hearings did not end citizen fears of black rebellion, and in February of 1742, when a slave was arrested for arson, attention turned once again to the possibility that civil war might erupt. The incendiary, long known as mentally incompetent, aggravated the situation by confessing that his act was part of a conspiracy by bondsmen on Long Island to kill all of Manhattan's white residents. Although the arsonist attempted to recant his admission, he was executed without delay.

Fears of a black-Catholic alliance were rekindled with the outbreak of the French and Indian War. Anxieties that their enemies might combine forces prevented whites from launching a total war effort. On the southern front, for example, only one half of all eligible militiamen from South Carolina were sent to the frontier to engage the Cherokees. The remainder were left behind to protect the citizenry in case a rebellion was attempted by slaves.

The pattern was set. The "intestine enemy," unlike a foreign power who could be vanquished in a single battle, could never be totally subjected. Black rebellion against government would remain an ever-present possibility as long as the institution of slavery existed in America.

# CHAPTER XIII

# Violence on the Frontier

B Y 1750, England's North American possessions were home to more than 1.1. million colonists. The population figure was far from stable, but was being constantly swelled by vast waves of immigrant Europeans. Like the seventeenth century pioneers, these new arrivals sought material betterment and escape from an economic system that made helpless victims of small farmers and artisans.

But unlike the first adventurers from the Old World, the eighteenth century immigrants were not English born and bred. Great numbers' were Germans from the war-racked Palatinate or Scotch-Irish Presbyterians from Ulster.

The reputation for tolerance justly earned by William Penn's Quakers made Philadelphia the preferred port of entry for refugees fleeing the injustices of Europe. Although the attractions of America had been widely touted by Anglo-American officials seeking to increase the working population, not all established residents were delighted with the seeming endless line of ships that sailed up the Delaware with their human cargos.

As early as 1729, Pennsylvania Secretary James Logan mirrored the resentment that griped many old timers. "It looks as if Ireland is to send all its inhabitants hither," Logan wrote, "The common fear is that if they thus continue to come, they will make themselves proprieters of the province."

Immigrants did continue to arrive. As many as two or three vessels put into the port each day, yet the Europeans showed no interest in capturing political leadership in Pennsylvania. Instead of moving into urban society, they pushed west into the wilderness. Here, close-knit communities were formed. Old customs and languages were preserved.

Expansion towards the mountains was inevitable, for land near the seacoast and the Delaware River had long since been taken up for cultivation. In rare instances when parcels were offered for sale, the market price was beyond the newcomers' modest means. Much more attractive was former Indian territory where soil was cheap and available. New Americans by the thousands clattered through the capital, pausing only briefly before setting out by cart, horse or foot to follow the sun.

Early arrivals from the Palatinate settled into land ajoining the original Penn communities, but subsequent Germans and the first Scotch-Irish, finding eastern lands already inhabited, pressed westward until the Appalachians blocked further progress. Prohibited from moving north because of the powerful Iroquois, the stream turned south along the foothills beyond the fall line. With each passing year the frontier was pushed back. Remote outposts became established communities. The border of Pennsylvania was left behind as immigrants poured into remote areas of Maryland and then into the Valley of Virginia.

At times it seemed that the clock had been turned back a century and a half. Pioneers in the mid-1700's were confronted by the same barriers that faced the first Jamestown adventurers. Virgin forests had to be cleared, crops planted in untilled soil and hostile Indians combatted. An ocean no longer separated the homesteaders from "civilization," but the imposition of seemingly unjust rule by absentee government was as trying to the patience of later day frontiersmen as it had been to the seventeenth century provincials. Just as the English officials had appeared to ignore the needs of colonists along the seaboard, so did provincial authorities in the east seem to disregard the interests of the mountain men.

In every province, colonial government was dominated by a seaboard clique. Whether controlled by merchants of New England or by tidewater planters in the south, legislatures and councils invariably relegated western concerns to positions well below the preoccupations of the old line. Equal apportionment in assemblies was unknown. In Pennsylvania, for example, twenty six of the thirty six member legislature represented the old counties of Bucks, Chester and Philadelphia. The remaining ten seats were allocated to the five frontier counties of Lancaster, York, Berks, Northampton and Cumberland.

The inability of frontiersmen to gain recognition was further complicated by the constant wrangling that took place between rival political factions. Among those struggling for governmental power were parties representing the Proprietors, the anti-Proprietors, the Quakers, Scotch-Irish, courts and Assembly. Resentments between east and west had existed since the earliest days, but the conflict did not become a life or death affair until the outbreak of the French and Indian War in 1754.

The battle between England and France burst forth with violent reality in America. Fire and destruction marked the frontier from New York to Georgia. As the European nations struggled to dominate the Old World, the fragile communities along the Appalachian chain became a battleground for an incongruous collection of belligerents. Redcoats from urban metropolises engaged warriors from the Mississippi and Ohio River valleys. Elegant Parisian grenadiers grappled with Palatinate farmers.

Local militiamen, whose fates were being partially decided by wigged aristocrats in continental palaces, left their cornfields for war. Women and children took the farmers' place at the hoe, or crowded into poorly defended garrisons for safety.

In Philadelphia, the politically astute Quakers, together with other pacifists: the Mennonites, Moravians and Amish, were waging a less violent, but equally passionate battle. Declaring that God and a "peace testimony" would protect the colony from all harm, the powerful sects refused to endorse legislative financing of frontier defense.

For generations, non-violence had indeed marked the relations between Pennsylvanians and the Indians, a truce credited to a remarkably successful treaty concluded by William Penn in 1682. While other colonies poured valuable resources into military appropriations, Quaker-controlled Pennsylvania concentrated upon more profitable activities. As a result, the capital grew from a small huddle of cave dwellers into a cosmopolitan city where life was pleasant and personal liberty was highly valued.

Only reluctantly did the Quakers recognize that individuals following other religions should be accorded the right to protect themselves by force of arms. The acknowledgment did not alter the strict code of non-violence prescribed for observance by the Friends.

Under religious practice, Quakers were not allowed to bear arms, vote financial approval of funds for war purposes or pay taxes to support any violent activity. Work on fortifications or non-combat positions such as guard duty was also forbidden to the sectarians. Believers who accepted the validity of the peace testimony also maintained that the sale or gift of food to the militia was an immoral abetment of war. Others claimed that even those in imminent danger should not seek safety in a fortified garrison, for to leave one's home for an armed refuge was an abridgement of faith in the power of peace to conquer the evil of violence.

The Quakers' refusal to support British efforts during war with France was a major factor in the temporary loss of charter rights in 1692. Throughout the two years in which provincial government was administered through crown appointees, the Assembly remained firm against approving defense measures ordered by the King.

Radical opposition to the pacifist faction surfaced repeatedly during the early decades of the eighteenth century and erupted into violence in the October, 1742, elections when proprietary and military interests attempted to wrest control of the Assembly away from the Quakers. During balloting in Philadelphia, militant parties hired idle sailors and ships' carpenters to intimidate Quaker and undecided voters at the polls. The result was a full scale battle between club-wielding mercenaries and the pacifists, who fended off the intruders with the help of lawmen and bystanders.

As the prospect of still another war with France became more certain, Benjamin Franklin sought to break the impasse between the frontiersmen demanding protection, and the easterners who refused to provide appropriations. Franklin devised a plan that would totally eliminate the need for government financing of the military. The doctor's scheme involved establishment of a voluntary "Association" of soldiers led by popularly-elected officers and funded through a colony-wide lottery.

The official Quaker solution differed radically from the doctor's program. Pennsylvania's anti-war elements endorsed a group known as the "Friendly Association for Gaining and Preserving Peace with the Indians by Pacific Measures." The aim of the Association, was to promote rational examination of various causes that underlay Indian uprisings. Supposedly, after the issues had been studied, non-violent solutions could be devised to satisfy all parties.

The Association's program attempted to replace the accepted western belief that all red men were naturally inclined to warfare, with the philosophy that Indians were forced into battle by corrupt white practices. It seemed logical that if the unjust actions of the pioneers were eliminated, then the need for war would disappear.

Sympathy for the passive faction wavered under intense pressure from neighboring colonies and English officials. In 1756 the legislature finally approved limited funds for establishment of forts along the frontier. Several Quaker members resigned rather than provide tacit approval of military assistance. The vacancies were soon filled by non-Quaker nominees willing to continue voting in the interests of the peace party.

After the conclusion of the French and Indian War, Pennsylvania returned to the policy of non-military support, a posture that brought instant disapproval from London. George III was annoyed by the inflexible stand of the province, and on October 19, 1763, the Earl of Halifax conveyed the monarch's displeasure to colonial Governor John Penn. Halifax wrote:

> His Majesty has commanded me to express to you his surprize and displeasure at a conduct so inconsistent with the security of the lives and properties of his subjects in Pennsylvania . . . I am further to signify to you His Majesty's pleasure that you do recommend it to the General Assembly . . . to make provision, without further delay, for raising and paying such a reasonable number of men as the actual state of war may require; to be employed, not only in protecting and defending the frontiers of Pennsylvania, but in acting offensively against the savages. . . . This is the conduct which His Majesty in such a time of general danger, has a right to expect from his colonies.

The King's complaints were not the only ones received in Philadelphia during the fall of 1673. From the frontier came demands that troops and funds be dispatched to combat Indians rumored preparing for massive invasion. In eastern Pennsylvania, protection of the pioneers from Indians was becoming of less concern than the shielding of friendly Indians from the western whites.

The importance of ''preserving'' friendly tribes who voluntarily renounced violence and lived as allies of the Pennsylvanians had long been stressed by provincial leaders. To insure that the unarmed red men would not become the prey of unpacified Indians, the government had moved large numbers of ''friendlies'' into white communities. Preserving was highly unpopular among westerners who feared that a rear guard attack might be launched at any time from the Indian enclaves in the east. The stereotype that red peoples were inherently devious and untrustworthy was widely accepted on the frontier, where most pioneers believed that the concept of non-violent Indians was ridiculous.

Despite backwoods opposition, Indians were lodged at private houses in Philadelphia and settled on Providence Island in the middle of the Schuylkill near the capital. Smaller contingents lived peacefully amidst white farms in other counties.

Among the most docile of the friendlies were the Conestoga, a tribe that had become christianized and lived under the protection of the Moravians in Lancaster County. By 1763, the once proud nation had been reduced to less than thirty members who lived by begging or selling brooms and baskets to neighboring whites. Life was hard for the Conestogas. On November 30, tribal leaders urgently petitioned Governor Penn for clothing so that the group's women and children might be covered during the forthcoming winter. Tragically, the garments would go unused.

On December 14, a mob of pioneers decided to end the policy of preserving, at least in the case of the Conestoga. During the early morning hours, fifty backwoodsmen from Paxtang Township rode into the Indian settlement. Because most of the Conestoga had already set out to sell their wares, only six Indians were found. Before an alarm could be raised, the Paxtang Boys killed and scalped the inhabitants, set fire to the village and rode away unidentified.

The massacre was viewed with revulsion in Philadelphia where cries for apprehension and punishment of the slayers poured forth. The uproar did little to change attitudes in the west where the raid was applauded with satisfaction.

On December 27, the vigilantes struck again. An even larger mob descended on Lancaster where the fourteen surviving Conestoga had been moved to the community workhouse for safekeeping. Pushing local defenders aside, the raiders broke into the jail and attacked the refugees with tomahawks, coopers' mallets and rifles. Within minutes, the entire contingent of Indians was dead. The victims included three men, three women and eight children.

A £200 reward was issued by the provincial government for the conviction of the Paxtang Boys' leaders, and Lancaster officials were called to the capital to explain why more diligent efforts had not been made to apprehend the murderers. By January, anger in the east rose even higher when reports were verified that frontiersmen from throughout the west were massing to invade the Quaker city. The insurgents' intention was to kill all the friendlies under official protection. The marchers expected to set out at any moment.

Philadelphians sent boats to the Indians on Providence Island in case an amphibious invasion was made, but the refugees considered the assistance to be inadequate and asked to be shipped to England. As an alternative, it was decided that the friendlies would be marched to New York and placed under the care of the crown's Indian agent Sir William Johnson.

The natives were herded together and ordered to begin the long northern trek on foot. Despite inadequate preparations, the group managed to reach the New York border, but here, the entire column was halted on the orders of Governor Cadwallader Colden. Labeling the refugees as "rogues and thieves" who were not to be trusted, the New Yorker refused to let the party cross through his jurisdiction. The weary Indians were turned back to Philadelphia.

By January 28, grave concern blanketed the City of Brotherly Love. No longer was the danger from the west directed only at the friendlies. Paxtang activist Robert Fulton had announced that westerners were of the same intention as the "blood-thirsty Presbyterians who cut off King Charles' head." In the spirit of rebellion, the insurgents had decided to destroy not only the Indians, but their Quaker protectors and the city that provided refuge.

Confirmation of the expanded objective was relayed to Governor Penn and the Council by Benjamin Kendall, a traveller who had met with Fulton in Lancaster. According to Kendall's intelligence, fifteen hundred westerners were preparing to march and another five thousand men stood in reserve in case additional forces were required. Kendall had been instructed to inform the government leaders that all who did not submit to the Paxtang Boys would be killed and their houses burned.

A call for volunteers to defend the capital was answered by one thousand Philadelphians. Many Quakers, refusing to be privy to violence, began departing, but not all the sectarians chose to continue the peace testimony. An estimated two hundred Friends joined the armed men vowing to turn back the invaders.

Noticeably absent from the defensive army were many of the city's Presbyterians and the disenfranchised poor who sympathized with the western challenge to established government. These elements formed a powerful fifth column which demanded that the sheltered tribesmen be surrendered so that no harm might come to whites. The proposal was ignored.

By February 5, Philadelphia was ready. Barricades were set up in the streets. Ferries were brought to the city side of the Schuylkill. Capital residents watched expectantly as the backwoodsmen took up positions on the opposite bank.

For two days the situation remained tense, but unchanged. It seemed that the Paxtang Boys who had moved so brutally against the defenseless Conestoga had lost enthusiasm for fighting when confronted by armed Philadelphians. Only about two hundred and fifty of the insurgents actually crossed the river.

Benjamin Franklin, condemning the westerners as "white savages" attempted to mediate the confrontation. Accompanied by government officials, the wily printer entered the enemy camp and successfully secured a face-saving solution. The western army would return home, but two representatives would be left behind to prepare a formal list of grievances. The document would be considered thoroughly at the highest levels of government.

On February 13, the petition was completed and presented to provincial leaders on behalf of inhabitants in the five frontier counties. The declaration alleged that because Indians were "perfidious" and naturally inclined to massacres, all contact between red peoples and private citizens should be prohibited. Other demands called for legislative reapportionment, trial of Indian murderers on the frontier rather than in eastern courts, publicly financed medical care for all settlers wounded in frontier fighting and reintroduction of bounties for Indian scalps. According to the document, the removal of the rewards had "dampened the spirits" of Indian fighters and eliminated a major incentive to western vigilance.

Authors of the petition made a limited attempt to justify the Conestoga slayings on the grounds that all Indians, whether they be men, women or children, were barbaric "enemies" of the crown. In reiterating the frontier code that war must be total and unmerciful, the document asked:

> In what nation under the sun was it ever the custom that when a neighboring nation took up arms, not an individual should be touched but only the persons that offered hostilities? Who ever proclaimed war with a part of a nation and not with the whole?

As Franklin had promised, the grievances were presented to the colonial Council, but no effective action resulted from the body's consideration. The temporary coalition between feuding interests in the east dissolved as soon as the physical threat to Philadelphia was removed. Although the government did agree to raise one thousand troops for frontier duty, a permanent solution to western grievances was not devised. The anger of the pioneers grew even greater when it became known that so many Quakers who had blocked defense appropriations to the west on the grounds of pacifism, had taken up guns when the safety of their own city was in doubt.

Incidences of violence continued to appear in the west until the outbreak of the revolution against England. During the 1776 rebellion, the worst fears of the pioneers were confirmed. Thousands of Indians, loyal to the crown, raided almost at will in the poorly defended back country of Pennsylvania.

No colony held a monopoly on the east-west conflict typified by the marches of the Paxtang Boys, for settlement of the back country bred dissension against governments from New York to Georgia. By the mid-1760's, European immigrants were located all along the foothills of the Appalachian chain. The farmers had been able to penetrate the territory, by means of an isolated throughway known as the Great Philadelphia Wagon Road.

For centuries, the road had been a primitive trace, used primarily by Indians going to war against distant tribes or by hunters following the buffalo migration. Decades after the English began planting the tidewater, the trail remained untouched, the silence broken only by the occasional tap of passing moccasins. A radical change occurred in the eighteenth century when waves of immigrants began flowing into America and treaties pushed eastern tribes beyond the first mountain ridge.

By the eve of the revolution, the road was the most heavily travelled passage in America. Each year, thousands of wagons creaked down the byway that stretched in an eight hundred mile semi-circle from Philadelphia to Augusta. Taverns and inns sprang up to serve passers-by, and small villages were formed to provide more permanent facilities. Forts were constructed at strategic intervals so that safety from foreign invasion could be assured.

Complete development of the road took nearly fifty years of slow progression from north to south. In the 1720's, immigrants moved out of Penn's colony into western Maryland where a welcome had been put out by Baltimore's agents. By 1735 most available land in the Chesapeake province had been claimed and wagons began moving into Virginia. By 1750, backwoodsmen were farming the North Carolina piedmont and only a few seasons passed before newcomers streamed into the South Carolina foothills.

Eastern interests originally encouraged frontier settlement, for expansion in the mid-Atlantic and southern colonies had been virtually halted at the fall line. The swamps and softwood forests that blanketed much of the territory beyond the point of navigation had proved impenetrable to all but the most hardy adventurers. Development of the wagon road area meant that a buffer of white settlers lay between Indian and French encroachment and the seacoast communities.

Eastern residents however, were somewhat wary of, and openly condescending about the pioneers along the wagon road. The gentility and English heritage that characterized villages on the Atlantic was noticeably absent on the rough farms of the west. Ethnic and religious differences were unmistakably apparent.

Small numbers of Swiss, highland Scots and English had begun the rugged trip southward during the early eighteenth century, and a significant troop of Palatinate Germans immigrated as far as the Shenandoah Valley, but increasingly, the back country was being peopled by independent, uncompromising Scotch-Irish.

Under the early Stuarts, thousands of lowland Scots had been transported to northern Ireland in an attempt to colonize the troublesome country and facilitate English domination. The Scots readily adapted to the new environment and became loyal supporters of the crown. In 1689, these Ulstermen were instrumental in defeating James' attempt to retake the throne with the help of a Catholic force based in Ireland.

Instead of receiving accolades for their service to England, the Scots in Ireland were increasingly subjugated. Most became virtual serfs on the grand estates of noblemen. The tenants were forced to pay exorbitant rents for the privilege of tilling the land. Economic disaster was a constant threat. Depressions and famines drove the standard of living to below subsistence levels. Instead of providing assistance, the English concentrated their activity on attempting to impose Anglican-ism on the zealous Presbyterians.

Just when it seemed that the situation could deteriorate no further, Irish landlords introduced the insidious practice of ''rack renting,'' a procedure in which farms were leased to the highest bidder. In a fran-tic effort to assure that they would retain some land, tenants agreed to return huge amounts of their harvests to owners of the farms. When it became obvious that the tenants could not survive on the remainder, mass evictions began. Like dominoes, less prosperous farmers who had been pushed from their plots, moved on to expel tenants on less desirable lands.

The prospect of beginning anew in America seemed the only alter-native to the Ulsterites. Reports from the colonies included glowing tales of the New World's promise. Across the Atlantic, land was so cheap that farmers could own their own property and no longer be dependent upon the dictates of nobles. English repression had not yet reached the western territory: all might practice their traditional re-ligion and folkways without molestation. The advantages were uncon-testable. The rush to immigrate began.

So many tenants left the Irish countryside for the plantations that landlords attempted to secure a Parliamentary ban on further immigra-tion. The effort was unsuccessful and before the outbreak of the 1776 revolution, as many as 250,000 Scotch-Irish or one-third of all Ulster-men in Ireland had immigrated to America.

The Scotch-Irish clattered down the Great Wagon Road in an end-less line, swelling the up country population as rapidly as the Irish communities had been emptied. From 1746 to 1753, the number of residents in North Carolina's three frontier counties rose from five hundred to fifteen thousand. In 1765, Governor William Tryon estimated that one thousand wagons passed through Salisbury in a single six month period. The flow increased and by 1770, it was reported that three thousand wagons were reaching the end of the road each year.

Polite and mannerly behavior did not often accompany the travellers of the Wagon Road. Britisher Nicholas Cresswell, who visited the backlands of Virginia, announced that only "whores and rogues" were in evidence. Disorder became so prevalent that in 1748 the Burgess made it a crime to gouge, pluck or pull out the eye of a fellow colonial. Also forbidden was the "biting or stomping" of another pioneer.

Anglican minister Charles Woodmason, an itinerant who attempted to bring religion to the back country, was initially repelled by the violence and questionable moral standards of the Scotch-Irish. Woodmason, himself unable to consummate marriage because of a misplaced horse's kick, found his congregations almost completely free of civilized restraints. He estimated that ninety-four percent of the brides he blessed in marriage were already pregnant and that nine-tenths of all settlers suffered from venereal disease. All pioneers, he suggested, were "rude, ignorant, void of manners, education or good breeding." Most repulsive was the frontier habit of wife swapping, a custom he announced was as common as the exchange of cattle or horses.

If an overabundance of moral uprighteousness was not a problem in the west, the lack of governmental order did create difficulties. Conditions were most critical in South Carolina where the frontier served as a magnet for a wide variety of lawless elements. The defeat of the Cherokee in 1761 attracted droves of adventurers who sought quick wealth. Unethical trappers and traders raced westward with supplies of liquor to capture the deer skin and fur traffic. Renegade soldiers, deserters from the French and Indian War and outlaws escaping from eastern justice also headed for South Carolina's backwoods. The cities, blighted by depression yielded up unemployed vagrants and the very poor who had nothing to lose by a drastic reordering of their lives.

After arriving in the up country, the unsavory elements formed outlaw bands and settled in organized renegade communities. The few legitimately appointed authorities were either intimidated by the superior force of the outlaws, or willingly joined in a corrupt alliance with the marauders. Murder, robbery and rape became commonplace. Young women were kidnapped from their homes and forced to serve as courtesans. Harvests were routinely stolen from the fields.

The situation was aggravated by the refusal of Charleston leaders to challenge the renegades' control. Pioneers reportedly begged the government to establish courts and other evidences of administrative oversight on the frontier, but all requests were ignored. The refusal of the provincial officers to provide funds so that justice might be extended to the frontier was probably rooted in the extreme financial sacrifices that had been made by easterners during the Cherokee uprising. After investing large amounts to subdue red men, the sea coasters may have been disinclined to provide still more for maintaining peace among the whites.

Without powerful spokesmen in the Assembly or economic leverage in Charleston, the up country farmers became the prey of ever enlarging squadrons of bandits. The helplessness of the pioneers weighed heavily upon Charles Woodmason, whose initial repulsion at the erring citizens of the frontier had been replaced by compassion. The clergyman emerged as the most vocal and influential defender of the Scotch-Irish; an erudite propagandist who bombarded Charleston authorities with petitions for assistance. His works left no doubt that on the frontier, renegades had assumed control. For example the minister wrote:

> Our large stocks of cattle are either stolen and destroyed—our cow pens are broken up—and all our valuable horses are carried off—houses have been burnt by these rogues, and families stripped and turned naked into the woods—stores have been broken open and rifled by them . . . private houses have been plundered; and the inhabitants wantonly tortured in the Indian manner . . . married women have been ravished —virgins deflowered, and other unheard of cruelties committed by these barbarous ruffians. . .
>
> No trading persons (or others) or with money or goods, no responsible persons and traders dare keep cash, or any valuable articles by them—nor can women stir abroad, but with a guard, or in terror—the chastity of many beauteous maidens have been threat[e]ned by these rougues. . . . And thus we live not as under a British Government (every man sitting in peace and security under his own vine, and his own fig tree), but as if [we] were in Hungary or Germany, and in a state

of war—continually exposed to the incursions of Hussars and Pandours; obliged to be constantly on the watch and on our guard against these intruders, and having it not in our power to call what we possess our own, not even for an hour; as being liable daily and hourly to be stripped of our property.

Conditions worsened in the spring of 1767 when an unprecedented reign of outlaw terror eliminated all pretenses of civilized control. Convinced that the colonial governor would offer no protection, residents of the back country formed vigilante mobs to expel the desperadoes. Homes of citizens suspected in cahoots with the marauders were burned. Criminals were apprehended and whipped unmercifully. Crime appeared to be decreasing.

Authorities in Charleston showered little thanks on the extra-legal enforcers. In early October, Governor Charles Montagu criticised the "rioting manner" in which the vigilantes, now known as the Regulators, had acted. Word that the farmers planned to march on the capital to press their grievances brought an even stronger reaction from the establishment. Officials ordered the Regulators to disperse. It was announced that those who refused to do so would be arrested.

It was incredible to the pioneers that provincial authorities would show more effort in apprehending law-seeking Regulators than had been expended to track down violent bands of murderers. Even more disheartening was a gubernatorial request that the legislature formally suppress the movement for acting "in defiance of government and to the subversion of good order."

Woodmason stayed a possible confrontation by writing and circulating an elegant petition called *The Remonstrance*. The minister's lengthy work was signed in the name of four thousand backwoodsmen and was submitted to the Assembly on November 7. The document included an extensive discussion of every pioneer grievance together with well considered suggestions for redress and subtle threats that retribution might occur if corrective action was not quickly applied.

Included in the list of needs mentioned in *The Remonstrance* was construction of churches and schools, appointment of better qualified officials and establishment of a welfare system. The need for a workable system of county courts was seen as particularly important, for the hearing of all criminal and civil cases in the east worked a dire hardship on pioneers. Because many were unable to undertake the costly and fatiguing trip, law in the west too often degenerated into solution by violence.

*The Remonstrance* also pled for equitable representation in the Assembly and the surveying of parish lines westward so that farmers would know precisely in which precinct their votes should be cast. Most important, Woodmason believed that a basic change in the disdainful attitude of easterners was necessary if the quality of frontier life was to improve. The arrogance of coastal authority was described as an evil that bred injustice and inhumanity. The minister wrote:

> . . . we are considered . . . hewers of wood and drawers of water for the service of the town: who treat us not as brethren of the same kindred—united in the same interests—and subjects of the same Prince, but as if we were a different species from themselves; reproaching us for our ignorance and unpoliteness, while they themselves contribute to it, and would chain us to these oars as unwillingly that either us or our prosterity should emerge from darkness into light. . . . What they waste and throw away, would lay for us the foundations of good things. The sums trifled away in a play house there, would have raised us fifty new churches. . . .

*The Remonstrance* was not enthusiastically received by the Assembly. According to Woodmason, opponents suggested that the document be burned by the public hangman and the proponents arrested. Yet despite the objections of conservatives, several conciliatory measures were put forth in Charleston. A limited court bill was reported out and it was agreed that two companies of soldiers should be organized to track down the remaining outlaws. Regulators were appointed to lead the military force.

Optimism that the eastern concessions would bring positive improvements was soon dashed. The arrests of the Regulators accelerated rather than ceased. In addition, it became evident that the court bill was a powerless instrument that would do little to bring justice to the frontier. By the spring of 1768, the dissident movement was again on the rise.

No longer were the pioneers concerned solely with ridding the land of ruffians. The threat of rebellion and perhaps permanent secession from the province had become a real possibility. Unwilling to place further trust in the good will of the government, the Regulators announced that they were assuming practical control of the western area.

Only those laws approved by the group would be enforced. Provincial taxes would not be paid. Eastern writs and processes that were deemed correct by the movement could be served, but measures not passing approval would be ignored.

On July 29, court deputy John Wood became one of the first to feel the new political power of the Regulators. While attempting to serve warrants, the lawman was seized by the backwoodsmen, beaten and tied to a post for two days before escaping back to Charleston. The furor created by the assault had not subsided when a group of Regulators met a large contingent of governmental deputies in pitched battle at Marr's Bluff. The pioneers easily vanquished the eastern lawmen.

News of the disturbances shook the capital.

Rumors suggested that as many as three thousand Regulators were rendezvousing for a mass march on the seat of government. To pacify the dissidents, the Governor ordered that writs be issued for a new election. Presumably the tensions of the irate Regulators would be eased if it appeared that positive action would be forthcoming from a new, more liberal Assembly.

The resulting legislature did indeed reflect the rising power of the west, for backwoodsmen in large numbers made their way to the seacoast voting places. But expectations that the people's representatives would act decisively to solve pressing issues was dashed by an entirely unrelated event. Parliamentary approval of the Townshend Acts had fanned citizen protests throughout the colonies. Royal officials were fearful that the riots and disorders that had accompanied the 1765 Stamp Act would be repeated, and to insure that the South Carolina legislature did not precipitate anti-British violence, the Governor prorogued the new Assembly. His action inflamed the west and the situation was even further provoked by word that the court bill had been disallowed in England.

Patience ended in the back country. The Regulators emerged stronger than ever and enjoyed near total support. Representatives of the eastern government were expelled or ignored. The remaining outlaws were dispatched with swift brutality. When the bandits had been eliminated as a source of concern, the movement turned on fellow citizens whose only crimes were unacceptable conduct. Women of loose morals were publicly humiliated. Vagrants were forced to work on pain of punishment and political opponents were targeted for severe retribution. Anti-Regulator John Harvey, accused of no crime, was thrashed by sixty men who flailed away with rods while fiddles played merrily.

The central government, realizing that a rival political force had gained dominance on the frontier, issued warrants for the arrest of twenty-five Regulator leaders. To bring in the suspects, a force of deputies was organized under the leadership of Joseph Coffell, a mercenary of unsavory repute. Though a small number of arrests were made, it proved impossible for Coffell's men to bring the prisoners through the Regulator-controlled back country for trial on the coast.

By some reports, Coffell's men were far more interested in private gain than public service. Instead of doing their assigned duty, the soldiers reputedly turned to plundering Regulator property. Frontiersmen who had only recently succeeded in expelling the outlaws, were in no humor to peacefully accept the imposition of another predator band. Believing that Coffell's supposed raids had been ordered by eastern conservatives, the insurgents prepared to invade the tidewater and destroy the property of high ranking opponents.

Critics claimed that the vigilantes had purposefully distorted Coffell's actions in order to discredit a growing, anti-Regulator movement known as the Moderators, frontiersmen who apparently had joined forces with the provincial representative.

On March 25, 1769, more than one thousand Regulators and Moderators gathered at Musgrove Plantation on the Saluda River. A massive battle was averted only when the rank and file of both organizations refused to fire.

The specter of massive internecine violence was unsettling to both the frontiersmen and the eastern establishment. Support for extension of government to the west finally materialized. Gradually, positive steps were taken to bring order to the frontier. A comprehensive court bill was approved. Plans were drawn up for construction of jails, schools and government buildings.

As evidences of legitimate authority appeared in the west, the insurgent movement declined. On October 31, 1771, the chapter of violence was closed when a full pardon for all acts of rebellion was issued to those who had dubbed themselves the South Carolina Regulators.

# Chapter XIV

# *Regulators Confront Tryon*

WHILE SOUTH CAROLINIANS were chafing at the reluctance of officials to extend government westward, pioneers in neighboring North Carolina were in open revolt for precisely the opposite reasons. The irony was not extraordinary, for although the two colonies had been founded under the same charter and peopled by immigrants of similar backgrounds, vastly different expectations of government had developed.

To the tar heels of the North Carolina piedmont, the eastern establishment had shown too great a proclivity in "civilizing" the frontier. Westerners complained that a burdensome, bureaucratic government, operating through prying officials, interfered in even the most minute aspects of private life. According to backwoods reports, the personal freedom that had made the Wagon Road area so attractive was being quickly eroded by strangling regulation.

The need for stable control had been obvious to North Carolina leaders since the first settlers began moving into the piedmont. In May of 1759, members of the provincial Assembly were forced to deal with dangerous riots that broke out all along the frontier. The legislature approved a £25 reward for anyone revealing the identity of the leaders in the "traitorous conspiracies." The payment went unclaimed.

A year later, the situation was even worse. The Assembly journal noted that uncontrollable mobs had congregated in roving pacts and had, "broke open goals, released malefactors, dug up the dead from the graves and committed other acts of rapine and violence. . . ."

In describing the turmoil that rent the colony, Moravian Bishop August Spangenberg declared: "there are many cases of murder, theft, and the like, but no one is punished. . . . If a man is imprisoned the jail is broken open; in short, 'fist law' is about all that is left."

The independent frontiersmen did not take kindly to eastern efforts to impose order. Wagon roaders saw the provincial government as a nonessential instrument dominated by plantation dandies who would be more comfortable with English lords than with fellow provincials. The gulf of misunderstanding between new immigrants and old was evident not only in philosophies concerning law and order, but in almost ever other facet of pioneer life.

Scotch-Irish Presbyterians resented the compulsory taxes paid to support Anglican churches on the seaboard. Eastern creditors, who required a stable economy based on gold or silver, felt threatened by frontier demands for cheap paper money. Westerners were angered that much of the choicest farm land was claimed by absentee owners. Easterners sent to the frontier as government officials resented being degraded by locals as greedy foreigners or representatives of corrupt courthouse rings. Pioneers, faced daily with threats from Indians, could not understand the reluctance of seacoasters to provide adequate defense measures.

Yet no issues stirred backwoods resentment so thoroughly as the eastern imposition of fees, quitrents and poll taxes. Unlike the Charleston government, the North Carolina establishment had quickly recognized that the piedmont could be exploited as a source of new revenue.

Unfortunately, little care was taken to assure that the fees charged by office holders for their services were either reasonable or legal. Attempts to impose schedules of maximum charges were completely ineffective and citizen animosity over inconsistent pricing was intensified by widespread illiteracy among the pioneers. Many settlers were convinced that government servants were extorting from the public in order to amass personal fortunes.

In some cases, piedmonters dealt with mounting fees by dispensing with the need for services. When costs for issuing marriage licenses rose to £15, settlers simply ignored the bliss of legitimate wedlock and lived together under common law. However most procedures such as registration of land titles and deeds, applications for probate and processes for lawsuits could not be so conveniently ignored.

Resentment was further increased by the problem of overlapping bureaucracies. To the helpless citizen, it seemed that swarms of unnecessary office holders, each with open palms, were involved in even the simplest service. Masses of clerks, registrars, surveyors, collectors, commissioners, inspectors, constables, treasurers and sheriffs depended solely upon fees for their livelihood. Most were appointed by the provincial government and few were natives of the locale in which they worked. In the public eye, these "foreigners" rarely deviated from a set pattern of behavior. The civil servants arrogantly swept onto the frontier, joined a local courthouse ring, intimidated local citizens into paying outrageous fees and then moved on with pockets overflowing.

A popular ballad commemorated the procedure by describing the rise to fame of Orange County official Edmund Fanning. According to the ditty:

> When Fanning first to Orange came
> He looked both pale and wan;
> An old patched coat upon his back
> An old mare he rode on.
>
> Both man and mare weren't worth five pounds
> As I've been often told;
> But by his civil robberies
> He's laced his coat with gold.

Fanning, a native New Yorker and a Yale graduate had little in common with the Carolina frontiersmen. He became one of the most detested fee takers and represented multiple officeholding at its worst. Fanning's control over Orange County was significant, for he served not only as an assemblyman, but as public registrar, justice of the peace, assistant judge of the Superior Court and commander of the county's militia.

In 1764, Governor Arthur Dobbs attempted to eliminate corruption by forbidding the collection of illegal fees, but the move resulted in slight improvement. Dobb's successor Sir William Tryon found the situation little changed. According to Tryon, local sheriffs and their deputies embezzled more than one-half of the monies collected in each county. A 1770 audit disclosed that in some areas taxes collected by the lawmen had not been turned into the central treasury for as long as sixteen years.

Closely akin to complaints involving illegal fees and collections, were backwoods grievances dealing with quitrents. Instead of levying charges according to the market value of the land, quitrents were generally set at a specific rate per one hundred acres. Under this system, the owners of inferior tracts were subject to the same payments as those whose land was far more productive. In addition, it was difficult on the frontier to discover exactly who was required to pay quitrents.

During the mass immigrant invasions, the taking up of land was a casual affair in which prior, legal ownership was given minimal regard. Some settlers claimed possession of all territory within an area bounded by their own tree blazing, a system known as "tomahawk right." More permanent was "cabin right," a custom in which newcomers might claim land that surrounded a personally constructed shelter. Under "corn right," pioneers agreed to recognize individual claims to one hundred acres of unimproved land for every acre under cultivation.

Easterners were not impressed with the extra-legal methods devised by frontiersmen to determine valid ownership. Instead, coastal dwellers began resurrecting old land grants that had been issued decades earlier to long deceased ancestors. For years, the property included in these forgotten patents had been considered worthless, but the arrival of the up country farmers dramatically altered the deeds' value. Piedmonters, who had toiled endlessly to tame supposedly unclaimed land in the wilderness, suddenly found themselves faced with eviction notices or bills for quitrents reportedly owed to absentee owners.

Convinced that the court system provided little redress for the poor against the rich, the tarheels unhesitatingly resorted to violence in order to halt the encroachment of seacoasters. In May of 1765, the brief, but decisive War of Sugar Creek was waged in Mecklenburg County over just such an attempt. In the fracas, more than one hundred armed countrymen attacked surveyors attempting to plot a parcel of land claimed by one Henry E. McCulloch under an eastern grant. In a May 9 letter to Fanning, McCulloch complained that he had only narrowly escaped harm from the mob. "They may be damned for a pack of ungrateful, brutal sons of bitches," McCulloch fumed. "I don't care. I will tomorrow make my will, and if they do [kill me] bequeath my revenge with my estate. . . ."

Fees and quitrents, although burdensome, were not as ideologically objectionable as the poll. The tax system worked an extreme hardship on new settlers who were invariably confronted during the first years of settlement by net losses or marginal profits. Because of the equal pay structure, however, hard pressed pioneers were assessed the same taxes as long established settlers and those more able to pay. Backwoodsmen, unable to remit the levies on time, routinely received eviction warrants signed by judges with special interests in the suits. All too often, the delinquents' lands were condemned and swiftly resold in private deals to court favorites who paid prices far below actual market value.

Dissension over the poll galvanized in 1766 when the Assembly approved construction of an elegant, three-story Governor's palace at New Berne. Supporters of the scheme promised that the structure would be the finest in the colonies. The brick and marble mansion would be graced with a vast dome, covered with costly glass. There would be galleries and a grand ballroom where the province's aristocrats might gather to socialize. Both a "great" and a "lesser" staircase were included in the plans, together with architectural luxuries that required the importation of trained artisans from Philadelphia. More than eight tons of lead would be needed for the indoor plumbing, a new innovation that would be installed by workmen from London.

The idea of a noble palace springing up in Carolina was unbelievable on the frontier where citizens lived in dirt floor shanties and slept three to a bed on corn husk mattresses. Equally disagreeable was Sir William Tryon, the major beneficiary of the mansion and a strong loyalist who had shown unconcealed disdain for the colony's inhabitants.

During the Stamp Act protests, the Governor had prorogued the Assembly and lectured the people for daring to submit petitions against the controversial law. He had dismissed the public printer for distributing anti-government broadsides and insisted that Lady Tryon be addressed with due respect under the title "Her Excellency." The extreme sacrifices required to house Tryon in a grand style were offensive enough to the backwoodsmen, but the resentment was magnified when it was learned that the £15,000 dwelling would be primarily financed by the poll.

Legislative endorsement of the mansion plan particularly rankled the pioneers, for the Assembly was held in little regard in the west. Gross malapportionment and the location of the capital on the eastern coast meant that people of the mountain area had little voice in the framing of public policy. The rapidly growing counties of the foothills received only token representation in the body. Orange County, for example, was allotted two seats in the Assembly, while five eastern districts with a combined population of less than that of Orange were represented by twenty five members.

Despite disapproval over the palace funding, piedmonters initially accepted the new poll without overt opposition. In February of 1768, however, the citizens' obedience was hard pressed when the Sheriff of Orange County announced that all taxes for the year would be collected in a single payment, on a specific day at five designated locations. Anyone who did not produce the entire levy would be charged a late fee of 2s 8d.

The sheriff's requirements placed a hardship on small farmers who traditionally paid taxes in installments whenever sufficient amounts of hard currency could be accumulated. The frontier had long suffered from a lack of specie, for although the population was increasing at a rapid rate, the amount of money in circulation was decreasing. The situation had been worsened by British currency restrictions on the issuance of paper money or bills of credit by provincial administrations. It was obvious that many of the pioneers would be unable to meet the tax deadline, either because they could not raise the total tax at one time, or because they could not secure sufficient tender to satisfy the bill.

For two years, a loosely organized group of Regulators had been publicizing pioneer grievances through a series of broadsides or "Advertisements." The movement had met with moderate success in Anson, Orange and Granville Counties, but after the lawman's decree new recruits poured onto the membership rolls. On March 22, the organization issued a recommendation that residents should continue paying the King's quitrents of four shillings, but should withhold all other taxes that collectors could not prove were legally authorized. Officials were urged to make their accounts public and verify that all monies being collected were actually being sent to the provincial treasury.

Orange County leaders were in no mood to cater to citizen requests. Instead of complying with the Regulator demands, Sheriff Tyree Harris confiscated the horse of a farmer who had refused to pay the taxes due. Reaction from the people was immediate. On April 8, nearly one hundred frontiersmen gathered at the county seat of Hillsborough to retake the animal. In the process, Edmund Fanning's house was fired upon.

Unrest spread to Anson County where Regulators swore oaths to reclaim any property confiscated because of non-payment of taxes. The men also pledged to break from jail anyone arrested for participating in the boycott.

Fanning was horrified at what he visualized as imminent anarchy. Instead of placating the population, the official called out the militia and notified Tryon that the region was in the "bosom of rioting and rebellion." According to Fanning, the west was inundated with "traitorous dogs," who were conspiring against the government, taking illegal oaths, threatening innocent officials and plotting mass violence. He predicted that a concerted attack would soon be made on law officers and announced that at least fifteen hundred Regulators were preparing to burn Hillsborough to the ground. Although Fanning had overemphasized the danger of the situation, he was correct in assessing the mood of the people. Citizens in his region had become so resentful of government that the militiamen refused to answer the call to arms.

In an attempt to quell the disturbances, Orange authorities organized a midnight raid on May 1 to arrest Regulator Herman Husband for "traitorously and feloniously" conspiring to instigate a rebellion. Husband, an early settler in the county, had been read out of the Quaker Meeting for disorderly actions, but he remained staunchly committed to non-violence as a means of protest. As a result, he had emerged as the philosophical mastermind and foremost pamphleteer of the Regulator movement. Arrested along with Husband was dissident William Butler.

When word of the apprehension reached the countryside, a force of seven hundred men organized to attack the jail. Hillsborough constables, intimidated by the large force, released the men on bail.

Tryon refused to be pressured into over-reacting and possibly escalating the widening dissent. Because the general aims of the Regulators were popular among segments of society that composed the militia, the Governor hesitated to risk his personal prestige by issuing a call that might not be answered. Instead, Tryon announced that if all dissident citizens returned home peacefully, he would consider any grievances that might be substituted.

The raucous westerners accepted Sir William's proposal. A petition signed by five hundred citizens was promptly forwarded to the Governor. The signatories assured Tyron that no protest against his authority or the King's supremacy was intended and that the disturbances were aimed only against corrupt, local office holders who used illegal methods to "squeeze and extort from the wretched poor."

Tryon's response was not as reassuring as the people had wished. He did order all officials to post printed lists of legal fees and promised to prosecute those who continued unlawful practices, but the Governor sternly informed the backwoodsmen that no further tax boycott would be tolerated.

When local officials ignored Tryon's call for reform, nervousness returned to the west. Four hundred Regulators assembled at George Sally's plantation on August 3 to swear a tax boycott and death for any who threatened their lives. A week later, a mob of five hundred backwoodsmen meeting at Peeds, announced that the town would be burned unless their grievances were met. Contributing to the restlessness, were rumors that Sir William had made a secret treaty with the Cherokees to attack the pioneers from the mountains while he invaded from the tidewater. The unsubstantiated tales probably sprang from the Governor's decision to bring fourteen hundred militiamen into Hillsborough to protect the fall session of the Superior Court. It was at this meeting that Husband and Butler would be tried. Also on the docket was the case of Edmund Fanning who stood charged with extortion for charging fees of 6s when the legal allowable amount was but 2s 6d.

In mid-September, as many as 3,700 Regulators poured into Hillsborough to assure that justice was done. None, however, was anxious to oppose the Governor's authority. The court cases were resolved in compromises designed to enflame neither faction. Charges against Husband and Butler were reduced to rout. Husband was found innocent and Butler received a suspended sentence after a guilty verdict was returned. Fanning, also deemed guilty, was fined one penny per count. After assuring that the situation was peaceful, Tryon disbanded the militia and returned to New Berne.

On October 4, Orange and Rowan County residents petitioned the Assembly for relief from ever increasing taxes and the resulting property confiscations that were becoming commonplace on the frontier. The settlers informed the legislators:

> . . . on your breath depends the ruin or prosperity of poor families, and so Gentlemen rolling in affluence, a few shillings per man may seem triffling, yet to poor people who must have their bed and bedclothes, yea their wive's petticoats taken and sold to defray [the taxes], how tremendous judge ye must be the consequences—an only horse to raise bread, or an only cow to give milk to an helpless family, by which in a great measure are otherwise supported, seized and sold and kept for a high levy, no part being ever returned. . . .

Two important responses were forthcoming from the Assembly: payment of taxes in barter rather than specie was approved and writs for a new election were issued.

Voters in the October, 1769 balloting chose Regulator candidates to represent the piedmont, but the exercise proved futile. Tryon, fearful that North Carolina legislators would join other provincial assemblies in protesting the Townshend Acts, adjourned the representatives for five months. Opposition to the bill did not abate in the interim. The Governor again believed it unsafe to allow the men to meet and further suspended the Assembly until December of 1770.

The delays acerbated the problems on the frontier and ended all hope that official solutions to problems could be devised. Local office holders resumed their illegal practices and it seemed clear that the situation would be improved only if residents acted on their own volition.

Public wrath was increasingly directed at the court system, the most evident symbol of provincial authority and the instrument by which the illegal actions of fee collectors were given legitimacy. Dockets of the Superior Court, the bi-annual body that handled all criminal cases and major civil suits, were routinely months in arrears. Citizens wishing to protest confiscations of goods or property found it virtually impossible to receive a ruling before the items were disposed of. Even when the cases were heard, there was no assurance that justice would be done. Jurists were largely uneducated and served at the pleasure of the King rather than for good behavior. As a result, corruption was widespread.

The situation was little better in the Inferior Courts where Justices of the Peace heard minor civil cases. Although their dockets were usually current, lower level jurists were deeply involved in the hated courthouse rings.

In Johnston County, an enraged mob attacked the sitting court and was repelled only by club-wielding jurists. In Anson County, one hundred armed Regulators invaded the bench in a spree of destruction. An even more unsettling confrontation appeared to be brewing for the fall, 1771 session of the Superior Court at Hillsborough.

A large number of cases involving Regulators were scheduled to be heard by the court and rumors alleged that the juries who would be deciding the suits were being packed with cronies of the local rings. Backwoodsmen were convinced that illegal confiscations and fee collections would be upheld and that the innocent defendants would be heavily prosecuted for involvement in the Regulator movement. On September 24, approximately one hundred and fifty Regulators under Husband, Butler and Regulator "General" James Hunter barged into the Hillsborough chamber. With sticks and clubs the rioters drove Judge Richard Henderson from the bench. Edmund Fanning was dragged into the street and beaten. Lawyers were forced to flee to escape whippings.

The following morning, insurgents reconvened the court and in mock session began to try the scheduled cases. According to reports, the rioters exhumed the corpse of an executed black prisoner and placed the remains on Judge Henderson's chair, suggesting that the dead man's action would be little different than the live judge's. Impromptu "juries" composed of Regulators, quickly found for their colleagues. When the docket had been totally cleared, the insurgents departed for home.

Any sympathy that may have formed in the east for pioneer grievances disappeared when news of the Hillsborough riot reached New Berne. Direct attacks on courts of justice were unconscionable crimes under English tradition. Resentment over the anarchist activity increased after Judge Henderson's house was subsequently burned.

Herman Husband, arriving in the capital to take his seat in the long delayed Assembly, was arrested and jailed. Amid rumors that the Regulators were planning a daring rescue, the legislators refused to act on even the most basic reform for the frontier. Instead, the delegates approved a drastic, arbitrary measure designed to eliminate all further protest. Several years later, the Privy Council would disallow this Johnston Act as "irreconcilable with the principles of the constitution, full of danger in its operation and unfit for any part of the British Empire." For the Regulators on the frontier in 1771, the repressive and arbitrary measure was in full effect.

Under the statute, death was decreed as the punishment for a long list of activities including assault on a court official, obstruction of a sheriff in his duties and arson of a courthouse, prison or church. The failure of ten or more persons to disperse when gathered in a riotous manner was also made a capital crime and lawmen were exempted from punishment if rioters were killed during apprehension. Any person escaping after indictment on any of the enumerated charges would be declared an outlaw and shot on sight. Finally, the measure specified that all Regulators who did not immediately disband were traitors to the King.

Frontier reaction to the Johnston bill was the exact opposite of that intended by the assemblymen. Instead of deterring further violence, the statute merely added to the discontent. Membership in the Regulators reached new highs. It was said that the pioneers were preparing to march en masse to the coast.

Citizens of New Berne began fortifying the capital for an attack. Tryon directed that a moat be built between two rivers bordering the village. The militia was ordered to stand by and the sale of arms was halted in an effort to keep war materials out of Regulator hands. The spring, 1771, session of the Hillsborough court was cancelled. Husband had been released unindicted, but the grand jury had returned sixty two true bills against other Regulators in connection with the Hillsborough riots. It was not anticipated that the trials would be peaceful.

On March 19, Tryon called out the eastern militia, but the soldiers were reluctant to move against fellow provincials. A 40s bounty stimulated recruitment, but the men straggling into New Berne were not enthusiastic. One soldier was accused of shooting himself in the foot. Another received one hundred and fifty lashes for attempting to "breed a mutiny" in the ranks.

With such men, Tryon hoped to succeed in a full-scale military action that would permanently crush the Regulators. The campaign's major thrust depended upon a western march by Tryon and one thousand men supported by swivel guns. A secondary troop of about three hundred men would be formed in the back country under the direction of loyalist general Hugh Waddell.

Only minor difficulties confronted the Governor as his army moved inland in late April. Waddell's progress was less satisfactory. Near Salisbury, the General's path was blocked by a large force of Regulators who forced the loyalists to turn back. News that the reinforcements would not be coming was a severe blow to Tryon, but equally depressing was word that a large supply of gun powder being rushed from South Carolina had been destroyed en route by Regulator commandoes disguised as slaves.

As Tryon continued forward, more than two thousand backwoodsmen were leaving their homes. In comparison with the eastern militia, the Regulators were an unorganized, leaderless mob with no tactical strategy. Though armed with muskets and rifles, most of the men undoubtedly believed that a compromise would be reached and that bloodshed would be unnecessary. Their presence was required only to lend an appearance of strength to the western negotiators. Tryon, however, had passed the point of compromise. His unwillingness to discuss the issues was buttressed on May 15 when insurgents captured and beat two militia officers.

Events far from the southern colony had transformed the confrontation into much more than a clash between mountain and seacoast interests. The forces converging on the piedmont had become players in a drama that reached across the Atlantic. From Boston to Charleston, the authority of royal governors was being threatened by unruly elements. The Stamp and Townshend Act protests were merely surface manifestations of deep-seated animosities that increasingly alienated Britain's overseas subjects. Although the Regulators were presumably fighting to secure improved local government, and the militiamen had taken up arms to defend their homes from western invasion, the Governor was performing his sacred duty to defend the mother country against dangerous rebels.

On the morning of May 16, the uneasy forces met about five miles from the Great Alamance River. Tryon refused to acknowledge peace feelers tentatively offered by the Regulators, a group Sir William had officially declared to be in "war and rebellion." Instead of agreeing to negotiate, the Governor announced that the insurgents must surrender totally, immediately and unconditionally. A one hour time limit was placed on the ultimatum.

The lines grew still as the minutes ticked by. Herman Husband, unwilling to participate in violence, left the field. The Regulator leadership broke the silence with the defiant cry: "Fire and be damned!"

At noon shots rang out from the militia. Reportedly the loyalists had opened up only after refusing several direct orders to fire. However, once the battle had begun, it could not be halted.

Initially the pioneers held their own, but after several hours, Tryon's superiorly trained force gained an unsurmountable advantage. In panic, the Regulators fled. Sir William took advantage of the disorder by directing that the forest containing rebel snipers should be set on fire. By early afternoon, smoke billowed across the piedmont. The battle was over.

The woods at Alamance were bloody as a result of the fighting. An estimated two hundred Regulators had been killed or wounded and casualties for the Governor's troops totalled seventy. The aftermath was also violent.

Tryon was determined that no prominent rebels would be left at large to reactivate the movement. In an immediate warning to all who would rise against the King, the Governor ordered the battlefield execution of James Few, a mentally deranged insurgent and a declared outlaw under provisions of the Johnston Act, who believed that God had anointed him for world leadership. In subsequent court martials, twelve Regulator prisoners were found guilty of treason against the crown and six were executed.

As a further warning, the remaining captives of the battle were chained together and marched across the back country. Tryon also offered rewards to militiamen for each horse, gun and saddle taken from the dissidents. The directive was intended to make counter attack impossible, but the measure merely served as an impetus for widespread looting.

On June 9, the dreaded stamp of "outlaw" was placed on four rebel leaders when Tryon proclaimed:

Whereas Herman Husband, James Hunter, Rednap Howell and William Butler are outlawed and liable to be shot by any person whatever, I do therefore, that they may be punished for the traitorous and rebellious crimes they have committed, issue this my proclamation, hereby offering a reward of one hundred pounds and one thousand acres of land to any person or persons who will take dead or alive and bring into mine or General Waddell's camp, either and each of the above named outlaws.

More lenient treatment was accorded those who had followed the ringleaders. A general pardon was announced for all low level Regulators who agreed to pay back taxes and take an oath to support the established government. By July 4, more than six thousand individuals in the west had sworn the required allegiance.

Reports of the battle sped throughout America and were seized upon by the radical press as a means for inflaming the people against the crown. Published accounts portrayed Alamance as a struggle between brave patriots and the oppressor minions of England. Publishers of the *Virginia Gazette* related a gory version of the battle in which Sir William was cast as a most bloodthirsty villain. Not only did the article accuse the Governor of treacherously slaying a Regulator during the truce, but the story suggested that Tryon had killed thirty rebels singlehandedly with as "much coolness as if hunting of squirrels."

Though the battle did stir the passions of political dissidents in other regions, it marked the end of the Regulator organization as a viable force. Defeated in battle, their grievances unsolved, thousands of backwoodsmen who had formed the nucleus of the movement chose to leave North Carolina for unsettled territory across the Blue Ridge. As many as fifteen hundred families may have departed the piedmont during 1772 alone.

Tryon returned to a hero's welcome in New Berne, but his stay was brief. Within four days, the official left the "palace built with blood," and set sail for Manhattan where he had been appointed the new royal governor.

Josiah Martin, Sir William's replacement, attempted to reconcile the rebels who remained in hiding. Martin journeyed to the piedmont and became convinced that the Regulators had been compelled by necessity into rebellion. The Governor wrote: "I now see most clearly, that [the people] have been provoked by . . . mercenary, tricking attorneys, clerks and other little officers, who have practiced upon them every sort of rapine and extortion. . . .'' Through Martin's efforts, all but one Regulator was pardoned. The exception was Herman Husband, the ex-Quaker who had refused to fight with a sword and had depended upon the pen for redress.

For a time, Husband lived with relatives in Maryland, but the outlaw was drawn back to the frontier, this time to western Pennsylvania. More than twenty years after Alamance, Husband again became involved in rebellion against government. This time, his opponent was not a governor in a great eastern mansion, or the King in an English palace. Instead, the old Regulator rose against the young American nation in the abortive Whiskey Rebellion. Husband was imprisoned for his part in the revolt, but was paroled because of advanced age and died before his trial could be called.

The passing of Herman Husband was little marked in the new republic, for citizens were preoccupied by the struggle to strengthen the union so that America might emerge as an independent power rather than a stepchild of foreign interests. The colonies had become states, and the states a federation which leaders hoped would shame the repressive monarchies that held sway in the Old World.

In addition, a new generation of rebels had captured the public's fancy. Attention was riveted upon firebrand dissidents from Massachusetts and Virginia who boasted the names of Adams, Franklin, Washington and Jefferson—men whose challenges to established authority had been total and successful. Even the most educated Americans had no cause to dwell upon long past revolts instigated by colonials who seemed more British than provincial.

In contrast to the 1776 revolution, the early rebellions seemed conservative and even reactionary movements. Rarely had the basic right of England to administer the colonies been questioned. Followers of insurgents such as Bacon, Leisler, Coode and Culpeper had not sought to alter the framework of government or achieve the power to determine who should rule. In most instances, the dissidents asked only a ''restoration'' of the ''ancient rights'' that protected English subjects against arbitrary Kings and Parliaments.

The goals of America's first rebels were indeed modest when compared to the wide-reaching demands of the late eighteenth century citizenry. But the need for relief from unresponsive government was far more urgent in the perilous lives of the original pioneers than to the established inhabitants of later days.

Despite the care taken by those who framed the Constitution, rebels would continue to rise up against the American government, for the severing of ties with England did not end the heritage of dissent that had been passed down from the first generation of western adventurers. There were new men and new times, but the causes of dissent seemed strangely familiar: officials were corrupt, laws favored the powerful, rights were ignored, the voice of the people was not heard.

# Selected Readings

## GENERAL BACKGROUND

*American Violence, A Documentary History,* ed. Richard Hofstadter and Michael Wallace, 1970; Charles M. Andrews, *The Colonial Period of American History,* Vols. I–IV, 1964; Hannah Arendt, *On Revolution,* 1963; G. E. Aylmer, *The Struggle for the Constitution 1603–1689,* 1963; Carl Bridenbaugh, *Myths and Realities, Societies of the Colonial South,* 1952, *Cities in Revolt, Urban Life in America, 1743–1776,* 1955, and *Cities in the Wilderness, The First Century of Urban Life in America 1625–1742,* 1960; *British Royal Proclamations Relating to America 1603–1783,* ed. Clarence S. Brigham, 1968; Wesley Frank Craven, *The Colonies in Transition 1660–1713,* 1968; *The Glorious Revolution in America,* ed. Michael G. Hall, Lawrence H. Leder and Michael G. Kammen, 1964; Willard A. Heaps, *Riots, U.S.A. 1765–1970,* 1970; Christopher Hill, *The Century of Revolution 1603–1714,* 1966; Douglas Edward Leach, *Arms for Empire—A Military History of the British Colonies in North America 1607–1763,* 1973; Leonard W. Labaree, *Royal Government in America, A Study of the British Colonial System Before 1783,* 1958; David S. Lovejoy, *The Glorious Revolution in America,* 1972; *Narratives of the Insurrections 1675–1690,* ed. Charles M. Andrews, 1915; Gary B. Nash, *Class and Society in Early America,* 1970; Clinton Rossiter, *Seedtime of the Republic,* 1963; *Royal Instructions to British Colonial Governors 1670–1776,* Vols.

I, II, ed. Leonard W. Labaree, 1967; *Settlements to Society, 1607–1763*, ed. Jack P. Greene, 1975; Julia Cherry Spruill, *Women's Life and Work in the Southern Colonies*, 1972; *Tracts and Other Papers . . .* , Vols. I, II, IV, collected by Peter Force, 1836; F. C. Turner, *James II*, 1950; C. V. Wedgwood, *The King's War, 1641–1647*, 1959.

## NEW ENGLAND COLONIES

Aspinwall Papers, *Collections* of the Massachusetts Historical Society, Vol. IX, 4th Series, 1871; Seventeenth century broadsides and personal accounts included in *The Andros Tracts . . .* , Vols. 5, 6, ed. W. H. Whitmore, 1868, 1869; Viola F. Barnes, *The Dominion of New England, A Study in British Colonial Policy*, 1923; Jeremy Belknap, *The History of New-Hampshire*, Vol. I, 1831; John R. Brodhead, *The Government of Sir Edmund Andros Over New England in 1688 and 1689*, 1867; Nathanael Byfield, *An Account of the Late Revolution in New-England . . .* 1689, reprinted Force's *Tracts;* Charles E. Clark, *The Eastern Frontier: The Settlement of Northern New England 1610–1763*, 1970; *The Diary of Samuel Sewall 1674–1729*, Vol. I, ed. M. Halsey Thomas, 1973; Everett Kimball, *The Public Life of Joseph Dudley: A Study of the Colonial Policy of the Stuarts in New England 1660–1715*, 1911; *The Hutchinson Papers*, Vol. II, 1865; *The Memorial History of Boston . . .* , Vols. I, II, ed. Justin Winsor, 1881; Perry Miller, *The New England Mind: The Seventeenth Century*, 1961; John G. Palfrey, *History of New England During the Stuart Dynasty*, Vol. III, 1864; *Provincial Papers of New Hampshire*, Vol. I, 1867; Anonymous, *The Revolution in New-England Justified . . .* 1691, reprinted in Force's *Tracts;* Harry M. Ward, *The United Colonies of New England 1643–90*, 1961.

## MID-ATLANTIC COLONIES

Mary L. Booth, *History of the City of New York*, 1859; *The Documentary History of the State of New-York*, Vols. I, II, ed. E. B. O'Callaghan, 1850; *Documents Relative to the Colonial History of the State of New-York*, Vols. II, III, ed. E. B. O'Callaghan, 1853; *History of the State of New York*, Vols. I, II, ed. Alexander C. Flick, 1962; Henry H. Kessler and Eugene Rachis, *Peter Stuyvesant and his New York*, 1959; Anonymous, *A Letter from a Gentleman of the City of New York . . .* , 1698, reprinted, O'Callaghan's *Documentary History;* Anonymous, *A Modest and Impartial Narrative . . . Of Jacob Leysler and his Accomplices*, 1690, reprinted Andrews' *Narratives;* Jerome Reich, *Leisler's Rebellion*, 1953; Mrs. Schuyler Van Rensselaer, *History of the City of New York in the Seventeenth Century*, Vol. I, II, 1909; *Minutes of the Provincial Council of Pennsylvania*, Vol. IX, 1852; William S. Hanna, *Benjamin Franklin and Pennsylvania Politics*, 1964; Brooke Hindle, "The

March of the Paxton Boys," *The William and Mary College Quarterly,* Vol. III, 3rd Series, 1946; James G. Leyburn, *The Scotch-Irish: A Social History,* 1962; Israel Acrelius, *A History of New Sweden . . . ,* 1966 reprint of 1874 translation; Jehu C. Clay, *Annals of the Swedes on the Delaware,* 1938; *Pennsylvania Archives—Papers Relating to the Colonies on the Delaware 1614–1682,* Vol. V, 2nd. Series, ed. John B. Linn and William H. Egle, 1877; J. Thomas Scharf, *History of Delaware 1609–1888,* Vol. I, 1888; Parke Rouse, Jr., *The Great Wagon Road,* 1973; Jack M. Sosin, *The Revolutionary Frontier 1763–1783,* 1967. Matthew Page Andrews, *History of Maryland: Province and State,* 1965, and *Tercentenary History of Maryland,* 1925; *Archives of Maryland,* ed. William Hand Browne, 1890; B. Bernard Browne, "The Battle of the Severn," *Maryland Historical Magazine,* Vol. XIV, 1919; *The Calvert Papers,* Vol. I, 1889; Lois G. Carr and David W. Jordan, *Maryland's Revolution of Government 1689–1692,* 1974; Richard A. Gleissner, "Religious Causes of the Glorious Revolution in Maryland," *Maryland Historical Magazine,* Vol. LXIV, 1969, and "The Revolutionary Settlement of 1691 in Maryland," *Maryland Historical Magazine,* Vol. LXVI, 1971; Edward Ingle, *Captain Richard Ingle The Maryland "Pirate and Rebel" 1642–1653,* 1884; Erich Isaac, "Kent Island," *Maryland Historical Magazine,* Vol. LII, 1957; Constance Lippincott, *Maryland as a Palatinate,* 1902; *Narratives of Early Maryland 1633–1684,* ed. Clayton Colman Hall, 1967; *The Old Line State A History of Maryland,* ed. Morris L. Radoff, 1971; Daniel R. Randall, *A Puritan Colony in Maryland,* Johns Hopkins University Studies in Historical and Political Science, 1886; Anonymous, *Virginia and Maryland . . .* 1655, reprinted in Force's *Tracts;* Henry F. Thompson, "Richard Ingle in Maryland," *Maryland Historical Magazine,* Vol. I, 1906; J. Thomas Scharf, *History of Maryland from the Earliest Period to the Present Day,* Vol. I, 1879; Raphael Semmes, *Captains and Mariners of Early Maryland,* 1937; Francis Edgar Sparks, *Causes of the Maryland Revolution of 1689,* JHUSHPS, 1896; Bernard C. Steiner, *Maryland During the English Civil Wars,* JHUSHPS, 1906, 1907, *Maryland Under the Commonwealth A Chronicle of the Years 1649–1658,* JHUSHPS, 1911 and "The Protestant Revolution in Maryland," *Annual Report* of the American Historical Association, 1898; Sebastian F. Streeter, *The First Commander of Kent Island,* 1868; "Captain Thomas Yong's Voyage to Virginia and Delaware Bay and River in 1634," *Collections* of the Massachusetts Historical Society, Vol. IX, 4th Series, 1871.

## SOUTHERN COLONIES

*The Aspinwall Papers,* MHS; *Bacon's Rebellion The Contemporary News Sheets,* ed. Harry Finestone, 1956; Philip L. Barbour, *The Three Worlds of Captain John Smith,* 1964; John Berry and Francis Moryson, *A True Narrative of the Late Rebellion in Virginia,* 1677, reprinted in Andrews' *Narratives;* Robert Beverley, *The History and Present State of Virginia,* 1947; Philip A. Bruce, *Economic History of Virginia in the Seventeenth Century,* Vols. I, II, 1896, and *Institutional History of Virginia in the Seventeenth Century,* Vols. I, II, 1910; "A Narrative of the Indian and Civil Wars in Virginia in the Years 1675 and 1676," the *Burwell Papers,* 1814, reprinted in Force's *Tracts;* Ann Cotton, *An Account of our Late Troubles in Virginia,* reprinted in Force's *Tracts;* the Eggleston Manuscript, *The William and Mary College Quarterly,* Vol. IX, 1900; Nathaniel C. Hale, *Virginia Venturer—A Historical Biography of William Claiborne 1600–1677,* 1951; *The Statutes at Large . . . Laws of Virginia,* ed. William W. Hening, 1969 reprint of 1823 ed.; *The Jamestown Voyages Under the First Charter 1606–1609,* Vols. I, II, ed. Philip L. Barbour, 1969; Anonymous, [Thomas Mathew?] *The Beginning, Progress, and Conclusion of Bacon's Rebellion in Virginia in the Years 1675 and 1676,* reprinted Force's *Tracts;* Ben C. McCary, *Indians in Seventeenth Century Virginia,* 1957; "Culpeper's Report on Virginia in 1683," the MacDonald Manuscript, *The Virginia Magazine of History and Biography,* Vol. III, 1896; Richard L. Morton, *Colonial Virginia,* Vol. I, 1960. *Narratives of Early Virginia 1606–1625,* ed. Lyon G. Tyler, 1907; Official correspondence dealing with the Plant Cutters Rebellion, *The Virginia Magazine of History and Biography,* Vol. XXVIII, 1920; *The Old Dominion in the Seventeenth Century A Documentary History of Virginia 1606–1689,* ed. Warren M. Billings, 1975; J. Mills Thornton, III, "The Thrusting Out of Governor Harvey: A Seventeenth Century Rebellion," *The Virginia Magazine of History and Biography,* Vol. 76, 1968; "Bacon's Rebellion," *Tyler's Quarterly Historical and Genealogical Magazine,* Vol. XXIII, 1941; Wilcomb E. Washburn, *The Governor and the Rebel A History of Bacon's Rebellion in Virginia,* 1972 and *Virginia Under Charles I and Cromwell, 1625–1660,* 1957; Thomas J. Wertenbaker, *Bacon's Rebellion,* 1676, 1957, *Patrician and Plebeian in Virginia,* 1910, *The Planters of Colonial Virginia,* 1922, *Torchbearer of the Revolution The Story of Bacon's Rebellion and Its Leader,* 1940, and *Virginia Under the Stuarts 1607–1688,* 1914; George F. Willison, *Behold Virginia The Fifth Crown,* 1952. Samuel A'Court Ashe, *History of North Carolina,* Vol. I, 1908; John S. Bassett, "The Regulators of North Carolina (1765–1771)," *Annual Report* of the American Historical Association, 1895; George Chalmers, *Political Annals of the Province of Carolina . . . ,* reprinted in Carroll's *Collections,* 1836; *The Colonial Records of North Carolina,* Vols. I, VII, VIII, IX, ed. William L. Saunders, 1886; Alonzo Thomas Dill, *Governor Tryon and His Palace,* 1955; *The Fundamental Constitutions of Carolina . . . ,* 1669; Francis L. Hawks, *History of North Carolina,* Vol. II, 1857–58; Marshall DeLancey Haywood, *Governor William Tryon and His Ad-*

*ministration in the Province of North Carolina*, 1765–1771, 1903; Arthur Palmer Hudson, "Songs of the North Carolina Regulators," *The William and Mary College Quarterly*, Vol. IV, 3rd Series, 1947; Mary Elinor Lazenby, *Herman Husband A Story of His Life 1724–1795*, 1940; Hugh T. Lefler and William S. Powell, *Colonial North Carolina: A History*, 1973; Hugh T. Lefler, *History of North Carolina*, Vol. I, 1956; *Narratives of Early Carolina 1650–1708*, ed. Alexander S. Salley, Jr., 1911; *North Carolina History Told by Contemporaries*, ed. Hugh T. Lefler, 1965; Mattie Erma E. Parker, "Legal Aspects of 'Culpeper's Rebellion'," *The North Carolina Historical Review*, Vol. XLV, 1968; William S. Powell, *The Proprietors of Carolina*, 1968, and *The War of the Regulation and the Battle of Alamance, May 16, 1771*, 1962; Hugh F. Rankin, *Upheaval in Albemarle, 1675–1689 The Story of Culpeper's Rebellion*, 1962; *The Regulators in North Carolina A Documentary History 1759–1776*, compiled and edited by William S. Powell, James K. Huhta and Thomas J. Farnham, 1971; *Ye Countie of Albemarle in Carolina A Collection of Documents 1664–1675*, ed. William S. Powell, 1958. Richard Maxwell Brown, *The South Carolina Regulators*, 1963; *The Carolina Backcountry on the Eve of the Revolution-The Journal and Other Writings of Charles Woodmason, Anglican Itinerant*, ed. Richard J. Hooker, 1953; Verner W. Crane, *The Southern Frontier 1670–1732*, 1956; *Historical Collections of South Carolina . . .* , Vol. II, ed. B. R. Carroll, 1836; Edward McCrady, *The History of South Carolina Under the Proprietary Government 1670–1719*, Vol. I, II, 1969; Francis Yonge, *A Narrative of the Proceedings of the People of South-Carolina in the Year 1719*, 1726, reprinted in Force's *Tracts;* William Roy Smith, *South Carolina as a Royal Province 1719–1776*, 1970; M. Eugene Sirmans, *Colonial South Carolina A Political History 1663–1763*, 1966.

## BLACK REBELLIONS

*American Slavery: The Question of Resistance*, ed. John H. Bracey, Jr., August Meier and Elliott Rudwick, 1970; Herbert Aptheker, *American Negro Slave Revolts*, 1970; John S. Bassett, *Slavery and Servitude in the Colony of North Carolina*, JHUSHPS, 1896; Jeffrey R. Brackett, *The Negro in Maryland-A Study of the Institution of Slavery*, 1969; *The Colonial Records of the State of Georgia*, Vol. XXII, ed. Allen D. Candler, 1970; William F. Cheek, *Black Resistance Before the Civil War*, 1970; T. Wood Clarke, "The Negro Plot of 1741," *New York History*, Vol. XXV, 1944; Joshua Coffin, *An Account of Some of the Principal Slave Insurrections*, 1860; Henry Scofield Cooley, *A Study of Slavery in New Jersey*, JHUSHPS, 1896; Marion D. deB. Kilson, "Towards Freedom: An Analysis of Slave Revolts in the United

States," *Phylon,* Vol. XXV, 1964; *Documents Relative to the Colonial History of the State of New-York,* Vols. V, VI, VII, ed. E. B. O'Callaghan, 1853; John Hope Franklin, *From Slavery to Freedom A History of American Negroes,* 1966; Eugene D. Genovese, *Roll, Jordan, Roll The World the Slaves Made,* 1974; Lorenzo J. Greene, *The Negro in Colonial New England,* 1971; Nicholas Halasz, *The Rattling Chains: Slave Unrest and Revolt in the Antebellum South,* 1966; Daniel Horsmanden, *The New-York Conspiracy or a History of the Negro Plot . . . ,* 1810; Winthrop D. Jordan, *White Over Black, American Attitudes Toward the Negro 1550–1812,* 1969; Frank J. Klingberg, *An Appraisal of the Negro In Colonial South Carolina,* 1941; Edward McCrady, "Slavery in the Province of South Carolina 1670–1770," *Annual Report* of the American Historical Association, 1895; Edgar J. McManus, *Black Bondage in the North,* 1973, and *A History of Negro Slavery in New York,* 1966; Edwin V. Morgan, *Slavery in New York,* 1898; Gerald W. Mullin, *Flight and Rebellion: Slave Resistance in Eighteenth-Century Virginia,* 1972; "The Negro Plot of 1712," *The New York Genealogical and Biographical Record,* Vol. XXI, 1890; Edwin Olson, *Negro Slavery in New York,* 1947; Ulrich B. Phillips, *American Negro Slavery,* 1918; Hugh F. Rankin, *Criminal Trial Proceedings in the General Court of Colonial Virginia,* 1965; William R. Riddell, "The Slave in Early New York," *The Journal of Negro History,* Vol. XIII, 1928; Kenneth Scott, "The Slave Insurrection in New York in 1712," *The New-York Historical Society Quarterly,* Vol. XLV, 1961; Wilbur H. Siebert, "Slavery and White Servitude in East Florida, 1726–1776," *The Florida Historical Society Quarterly,* Vol. X, 1931; Ferenc M. Szasz, "The New York Slave Revolt of 1741: A Re-examination," *New York History,* Vol. XLVIII, 1967; Thad W. Tate Jr., *The Negro in Eighteenth-Century Williamsburg,* 1965; R. H. Taylor, "Slave Conspiracies in North Carolina," *The North Carolina Historical Review,* Vol. V., 1928; Harvey Wish, "American Slave Insurrections Before 1861," *The Journal of Negro History,* Vol. XXII, 1937; Peter H. Wood, *Black Majority Negroes in Colonial South Carolina from 1670 Through the Stono Rebellion,* 1974.

# Index

agents, colonial, x, 19, 90, 99, 122, 124, 127, 146, 159, 160, 162, 191, 198, 217

Alamance, Battle of, 283-285

*An Association in Arms . . .,* 211-217

Andros, Sir Edmund, 164-171, 173, 175-180, 183, 184, 186, 187, 190

Anne, Queen of England, 172, 173, 174, 219, 223, 237

Argyll, Earl of, 155

Argyll's Rebellion, 155, 172

arrests for rebellion, 71, 72, 79, 143, 144-145, 177, 199, 224, 277, 281, 285; slaves, 232, 233, 237, 241, 248; in Virginia, 4, 6, 17, 20, 102, 138, 139, 233. See Regulators.

assemblies, disolved and prorogued, 18, 62, 101, 137, 143, 149, 202, 209, 227, 269, 275, 279

Bacon, Elizabeth, 97-98, 99, 101

Bacon, Nathaniel, Jr., 97-108, 113, 285

Bacon's Rebellion, 93-113, 117, 123, 126, 134, 135, 136, 137, 138, 149, 203, 225

Baltimore, Second Lord (Cecil Calvert), 24, 32, 46, 47, 90, 93, 94, 121, 134, 138, 201, 203, 205; and the Commonwealth, 53-58, 60, 62-63; settles Maryland, 16, 25, 28, 29, 30, 44, 116

Baltimore, Third Lord (Charles Calvert), 202, 203, 206-212, 214, 216-218

Baltimore, Fifth Lord (Charles Calvert), 218

Baltimore, First Lord (George Calvert), 22-24, 27, 116

banishment of rebels, 20, 34, 53, 63, 72, 128, 130, 232, 252

Barbados, 51, 123, 128-129, 147

Barefoote, Walter, 147, 160

barred from office, 63, 103, 124, 128, 139, 151, 204

Bayard, Nicholas, 182-183, 190, 192, 196, 199

Bennett, Richard, 51-53, 55-58

Berkeley, Lady Frances, 97, 99, 123

Berkeley, Lord John, 89, 116

Berkeley, Sir William, 46, 50, 52, 62, 63, 86, 90, 92, 93, 116; and Bacon's Rebellion, 94-112, 117, 137, 203-204

Berry, Sir John, 110, 112

Beverley, Robert, 108, 137-139

Biggs, Timothy, 122, 125-127

Birkenhead's Plot, 86-87, 231

Bishop of Durham Clause, 24

Bloody Assizes, 155, 171, 178

Board of Nine Men, 73

bodyguards, 18, 90, 124, 195

bonds, good behavior, 63, 102, 124, 169

bounties, 96, 239, 244, 262, 281. See rewards.

Bradford, William, 33, 34

Bradstreet, Simon, 142, 161, 177

branding, 80, 109, 206, 232

Brent, Giles, 43-45, 45-47

British investigators, 51-53, 55-60, 97, 110-112, 157-158, 204. See Edward Randolph.

British military intervention, 51-52, 53, 75, 78, 104-105, 108, 110-113, 143, 150, 158, 159, 164, 196-198, 225

Buckingham, Duke of, 39, 41

Burton, Mary, 247, 248, 251, 252

Butler, William, 277-279, 280, 284

Byrd, William, 98, 99

Byrd, Valentine, 122

Cabal, 83

Caesar, 247-248, 252

Calvert family. See Baltimore.

Calvert, Leonard, 25, 26, 28-31, 43, 45, 46

Calvert, Philip, 63

Canada, xii, 69, 71, 73, 170, 193-194, 197, 232, 235, 241

Carteret, Sir George, 116

Carteret, John, 228

Carteret, Peter, 119

Cary, Thomas, 222-225

Cary's Rebellion, 222-225

Catherine of Braganza, Queen of England, 83, 152, 153

Catholic conspiracies, 16-17, 59, 83, 151-152, 171, 176, 185, 187-188, 193, 197, 201, 212, 214-215, 250-251

cessation, 134-137, 140

Charles I, King of England, 19, 30, 35, 50, 53, 55, 57, 64, 68, 98, 115, 151, 171, 217, 260; and Maryland, 22-24, 26, 27; civil wars, 39-44, 46-48

Charles II, King of England, 81-84, 96, 104, 108, 112, 115, 116, 121, 122, 125, 136, 142, 143, 148, 150-151, 157, 160-162, 174, 207, 208; and civil wars, 48-52, 55, 62, 63; and Restoration, 64-67, 69, 74

Charles XI, King of Sweden, 78

*Charter of Liberties and Privileges,* 184-185

Chicheley, Sir Henry, 95, 135-139

civil wars, English, 38-43, 46-49, 50, 51, 68, 70, 81, 95, 110, 120, 154, 155

Claiborne, William, 26-32, 43, 45-47, 51-58, 63, 104, 204

Clarendon, Earl of, 115, 126

Clarke, George, 246, 249, 250, 252

clergy; Anglican, xii, 20, 163, 172, 209, 213; Puritan, 33, 35, 142, 146, 156, 160, 167-169, 177, 178, 201-202; Reform, 195-196. See Charles Woodmason.

Cloberry and Company, 27, 31, 32

Colleton, James, 129-131

Colleton, Sir John, 116, 127

Commissioners for Foreign Plantations, 18, 19, 32, 37-39, 67, 81, 84, 127

Commonwealth, 48-55, 57, 60-61, 64, 65, 67

confiscation of dissidents' property, 20, 32, 43, 63, 80, 109-111, 113, 200

Connecticut, 74-76, 133, 161, 165, 178, 184, 194

consolidation, 36, 158, 161, 180. See Dominion of New England.

Coode, John, 193, 206, 211-218, 285

Copley, Sir Lionel, 217-218

corrupt administration, 15, 16, 91, 101, 102, 110, 112, 125, 128, 130-131, 176, 183, 195, 207, 221, 272-275, 278-280, 284-285, 286

Cranfield, Edward, 141, 142-147, 148

Craven, Lord William, 116, 127

Cresswell, Nicholas, 265

Cromwell, Oliver, 47-48, 57, 58, 60-61, 68, 108, 156

Cromwell, Richard, 61

Culpeper, John, 123, 125-127, 285

Culpeper, Lord Thomas, 89, 113, 114, 134-136, 138-140, 148

Culpeper's Rebellion, 123-127, 128, 225

customs, xii, 66, 88, 112, 121-127, 135-136, 139, 140, 208, 217. See navigation acts.

customs collectors, 91, 121-122, 123-125, 126, 159, 160, 161, 163, 184, 186, 190, 208, 215-216

Davyes, William, 203, 204

*Declaration of the Gentlemen . . . of Boston . . ., The*, 176, 183, 188

*Declaration of Indulgence*, 151, 172

*Declaration of the Inhabitants . . . of New York, A*, 188

*Declaration of the People*, 104

*Declaration of the Reasons and Motives . . .*, 211-212

*Declatation of Rights by Charter*, 157

De la Warr, Lord, 10, 19

defense expenditures, 91, 170, 202-203, 226-227, 256-258

defense strategy, frontier, 46, 91, 95-97, 102-103, 170, 180, 183, 194, 197, 209-210, 225-226, 256-258, 262, 272

disenfranchisement, 58, 90, 202, 213

divine right, 15-16, 33, 64, 209, 219

Dobbs, Arthur, 273, 274

Dominion of New England, 162, 164-171, 173-181, 182, 183, 185, 211, 219, 221

Dongan, Thomas, 185-187

Donne, John, 86

Dover Plots, 83-84, 151

Drummond, William, 102, 108-109, 112, 117

drunkenness and rebellion, 97, 145, 177, 189, 190, 224, 243

Dudley, Joseph, 142-143, 160, 162-164, 177, 180, 199, 200

Durant, George, 122, 124, 125, 128

Dutch West India Company, 69-70, 73, 75-76, 189

Dyer, William, 184

Eastchurch, Thomas, 122, 123, 125-126, 127

Edict of Nantes, 172, 185

Eleven Years Tyranny, 41

Elizabeth I, Queen of England, 39, 115

English-Dutch Wars, 72, 75, 83, 84, 89, 151, 158

Exclusionist Movement, 152-153, 154

executions for rebellion, x, 7, 59, 68, 87, 139, 155, 199-200, 203, 216, 283; Bacon's Rebellion, 107, 108, 110, 117, 204; slaves, 233, 237-238, 241, 243, 244, 248-252, 253

extra-legal communities, 86, 110, 235, 239-240, 244, 265. See plantation covenants.

Faction, the Puritan, 161, 180, 181
Fanning, Edmund, 273, 275, 277-280
fees and fines, illegal, 16, 20, 40, 72, 102, 207, 210, 212, 272-275, 278, 285
Fendall, Josias, 60, 62-63, 204, 206, 211
Fifth Monarchy Saints, 82
Fire, Great of 1666, 82-83, 84, 158
Fleet, Capt. Henry, 28, 29
Florida, 69, 115, 129, 226, 241, 244
foreign invasion, 69, 123, 171, 174, 183, 186-187, 190, 193-194, 210, 216, 231-232, 245, 251
Fort Moosa, 242, 244
France, xii, 25, 38, 69, 71, 76, 78, 105, 121, 135, 150, 151, 170, 171, 172, 174, 178, 180, 186, 190, 193-194, 197, 200, 210, 214, 216, 226, 231, 235
Franklin, Benjamin, 257, 261, 262, 285
French and Indian War, 253, 256, 257, 258, 265
Friendly Association for Gaining and Preserving Peace . . ., 258
*Fundamental Constitutions, The,* 118-120, 127, 128, 130, 131

George III, King of England, ix, 258
Georgia, xiii, 242, 256, 262
Gillam, Zachariah, 124-125, 127
Glorious Revolution, 173-174, 175, 177, 218, 219, 231
Glover, William, 222-223
Gove, Edward, 143-145
Gove's Rebellion, 143-144
governors, appointment of, 220-221
Great Philadelphia Wagon Road, 262-263, 264, 271
Great Seal, 24, 28, 36, 47, 56, 75, 115
Greene, Thomas, 54-56

Halifax, Earl of, 258
Hartford, treaty of, 71
Harvey, Sir John, 14-21, 28, 29, 30, 31
Hatch, John, 63
Henderson, Richard, 280-281
Henrietta Maria, Queen of England, 23, 42-43, 82
Hill, Richard, 214, 216
Holland, xii, 27, 38, 42, 51, 56, 69-78, 81, 83, 84, 89, 121, 135, 150, 151, 153, 155, 174, 195
Horsmanden, Daniel, 248, 249, 252
Hughson, John, 247-248, 250, 251-252
Hughson, Sarah, 251
Hunter, Robert, 236, 237, 238
Husband, Herman, 277-281, 283-285
Hyde, Edward, 223-225, 234-235

indentured servants, 12, 13, 14, 47, 73, 80, 86-87, 88, 89, 106, 133, 230, 238
Indian tribes, Anacostans, 29; Catawbas, 226; Cherokees, 227, 239, 253, 265, 266, 278; Chickasaws, 227; Choctaws, 226; Conestogas, 259-262; Creeks, 226, 239; Doeg, 93-94; Esopus, 75; Iroquois, 70, 112, 170, 194, 235, 255; Maqua, 179; Occaneechee, 100, 101; Pamunkey, 106; Paspahegh, 11; Patuxents, 29, 30; Mohawks, 192; Senecas, 93, 210; Susquehannah, 27, 31, 43, 93-95, 100, 101, 105, 112; Tuscarora, 223, 225, 226; Weskeskek, 179; Yamassees, 226, 227, 239
Indians, 4, 5, 8-9, 10, 13, 17, 29, 59, 77, 79, 170-171, 193, 225; Indian-Catholic conspiracies, 171, 175, 179, 186-187, 205, 210, 211, 214; massacre of Indians, 11, 29, 70, 94, 100, 105, 106, 259-260, 262; peace